COLLEGE LIBRARY

**Please return this book by the date stamped below
- if recalled, the loan is reduced to 10 days**

Fines are payable for late return

THE
MANAGER'S
HANDBOOK

THE

MANAGER'S

HANDBOOK

The practical guide

to successful management

Fully Revised

ΞII ERNST & YOUNG

WARNER BOOKS

Conceived, edited and designed by
Marshall Editions
170 Piccadilly, London W1V 9DD

Editor: Erica Hunningher
Revisions Editor: Maggi McCormick
Revisions Art Editor: Lynn Bowers
Picture Research: Sarah Wergen,
Richard Philpott
Research: Jazz Wilson
Editorial Director: Ruth Binney
Production: Barry Baker, Janice Storr

First published in Great Britain by
Sphere Books Limited 1986
Copyright © 1986 Marshall Editions Limited
Revised edition published 1992

This edition published 1994 by Warner Books
A Division of Little Brown and Company (UK)
Brettenham House, Lancaster Place, London
WC2E 7EN

Copyright © 1992 Marshall Editions Developments
Limited

Filmset in Century Schoolbook by MS Filmsetting Ltd,
Frome, UK
Origination by Reprocolor Llovet SA, Barcelona, Spain
Printed and bound by Usines Brepols SA, Belgium

# CONTRIBUTORS

Ernst & Young is one of the world's largest
international consulting and accountancy
firms. E & Y specializes in helping
companies resolve a broad range of
business problems, particularly in the
fields of Finance, Audit, Tax, Management
Consultancy, Information Technology,
Corporate Recovery and Education.

Consultant editors
Peter O'Neill, BSc, FCA
Joe Liddane, BA, FCA
Brian Chandler

Authors
Judith Ashton, BEd, ACA
Leslie Atkinson, MA, FIPC
Liz Baltesz, BSc, MSC
Joseph M. Berry, DipCom
Moira Blair
Stephen Bright, MIPM
Richard Buckley, BA, FCA
Brian Chandler
Tim Chessells
Mike Cookson, BSc, ACA
Keith Davis
John M. Duncanson, BSc
John Gibson, BA, FCA, FIPA
Angus Goodenough, BSc, ACA
Lynne Gordon, MA, CA
Alistair Gray, MA, FInst, M, MBIM
Gerard M. Gray, BA (Econ), ACMA,
  MBIM
Oliver Hegarty, BSc
Toby Hoskins, BA, ACA

Timothy E. R. Jacobs, MICE, MIMC,
  Ch Eng
David Jardine, CA, ACMA
Colin Jones-Evans, BSc, GIPM
Joe Liddane, BA, FCA
Niall Lothian, BA, CA
Tina Mason, BA, ACA
Guy Millward, BA, ACA
Mike Mister
Mahesh Patel, BA (Econ), ACA
Barry Ricketts
Martin Russell, ACA
Owen R. Scott, MA
Ronald S. Smith, MIIM
Colin Suter, MBA, BTech, DipM, DipPM
Ruth Wellin, BA Cert Ed
Tony Whelan, HCIMA
H. Beric Wright, MB, FRCS, MFOM
Iain Wylie, MA, DipPM

CONTENTS

INTRODUCTION

There is something of a revolution going on in the world of management education and training in the UK. Managers at all levels and at all stages of their careers need to be aware of this and seek out ways of capitalizing on the new and exciting opportunities for developing their managerial skills that are now becoming available.

I am pleased to have been a part of this changing process. As Chairman of the National Forum for Management Education and Development, the parent body of the Management Charter Initiative, I have been delighted by the progress that MCI has made since its launch in July 1988. As a result of considerable wide-ranging research over a lengthy period, MCI was able to define, for the first time in the UK, competence-based standards for first-line and middle managers.

With these now in the public arena and with other MCI processes also in place – Qualification Criteria, Crediting Competence, Endorsed programmes and developing National Vocational Qualifications with Awarding Bodies – British managers now have greatly enhanced means of improving their managerial competence.

We are moving into an era where the combination of the knowledge and understanding acquired by way of formal education and training, together with its practical application in the workplace, will be the measure of competent managers. If the UK is to improve its international competitive position, then the enhancement of managerial competence at all levels is the key.

I would like to recommend *The Manager's Handbook* to both young and experienced managers as a valuable addition to their toolkit and as an excellent reference book on all managerial topics.

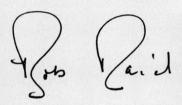

SIR BOB REID
CHAIRMAN, BRITISH RAIL

Who are you?

Self-knowledge is invaluable to any-one seriously intent on choosing the right life-path. If you, as a manager, don't know yourself, you will be led into making ill-advised decisions about your life and work from which it may be difficult or impossible to extri-cate yourself.

It would be wrong to suggest that self-knowledge is the key to manager-ial success. A good manager will need a range of skills and knowledge which come with experience. You will need to practise skills, take advice, use others' strengths and work hard. But self-examination is a good starting point and is rarely stressed when it comes to choosing the right job for you and doing your present job best.

The problem is that there is rarely time to stop and think: 'Hold on, do I *really* want to do this?' There are powerful pressures to go straight from school into a job; these stem from a perceived shortage of good jobs, the need to pay the rent, the need to be socially acceptable, the desire to be of value to the community and the desire to finance outside-work activities.

Job mismatch can also happen if your natural areas of skill and enjoy-ment are obscured by the desire to achieve simply for achievement's sake; by a natural competitiveness; or be-cause it seems somehow wrong to con-centrate solely on what is enjoyable or comes naturally. Companies now spend more time on matching people with jobs, using sophisticated tests, assessment centres and career coun-selling. Their costs, when they get it wrong, are great; yours could be inestimable.

If you are not enjoying your job, look at situations in the past where you have enjoyed yourself and done well at something. The chances are that you have strayed away from your natural abilities and a move to recap-ture them will be rewarding for you and the company you work for.

Am I in the right job?

People's values and interests change. Every so often you should ask your-self the following questions to find out whether you are still satisfied with your job. There is no 'right' answer except the truthful one.

● Do you begin to feel anxious in the evening at the prospect of work the next day?
● Do you talk obsessively to your partner about your work or about a member of staff? Or are you un-naturally reticent about them?
● Do you find yourself working late regularly or not taking your lunch hour because you feel you need to impress or because you have been given, or taken on, too much work?
● Are you offhand or short-tempered with your subordinates or peer colleagues?
● Are you enjoying your job and clear about where it is taking you?
● Do you feel your boss is incom-petent and that you could do his/her job just as well?
● Do you have pangs of envy when you hear your friends talk about their jobs? What do you envy? Their freedom? Responsibility? Opportun-ity to travel? Salary?
● Are you sick of being delegated to and not delegating?
● Do you feel run-down or stressed?
● Have you had to give up hobbies or interests because of work?

The Ancient Greeks thought self-knowledge so crucial that they had the phrase 'Know Yourself' carved above their temple entrances.

Is the job right for me?

If you feel dissatisfied in your work, ask yourself what you need:

- More money?
- Longer holiday allowance?
- Better contractual terms?
- More recognition for your efforts?
- More time for outside interests/ hobbies?
- An office or a bigger office to yourself?
- A personal assistant?
- More challenging tasks?
- More responsibility?
- More variety in your work?
- An expense account?
- Less travelling for extended periods?
- Better refreshment facilities?

It may be that your current job cannot give you, say, more money or more responsibility. But the task of analysing and focusing on what your needs are is crucial to an understanding of yourself.

Analyse your needs

To be an effective manager you must realize that your satisfaction requirements *change*. In the mid-1950s, A. H. Maslow, a pioneer in management psychology, put forward the theory that there are five basic needs which people aim to satisfy. How many of Maslow's needs does your job fulfil?

1 Physiological needs: the basic need for food, clothing, shelter

2 Safety needs: the need for security, continuity, protection against anything that threatens an organized orderly existence

3 Social needs: the need to belong and be accepted in a social context

4 Esteem needs: the need to have status and others' respect

5 Self-fulfilment needs: the need to feel fulfilled through the creative use of your natural aptitudes and practised skills which leads to 'self actualization'

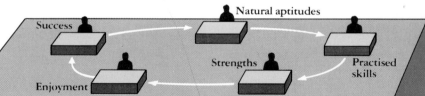

Success · Natural aptitudes · Strengths · Practised skills · Enjoyment

What are you good at?

If you are unhappy in your job, get back in touch with what you enjoy and are good at. What are your natural aptitudes and skills? Try to list, analyse and grade them. Then ask yourself whether you are concentrating on the most important. It is not easy, so where do you start? At the beginning.

All of us are born with a natural aptitude for something, whether it be a fascination for words or a flair for ball games. We are encouraged to practise and develop that particular talent. As a result, we come to have a definite strength; it might be a technical skill such as playing chess, tinkering with cars or something like being a good talker, getting on with people, taking responsibility. Whatever it is, we are bound to get enjoyment and a sense of satisfaction from doing it. This, in turn, naturally leads to success.

What type of person are you?

To know how you function in the office, what you are best and worst at, is all part of knowing yourself. Some managers deal with people in just the right way: neither too bossy nor too appeasing, they handle staff with tact and sensitivity, careful not to overlook individual needs while ensuring that the team or the department thrives as a whole. They also tend to get the job done and everyone benefits.

'With your creative ability, Peter's methodical approach and my analytical thinking, we make a great team!'

Others are great at thinking, solving problems but don't know how to handle people. No two managers are alike. What type of manager are you?

Carl Jung pioneered the study of personality types at the beginning of the century. He thought that people oriented themselves toward the world in either of two basic ways. 'Introverts' are most happy when they are by themselves doing their own thing; they do not pursue social activity and often feel uncomfortable in it.

'Extroverts' give their lives meaning from interaction with people and can feel at a loss when by themselves. Human beings are complex and don't fit into boxes. But some theories are a useful starting point for the difficult task of self-analysis.

Jung thought that we receive and process data via four functions: thinking, intuiting, feeling, sensing. Each person has one predominant function, one or two that are semideveloped, and one that is underdeveloped. As a 'thinker' you will be strong on clear, logical thinking; you will be methodical and be able to analyse problems.

As an 'intuitor' you will be good at ideas, creative or lateral thinking – the imaginative approach. The 'feeler' will see things according to personal values and not from a dispassionate weighing up of pros and cons; 'feelers' are warm, outgoing and thrive on social interaction. The 'sensor' is down-to-earth, energetic and practical, preferring action to words or ideas. The 'sensor' likes to get things done.

Concentrate on your strengths

● Try to recognize your basic bent or direction: it will give you belief in yourself, which in turn leads to motivation and energy.

● Work out what your strengths are – doing, organizing, analysing or what? You will then be in a good position to avoid a job mismatch.

● Ensure that your weaknesses are covered. If you are part of, or running, a team, make sure that there are those whose strengths can compensate for your weak points.

● Keep out of situations in which your weaknesses are likely to be continually exposed.

● If you have been given a specific task that will show you up, pick the brains of a colleague or delegate the job to someone you can trust.

● Remember, however, that you cannot avoid all situations that challenge your weaknesses: sometimes you must cope the best you can or learn to improve.

● It may be necessary to make fundamental changes to your situation if you are continually under pressure and your natural strengths are not being exploited.

● If you decide that you lack challenge or are going in the wrong direction, it may be that the only solution is to change jobs. If so, seek advice and reflect long and hard on the wisdom of such drastic action.

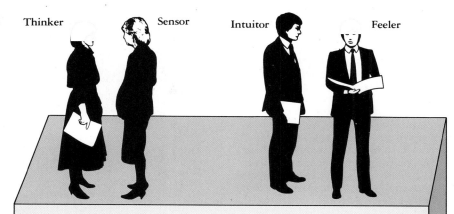

Thinker   Sensor   Intuitor   Feeler

Jung's four functions

As a manager it is useful to know whether you are an introvert or extrovert and which of the four functions is your strongest and which the weakest. Also, if you can spot the strong and weak functions of your subordinates, it will help you decide who will be most useful for different tasks and enable you to build effective teams.

Thinker
● Enjoys tackling problems with logic.
● Is strong on analysis but weak on implementing solutions.
● Is a methodical worker.
● Is sceptical of projects unless backed up with sound, rational arguments.
At work:
Good with facts and figures; researching; systems analysis; accounting; financial side of business.

Sensor
● Is good at getting things done, often impatient with the planning stage.
● Feels at home with routine work.
● Has a lot of common sense and is practical.
● Works hard and is usually well organized.
● Is energetic and single-minded.
At work:
Good at initiating projects; setting up deals; negotiating; troubleshooting; converting ideas into action.

Intuitor
● Enjoys playing with ideas and theories.
● Is good at seeing the 'overview' but misses the detail.
● Is creative and has a strong imaginative sense.
● Will often get hunches about things that turn out correctly.
At work:
Good at long-term planning; creative writing; lateral thinking; brainstorming.

Feeler
● Enjoys human company.
● Assesses on personal values not technical merit.
● Is warm and sympathetic.
● Is perceptive about peoples' moods, feelings and reactions.
● May overlook blatant facts in favour of 'gut feelings'.
At work:
Good at cementing team relationships; counselling; arbitrating; public relations; will talk as easily with a clerk as with an executive.

What do you value?

'My aim is more money.'

'I don't care what else the job has to offer, as long as I get to travel.' 'I started in Personnel, recruiting technical staff but realized I just had to get out to where the technical problems of production were actually being solved.'

To what extent values are innate or brought about by social conditioning is a vexed question. As children we are bombarded with other people's values. What makes us absorb some and not others is probably due to our psychological make-up. What is clear is that everyone has a personal value system and to be a good manager you should have a fair idea what yours consists of.

This is not always easy. It can take quite a time for dominant values to emerge. Also, people have many values and so it is necessary to work out your priorities – experience will help to show what they are. But be open to their changing.

Add your values to your natural aptitudes and strengths. Then you are well set to begin or continue a successful, happy career.

Review your personal balance sheet regularly and above all with an eye on tomorrow.

What do you value in your job?

- An ordered environment and security?
- The chance to help others?
- Freedom and flexibility?
- Being your own boss?
- The chance to achieve?
- Power, recognition or authority?
- A tangible finished product?
- Facts and figures to work with?
- Congenial people to work with?
- The chance to travel and meet people?
- A glamorous lifestyle?
- A high salary?
- A company car and other perks?

Do you value conformity and structure?
Conformity has negative connotations but many would admit to wanting it to some degree. To value conformity, order and structure is really to value security; a job that has a regular routine, in which roles are clearly defined and set procedures are used, can provide it. If you value security, look for a well-defined job that gives company benefits, such as health insurance and an adequate pension scheme.

Do you value helping others?
It could be said that all jobs benefit mankind, if only in the smallest way; but clearly some do so more directly than others. If you want to help others but don't want to be a nurse, doctor, teacher or social worker you could join the personnel or training departments of large companies: all organizations need their share of 'people' managers. Alternatively, you could use your managerial skills in the service of a charitable organization; philanthropy can compensate for a low income.

Do you value freedom and flexibility?
Some people hate regimentation in any form. A commuter-style routine, clocking in and out at specific times, may fill you with horror. If you value your freedom then make sure your job allows you a tolerable amount of flexibility. Can you come in 30 minutes late and make it up after hours? Can you wear more or less what you want? Does your boss fret every time you make a phone call?

'I'm going for the top job.'

'Security matters most to me.'

Do you value achievement?

The need to achieve is often instilled in a child by parents and the need for parental approval can last into adulthood as an unconscious drive: a desire to achieve without really knowing why and without being satisfied. If you do value achievement, make sure it is recognized and rewarded. If it is not, are you in the right job? Realize, however, that you cannot achieve everything at once. Set your sights on short-term attainable goals.

Do you value power?

Most people value power but few will admit it. To want power may disguise a need to be in control of your immediate environment and therefore your destiny: to be responsible, independent, to give orders rather than receive them. If you value power, choose an industry or company where power is recognized as a legitimate goal. But be careful not to alienate yourself through manipulation and unscrupulous behaviour.

Do you value a tangible product?

If, as a child, you loved making models, drawing pictures, building sand-castles, you may find that one of your priorities at work is to see something tangible produced. If you need the satisfaction of turning raw material into a finished product, avoid jobs, such as the Civil Service, that don't provide tangible results: you will be better off in an industry such as manufacturing, engineering or publishing.

Do you value facts and figures?

Accounting, computing and research oriented jobs are attractive if you prefer dealing with data to people. It may be that outside the office you have a rich, emotional, if not turbulent, personal life and that in your job you need something that makes no demands on your inner resources. Or you may be an introverted 'thinking' type who likes to work methodically through the day with minimal social interaction.

Do you value working with people?

For many, working with compatible colleagues has as much or more value than a high salary. If you interpret quality of life in terms of communication of ideas and rewarding friendships rather than material perks and incentives, you will be happiest in a job where it is no sin to chat with those around you. You might find journalism, public relations or local politics suitable.

Do you value financial success?

Some people grow up knowing nothing more than that they want to be rich. Money, what it can buy, the opportunities it affords are uppermost in their plans. If getting rich is your first priority, go for the big salaries and generous perks offered by large corporations or set up in business on your own. You are unlikely to become wealthy by working in public administration or the people professions.

15

Be aware of the future

In the final analysis, knowing yourself, and therefore arming yourself with the equipment to make correct choices concerning your life and job, is not something easily acquired.

It is *not* simply a matter of answering questionnaires, adding up your scores and drawing glib conclusions. Self-knowledge, as sages from Socrates to the Zen masters have avowed, is a process that continues as long as you are alive. There is no beginning or end.

Questioning yourself about your needs, personality type, strengths and weaknesses, and your values, is just a start. You should now try to develop a day-to-day awareness of your behaviour and attitude toward the myriad aspects of your life and work. Ultimately it is perception and sensitivity that determine whether you, as a manager, will be able to motivate, delegate, reprimand, negotiate, communicate and perform all the other managerial tasks.

Since life is a continuously flowing river and not a static pond, you should be aware that you are changing – your body, your thoughts, your attitudes – every moment. It is important, therefore, to keep up to date with yourself; to keep breaking the habit of thinking that you fit a particular mould.

You should keep a personal balance sheet, listing your strengths and weaknesses, values and desires, and then review it at a set date, every year or two years, to see how you have progressed. You may find, for instance, that on the debit side you listed 'Take things to heart too much and am too stressful' and then wondered, when reviewing it after a year, why you ever thought it was a problem.

Be prepared to change. After gaining better awareness of your strong and weak points, concentrate on your strengths: winning is about giving your strengths full rein. That is not to say that you should ignore an obvious weakness. It will have to be dealt with. Through effort, training and experience, most managers can become competent at all the managerial skills.

Finally, be aware that the rate of social change is increasing and that in

Facing up to the future

You should be aware of the fundamental changes in life that will affect you and your work, and be prepared to adapt accordingly

Starting out
After leaving school or university, you face the challenge of trying to establish yourself in the outside world. It is likely that you will be relatively fit and eager to get on with making money to pay for your rent and leisure activities. You will probably have lots of confidence and energy born from a lack of experience of failure, and these provide the necessary impetus to get you into your working life.

Getting established
Later on, perhaps from the age of 25 to the early 30s, you will start focusing outside work on your personal and emotional life. Your job may not be as exciting as it first was but you have begun to establish a financial base and are now looking for a partner to share your life and a house to buy. Now is also the time when you may start looking for an alternative job.

Consolidating
From late 20s to late 30s you will probably be fairly set in your job, even if you have changed careers,

the future more people may be working at or from home, and there will be more leisure time and job sharing. Change and impermanence are part of tomorrow's world. Be ready to accept the challenge.

and may be living with your partner in bought accommodation. Security will be high on your list of needs and you will still be ambitious, having been promoted but with more rungs to climb. You might have started a family. If so, you might find that your job, at least temporarily, becomes of secondary importance.

Staying on course
You might also find that babies mean sleepless nights and, coupled with a tailing off of your leisure activities, it is harder to cope and more stressful at work. If this happens to you, check to see whether your workload can be lightened by, say, delegating more. Also, make sure that you are using your talents and have not strayed away from using your natural core strengths.

Midlife turbulence
In their early 40s, men and women experience a phase of transition. The infamous midlife crisis may result in turbulent change for you and your partner. You may have anxious feelings about fulfilment, linked to concern about your career development.

Marriages can come under stress during these middle years. Couples may already have grown apart by this time: a jet setter on expenses, for example, is likely to grow away from a spouse with a less glamorous lifestyle; a middle-manager, dissatisfied with a humdrum job, may compensate by seeking excitement at the expense of family commitments.

If you have children, their adjustment to adolescence may coincide with your problems at middle age, heightening domestic conflict.

Planning for retirement
If you have weathered the storm that follows the midlife crisis, you should be able to cope with the next phase of readjustment. Now you should have settled for your position in the company and be making the best of it. Retirement will be increasingly on your mind: 'How will I cope? Should I be saving more? Shall I try to carry on working or negotiate a consultancy? Will I have the leisure interests to fill my day or will I be at a loss?' You will begin to take stock of your career and what you have and have not achieved.

Public image

If you know your basic direction, recognize what you need and value and are aware of your strengths and weaknesses, you will be in a position to sort out what kind of organization you should work for. Most important is to try to match your strengths with the company's needs.

Success in one company does not guarantee success in another. The management whizz-kids of the UK who did well in the orderly environment of Ford were unable, for example, to cope with the turbulent scenes at British Leyland when they were recruited into that troubled company in the 1970s. There is a world of difference between working for, say, Bank of America, British Steel Corporation, Sinclair Research or Pan Am.

Each organization needs different kinds of people to run it: some thrive on the intellectual challenge of systems administration, while others prefer the more human aspect of the personnel department.

Thus you should look at an organization and the job it offers and consider whether it suits you: is it a large conglomerate or a small family-owned business? Will it provide you with scope to gain experience or move up the promotion ladder? Will you fit in with the corporate 'culture'? How far does it match your strengths, weaknesses, values and needs?

The way a company is regarded by its competitors, its customers, the general public and by its employees tells you a lot about the organization and its style of management.

Many employees in large companies do not understand the complexity of the organizations for which they work. They work in specialist departments and see only the details which make up their particular contribution to the whole activity. To them the detail *is* the company: the more ambitious you are, the more you should keep the wider perspective in mind.

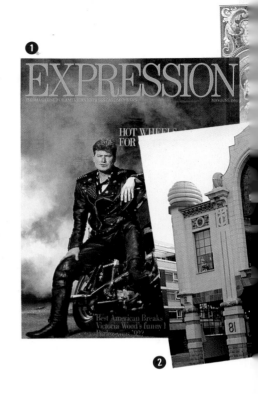

The corporate image

It is difficult to assess a company accurately from its outward manifestations. The products or services, the style of advertising, the buildings may all give a false or superficial idea of what life is like on the inside. You cannot tell what it is like to work for American Express simply from looking at its credit cards.

1 A company's literature is a poor indicator of corporate personality. Literature is often produced by groups outside the company whose job it is to create a desired image. But a company does not change every time a new advertising campaign is introduced.

2 A company's physical premises – its offices or factories – can indicate corporate personality. Small, spartan offices may show a down-at-heel company, but they could also be a sign of an efficient management anxious to keep

overheads to a minimum. The flamboyant Michelin building suits the image of the Paul Hamlyn publishing empire of which it is the headquarters.

3 It is important but difficult to assess what a company is like from its staff. At an interview, you should try to meet as many people as you can. Be aware of the back-up staff of secretaries, receptionists, telephonists. How a company treats those on the bottom rung is a good pointer to how they treat those at the middle/top.

4 A company with an advanced technological service/product does not necessarily have a progressive attitude to management.

More important are the price, quality and reliability of that service/product. Is it the best in its field? Does it deal in a high volume of small transactions or a small volume of high-quality transactions? What future does the service/product have?

Does the organization suit you?

● What reputation does the organization have? Is it, for example, known for high-quality goods or for giving good value for money?
● How is it regarded by its competitors and by the financial press?
● What sort of people work for it? Is there an old-boy network? Will you suit the profile of those at senior levels?
● Is it optimistic, go-ahead and expanding? Or the reverse?
● Do employees seem to be happy? Are there good conditions of employment?
● Is there a history of good or bad industrial relations?

19

First impressions

The first link with a company often occurs when you read its recruitment advertisement in a newspaper. Such ads tend to glorify the company, the job and the person needed to fill the post. You need to find out much more about a company you are considering joining.

Talk to friends, colleagues, people who have left the company and, if possible, those who are currently working there. You might pick up some company gossip from the local bar. Keep your eyes and ears open to the media and especially the pages of the financial press.

Get hold of the company's annual reports from the last two or three years and those of its chief competitors and compare them.

Remember, however, that the report is prepared primarily for shareholders or potential shareholders, bankers and financial institutions and the financial press. Consequently, it tries to show the company in the best possible light.

If, for example, the company feels it necessary to present a balance sheet that shows a lot of cash, it will manage its transactions near the year end to produce such a situation. Read the financial press for a more objective view of the company's performance and management.

Company reports will contain much accounting jargon; don't let it put you off. With a careful read through and some common sense, you should be able to deduce a considerable amount about the company's products, people, customers, markets, physical location, objectives and financial strength.

The comparative analysis over several years is often the richest source of information. Is the company achieving what it sets itself as a target? If the profit graphs show increasing earnings, are they increasing as fast as those of competitors?

1 What is the company's reputation in the market place? Is it well known and successful? What does the financial press say about it?

2 How significant is the expansion into Europe? Does the European flag give a true impression of the direction in which the company is heading?

3 What exactly does the job require? How many staff will it involve managing/ supervising? What happened to the previous incumbent? Was he/she promoted or fired?

4 Don't be put off by high demands. You may not be perfect, but nobody else is either.

5 Does the company have a reputation for efficiency and profitability? Will you have the resources to achieve the expected results?

Expo

Part of our professio our European sales ta motivation of our dis **High performance pr** The selected candidate and marketing to date for enthusiasm, a level Lotus at international le The lifestyle and the rev Telephone Nick Kemp, Norfolk NR14 8EZ on (0

LOTUS

Handlin

1 **How big is** the organizational unit in which you will work? How big is the management team in your unit?

2 **Does the ad** tell you the full extent of the duties you will be expected to perform? Have you really got the right type and level of skills for the job?

3 **To what extent** will you be working on your own? Who will you have to report to? What future career prospects does the job offer?

4 **How generous** is the remuneration package in comparison with your current job, or with similar vacancies? What do you think you are worth?

The annual report

From two or more annual reports you should be able to acquire the following basic information about a company:

● Ownership: who are the owners? What is the profile of those at the top?

● Corporate values and objectives: read the chairman's statements, bearing in mind what is not said.

● Products, services and investments: what exactly are they?

● Future plans and expectations: is it likely to diversify or take over another company?

● Financial position: study the accounts and the audit opinion.

● The relative profitability of the different business segments.

● Growth record: is it expanding? Is its market shrinking?

Size and scope

When it comes to choosing an organization to work for, size is important.

There can be a world of difference between a small family company and a giant multinational conglomerate. The accepted wisdom is that there are more opportunities in larger companies but a greater variety of work in smaller companies; large companies are formal and heavily bureaucratic, while small companies permit a high degree of flexibility and freedom.

In fact, there is only one rule: 'Don't make a judgement on size alone – investigate'. Giant organizations, such as GEC, may be split into small vigorous units. Small stagnant companies are just as common as large monolithic ones. Size is relative and not static: Apple Computers, for example, employed only a handful of people in 1977. By 1985 they had a workforce of several thousands.

Choosing an organization also depends on yourself: what stage of your career are you at? Are you building or

Organization A produces bathroom suites for the wholesale trade. It has a workforce of 500 people. It started life as a family-owned company but was taken over by a large overseas organization, involved in the same trade. The parent company operates worldwide and has its base in its home country's capital city. Three members of the family are still employed at senior levels: the father, a well respected local man, is still the chairman.

A number of expatriates have been installed at different levels. This local unit believes that it has autonomy and the authority to approve its own capital expenditure programme. The production facilities have been slightly modernized as a result of the takeover.

Questions you might ask yourself include:
● How many expatriates are there and is the company merely a place to gain experience for them?
● What influence and power do the expatriates have? Is the chairman just a nominal head kept on for good public relations with the local community?
● What exactly is the relationship between the expatriates and former senior figures/family members/other employees?
● What management practice does the parent company believe in? Does it understand the local mentality and attitude?
● Is there a point at which you are likely to go no further in the company?
● Is the local unit safe if something drastic happens to the parent company?
● Are the local unit's profits measured in the currency of the parent? If so, what is the risk of a damaging currency fluctuation?
● Have the modernized production facilities contributed to profits? Will there be more modernization and, if so, is there a risk of redundancies?
● Can the local unit really authorize its own capital expenditure programme?

consolidating? You must ask yourself exactly what you want: money, experience, a prestigious name to work for or a chance to develop new skills. Maybe you can find them all in one company.

It is more likely that you will have to compromise. If you want to build a career as quickly as possible, it may be best to go for a large company with a household name for an all-round training. Having got your blue-chip credential, you may then wish to take a risk with a smaller, less well-known firm where you are likely to have a greater degree of power and influence. But don't be put off by an unknown name: all the best-known companies have been unknown quantities at some stage.

Before making a decision about joining a company you should try to find out about its size and scope. Look at the two examples of organizations below and ask yourself the questions that follow.

Organization B deals in life insurance. It is publicly held and has a workforce of, 1,500 people. The head office is based in a capital city. It has prestigious premises: a marble entrance, plush carpets, canteen and executive dining suite. It has grown rapidly in the last ten years, with turnover and profits increased by 500 per cent. It has offices in every major city in the country and an extensive overseas network. The chairman came up through the ranks and is knowledgeable about the business. He is now 58 years old and due to retire.

Questions you might ask yourself include:
● How did the organization grow so fast – by merger/acquisition/real growth?
● What happens when the chairman retires? Is he the driving force behind the company? Does he set the management style? Has his succession been planned for?
● Is there a chance of the company being decentralized?

● Will you be based at head office or sent out to the provinces?
● Does its size suit you? Is it strong on systems? Does it have a bureaucracy that works?
● Does it have a formal, hierarchical structure?
● Will you get an overview of all the operations or will your knowledge be restricted to a few?
● Will you be near the seat of power? Will you pick up the rumours and undercurrents?
● Is there an old-boy network operating at senior levels? Do you match the profile of those at the top?
● Does the company practise equal opportunity? How many women are there in senior posts?

Corporate culture

As a manager, it is important for you to know the official company culture and to compare it with reality. Look at your company's recruitment brochure or annual report – it will be full of fine words giving a glowing picture of the company's performance and policies. But have these establishment values really permeated through the company? Are they shared by top executives and middle managers? Are they just for public relations?

A company may state clearly that it believes in equal opportunity between the sexes. The presence of women in top management provides more compelling evidence of its objective.

Company values take time to evolve into a shared, unwritten code of behaviour. Although hard to define, this corporate culture *is* recognizable in management style, budgets, priorities, attitudes to employees and customers, even notepaper.

There is a world of difference between the culture of an advertising agency and a local government office, for example, which shows not only in dress and language but also in the pace at which business is conducted.

You should know the culture of your own company as well as that of its rivals. The IBM corporation has a paternalistic culture: as an employee you are expected to devote yourself totally to the company and, in return for hard work and loyalty, you are looked after and well rewarded – both financially and with other substantial benefits.

By contrast, Apple, the computer company that has grown dramatically over a short time, has a forward-looking, optimistic culture, seeing itself as a David growing in strength at the expense of a Goliath.

Some companies have a customer-oriented culture: Marks & Spencer, for example, ensure that a customer can change a sweater or a pair of socks without question.

Are you aware of your company's culture?

- Is there a high turnover of staff?
- Is there a fast-moving, high achievement atmosphere?
- Are important decisions made at the top or does middle management run its own show?
- Is it bureaucratic or is there a high degree of freedom?
- What is its market strategy – to be a leader, follower, specialist?
- Is it R & D-oriented? Is it risk-oriented?
- Does it have a relaxed, first-name terms policy?
- Does it have a traditional, hierarchical structure?
- Does it have a systematic, predictable approach?
- Is it product-oriented and quality conscious?
- Is it bright, forward-looking and optimistic?

Culture clash

An example of the importance of 'management culture' was illustrated by the proposed merger in late 1983 between A. G. Stanley, the paints and wallpaper group, and Jacoa, the paints manufacturer.

The merger seemed to make business sense and would have created the largest home-decorating retail group in the UK. The merger was called off at a late stage in the negotiations.

The chairman of Stanley said, 'On the face of it the merger looked right, but when we got down to the nitty-gritty there were big differences in trading philosophy. I am not sure our management and theirs were quite convinced we could work with each other. There was a clash of personality.'

Shared values

Corporate culture at McDonald's is summed up in their motto: 'Quality, Service, Cleanliness and Value'.

Employees get precise instructions on the McDonald's view of QSC & V. Everything is spelled out – from choosing prime lean beef to requiring cashiers to make eye contact with and smile at every customer.

The result is a workforce steeped in the company's philosophy, enabling McDonald's to run thousands of successful restaurants with a relatively small number of corporate managers. The formula works internationally, as Muscovites will testify after consuming a Big Mac just like those sold in London, New York, Paris or Tallahassee.

This kind of employee involvement cannot be achieved through management controls but only through a system of shared values.

Unilever

BIRDS EYE

Timotei shampoo

Brooke Bond
PG tips

Persil
biological action
automatic

Cultural identity

What do Captain Birds Eye fish fingers have in common with a Cornetto, Flora margarine and PG tips? And with Vaseline, Signal toothpaste, Persil, Harmony hairspray and Lux soaps? Along with a host of other well-known household brands, they are all products of the Unilever group of companies.

Unilever's long story of success goes back over a hundred years in the UK to William Hesketh Lever, founder of Lever Brothers and of Port Sunlight village on Merseyside. Unilever itself was established

in 1930, when Lever Brothers merged with Margarine Unie of the Netherlands. Today, Unilever is one of the largest consumer goods businesses in the world.

As well as promoting the Unilever name, the company clearly understands the need to develop and market strong brand names. The corporate culture is doubly successful in that we admire the parent Unilever and we admire the brands, but we may not always make the association that the parent and the brands are both Unilever.

Who really has power?

If you function entirely within the outlines of your job description, operating within a standard area of activity, handling routine crises, there may be no need for you to know who has power.

But if you want to extend your sphere of influence by, say, doubling your department's staff, or getting new policy agreed and implemented, you need to find out who has command of resources. You have to know where the real power lies.

An obvious starting point is your company's organization chart: a typical chart consists of a series of functions set in boxes of the same size with neat connecting lines showing how power and authority flow downward, through departmental heads to the lowest levels.

To find out who actually has power, you need to read between the lines, checking out the links between powerful figures. No organization chart shows who generates ideas, which managers are related to each other, who play golf together, or who was recruited or trained by whom. Power rarely lies with one person; there is usually a group, linked by common experience or values.

Power may lie outside the organization chart if your company is a subsidiary or if the chief depends on outside advisers. The owners may have the whip hand; but if the number of shareholders runs into thousands, power will be diluted and will, in effect, revert to the directors.

The clever company allows itself to be driven by people who have key knowledge and/or up-to-date skills. In not-so-smart organizations the boardroom is filled with people whose power bases were built in the past. During a recession, financial control is needed at the top; when the economy is growing, it is ideas people who should be holding the reins.

To get new ideas implemented, you need to know who has influence and who has access to those with power. The chief executive's secretary may have little power but enormous influence. As well as knowing who makes the decisions you need to find out who influences decision-making.

Before planting your idea, ask yourself whose opinion the boss is going to seek. An approach from the side, via someone whose views the chief executive respects may be more effective than dropping a proposal directly on the boss's desk.

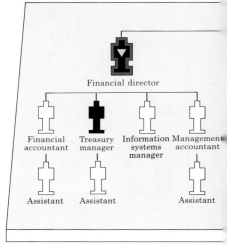

Financial director

Financial accountant

Treasury manager

Information systems manager

Management accountant

Assistant

Assistant

Assistant

Find out who has the power

● Which ideas are going to prove easy or difficult to get accepted?
● What criteria will be used to evaluate your ideas (and you)?
● Is the direct approach, via your immediate superior, always going to be the best one?
● With whom can you test ideas before launching them?
● Who should you get on your side before attempting to implement your ideas? Who is likely to be against them?
● In what order should you approach the people from whom you need support?
● Who is it best to speak to personally and who prefers memos?

Holders of power and influence

Imagine you have recently arrived in the sales department, recruited by the sales manager, interviewed by the sales and marketing director. You saw the chief executive for five minutes before your appointment was ratified.

To operate effectively, you need to consider the realities about power and influence in the organization chart. Many of these will not become apparent, in the normal course of events, for some time.

A complex triangle of relationships and influences will emerge. You will need to study it and test it before you can begin to plan how to get your best ideas agreed and implemented.

You should also try to discuss where the tensions are. Who fails to get on with whom? Which people have mutual respect for each other? You will need to add what you know about the personalities of the key figures.

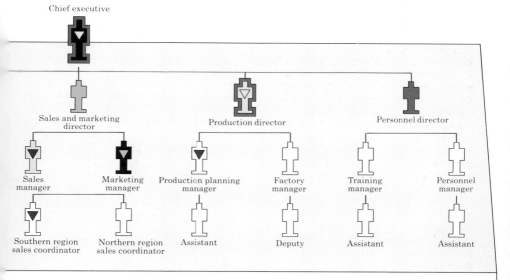

● **1 Social links**
The chief executive, the financial director and the personnel director's husband play golf at the same country club. The three wives socialize with the production director's sister and are members of the same local political party.

● **2 Education**
The sales manager, production planning manager and southern regional sales coordinator went to school together.

○ **3 Family ties**
The sales manager is married to the production director's sister.

○ **4 Company history**
The chief executive, the financial director and production director have each spent more than 25 years in the company. In that time it has grown substantially and each has a 4 per cent shareholding. The chief executive is an accountant and was formerly the financial director.

○ **5 Training**
The marketing manager was hired (seven years ago) by the sales and marketing director, when the latter was marketing manager.

● **6 Key skills**
The treasury manager's position is a recent creation. Cash flow questions are discussed every Monday by the chief executive, the financial director and the marketing manager. The chief executive's secretary usually takes notes.

27

Different departments/different tribes

No organization is just one huge homogeneous mass of individuals who look alike and speak exactly the same language. Rather, there exists within it a number of different departments with different functions to perform.

These 'tribes' develop their own collective identities and protective mechanisms; they have their own common language, dress, culture, rituals and 'watering holes'.

None of this is overt. On the face of it the tribal differences are unspoken and largely unrecognized. Nevertheless they do exist and you should try to understand the make-up of different tribes and ask yourself whether your own tribe is in a healthy, productive state. Is there good communication between tribal members, with a common language evolved from working together?

Even physical location can be important. If a department is hived off in a separate building down the street, it becomes even more isolated from the other tribal groups in the company. Isolation may mean that the tribe is removed from the centre of power and is forgotten. But it can also give that tribe a sense of identity and the feeling of being an élite corps.

Knowing your organization means understanding which tribes exist, what functions they perform, which are the most powerful, the most and least efficient, which tend to get the biggest slice of the budgetary cake, and so on. You should know which tribes are central to the company's operations and which are peripheral.

You should learn what differentiates one tribe from another – in function, educational background, and language – so that you can overcome the barriers when having to deal with members of different tribes.

On a day-to-day level, you should establish contacts in other departments – people you can draw on for information or help. By trial and awareness you should ensure you know the politics of other tribes. Who is the chief? Who is waiting to become chief? Who is excluded from the inner circle? If you know the politics, you will deal with them more effectively.

Be prepared, if you want to get something done, to listen to the ritual tribal moans. It may mean that you have to massage the ego of a salesperson, reassure a production chief that you know he/she is overworked or let Finance know that you respect their painstaking approach.

Tribes make up the organization and the link between a tribe and the company's power structure can have an impact on promotion prospects. If the head of your tribe becomes head of the company, everyone in the tribe will feel more important. If no one from your tribe ever gets anywhere near the top, ask yourself why.

What Finance may think of themselves	What others may think of Finance
'We are the custodians of the company's money; we control costs and protect the profits. We are meticulous and prudent and stop the company from making costly mistakes. If Production had their way, we would have ever-more expensive machinery eating up profits; as for Sales, they would pour far too much into unprofitable advertising.'	'They are routine-minded plodders who lack vision. They are far too cautious and obsessed with the business of measurement. They might be good at controlling costs, but they don't make the profits.'

Tribal stereotypes

'We sell to the customers and know exactly what they want.'

'The company's survival hinges on Sales.'

'Those customers modifications agreed to by Sales will be impossible to implement.'

What Production may think of themselves

'We are in the boiler room of the company, getting our hands dirty, making it happen. We are constantly being dictated to by Sales and Finance, who don't appreciate the problems we have, nor that the buck stops with us. We work hard, uncomplainingly, but without enough recognition. After all, we actually come up with the goods; without us there would be no business.'

What others may think of Production

'They are obstructive and obstreperous; closeted away in their own self-centred world, they are ignorant of the real needs of our customers. Their myopic outlook prevents them from seeing that the company survives because of other tribes apart from theirs. They're obsessed with deadlines, schedules, raw materials, quality control and goodness knows what else!'

What Marketing may think of themselves

We *are* the business. We look at the direction it's taking and make the decisions to steer it on course for prosperity. We have the necessary vision to cope with the ever-changing environment and plan for future success. We have to fight against the entrenched, obstructive attitudes of Finance, Sales and Production who can't see beyond today. The company's future is safe with us.'

What others may think of Marketing

'They are the visionaries who are so busy looking at the stars that they don't see the pot holes ahead. They're out of touch with the day-to-day reality of the business, so busy are they planning for its future. They could do with rolling their shirt sleeves up and getting down to some honest work.'

29

What are the rules?

When you join an organization, you cannot survive as a manager without knowing the rules and norms by which it operates.

To begin with you should read and follow the organization manual, if there is one. Note the physical manifestations of your company's corporate culture: use of first names, expected style of dress, executive dining-rooms, makes of company car etc.

You need quickly to gather enough verbal and non-verbal information to know the ropes. The more you value security, the more important will be the rapid establishment of your exact role – agreed objectives, precise tasks to perform and codes of behaviour.

Different organizations have different conventions and, within them, departments and employee levels have their own operating codes. Even individuals can have their own personal rules. At first, you may question the relevance of certain practices, but it may be wise to conform initially so as to be accepted by your colleagues.

Soon, you will be able to work out the norms particular to your department. But keep an eye on those who are in a position to promote you. If, say, you wish to be treated as an executive, think and act the part.

Once you feel in tune with your colleagues, you should try to distinguish the important rules and

Anita Roddick

Founder and managing director of The Body Shop, Anita Roddick opened her first shop in Britain in 1976, offering natural skin and hair products sold in specimen bottles to save costs.

Fifteen years later she controls a company with £20m profits and over 600 shops and 2,000 employees worldwide. In 1987 The Body Shop was voted the Company of the Year, and a year later Anita Roddick was awarded the OBE.

She attributes her success to 'energy, curiosity and breaking the rules'. The name The Body Shop was chosen because Roddick had seen the name above a car repair business in the US and 'liked it'.

Richard Branson

Ruler of the Virgin airline, record and entertainment businesses, Richard Branson has a reputation for unconventionality and derring-do. His houseboat lifestyle and record-breaking feats in boats and balloons are well known.

At 16, he started producing *The Student* magazine. In 1971 he opened his first record shop, and started the airline in 1984. By the late eighties he had not only taken Virgin into public ownership but then had the audacity to buy it back.

As Branson challenges the monopolies of the major airlines on the world's most profitable routes, he holds his basic beliefs in youth, controlling costs and entrepreneurship.

norms from the insignificant.

Be sure you know which rules are considered so important that breaking them would get you into real trouble. Many companies, for example, are fairly relaxed about checking employees' expenses but, in others, irregularities in claims may get you fired.

In some organizations, such as banks, you will not go far unless you are prepared to follow the rules, both official and unofficial. In others, there will be a better chance of succeeding if you break the rules ... carefully.

In all organizations, there are times when more damage is done by slavishly adhering to the rule book than by disregarding its contents.

Breaking the rules

If you plan to break an important rule, weigh up the risks and/or seek approval or protection from influential people. Ask yourself:
● Will flouting convention cause disapproval among those in a position to promote you?
● Will non-conformity draw attention to your innovative qualities?
● Will breaking the rules be interpreted as rebellion or creativity?
● Will breaking the rules bring trouble from your subordinates?
● Could you increase your influence by setting personal norms and expecting others to conform?

Robert Horton

An interest in politics and the Suez crisis steered Horton, who trained as an engineer, towards a career in the oil industry. At BP he acquired a reputation as a trouble-shooter, sorting out the company's tanker over-capacity in the 1970s, and its chemical business in the early eighties. He became head of Standard Oil of Ohio in 1986, and continued as CEO after BP acquired the company in 1987. He went on to become Chairman of BP in 1990.

Three years later, in February 1993, Horton was appointed Chairman of Railtrack, where his ambition remains undiminished. 'Our vision is to create a modern network equipped to meet Britain's needs in the 21st century.'

Steve Jobs

In 1977, Steve Jobs and Apple co-founder Stephen Wozniak set out to change the world through computers. Their employees produced the Apple MacIntosh and Apple grew from a capitalization of just over $5,000 in 1977 to $1.7 billion four years later.

Then problems began to set in. Apple's idealistic engineers came into conflict with the need for profit. The market called for new products, but production fell behind schedule. Jobs disagreed over strategy with the chief executive he had hired, and was fired by him. Jobs sold his Apple shares and set up a new company NeXt with backing from, among others, the Canon Corporation.

The winning team

If you are building a career in a company, you want to be associated with success. Winners will often be working for the team whose function is critical to the company's success. Winning teams have strong, visible leadership.

Look carefully at the departments in your organization. Work out which function is dominant.

Don't be misled by fashions in organizational thinking. A company may decide that better marketing is the key to success. The marketing department is expanded, budgets increased, and promotion prospects enhanced. Meanwhile, in purchasing, staff are unable to get authorization for the new typewriter they need. But fashions come and go. Don't commit yourself to a department without questioning whether or not it is a long-term winner.

Star billing, like fashion, has nothing to do with efficiency, nor with justice. A department that is doing its job well and making no demands on top management may be taken for granted. A less efficient department which is good at selling itself to top management may get both kudos and a bigger budget. If it is also coming up with good creative ideas, it may deserve its privileges.

Success may lie with the department that is on the up rather than the one at the top which is about to peak. What would happen if it lost its leader? A declining department may offer better opportunities if it has a potentially important contribution to make to the business. An effective leader may be able to build it up to become a winner.

Above all, it is department leaders who set the style. The best leaders marshal the functional expertise without losing sight of the corporate mission. They make winners of all they lead. To win, you need to be a good leader, or to work for one.

How to be in the right place at the right time

Consider which functions/departments in your organization:
● Are growing and which are declining in importance.
● Have been set up recently.
● Have the easiest time getting their budgets approved.
● Provide top people.

Ask yourself:
● Is this emphasis right for the company?
● Is it in line with its critical success factors?
● Will it take the company into the future?

Then ask yourself:
● Do you have the key skills/ knowledge the organization needs?
● Am I able to use them as a manager in a department that is, or should be, growing in importance?
● If so, get your act right and build your department to win.

Create a winning team by:
● Recruiting employees of high calibre. (But remember that moderate people can perform miracles if correctly led – and conversely a collection of stars is not necessarily a team).
● Generating enthusiasm so that they believe in themselves.
● Believing in yourself and your people.
● Using your management skills to build a team where individuals work for one another.
● Establishing high standards.
● Making sure that your department delivers what it promises and does not welch on commitments.
● Avoiding empty publicity which is not backed by solid achievement.
● Taking time to have your group's successes known and talked about throughout the organization.
● Building relationships with influential people.

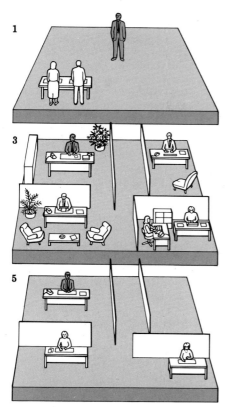
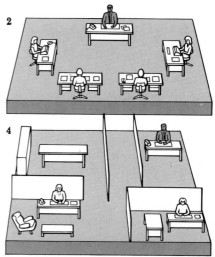

The rise and fall of a department

Consider the following scenario. Use this example to test whether your department is rising or falling.

1 The information systems (IS) department of a large organization had sunk to an all-time low: it lacked strong leadership, there was a high turnover of staff and morale was rock-bottom. But then the chief of the department left, and his successor, a dynamic, inspirational type, breathed new life into it. Its bad reputation was arrested, and it began to recruit high-calibre graduates attracted by the leader's vision.

2 The department's efficiency improved dramatically. Optimism pervaded the air. On the strength of its results, it managed to secure better offices, budgets, equipment and recruits of an even higher standard.

3 IS then became *the* department of the organization. The leader was the golden boy of the company and the envy of others. IS now had the plushest premises, the best recruits and a sizeable budget. But then, with his department on the crest of a wave, the leader decided to leave the company.

4 The new head of IS was competent but unable to match his predecessor. Earlier achievements could not be reproduced and top management became less well disposed. Budgets were reduced, staff began to leave and recruits were no longer high-calibre.

5 IS had sunk back to mediocrity. It was becoming stagnant and moribund. There was no sense of tribal identity. The few remaining long-serving staff romanticized about the 'good old days'.

The heart of the business

The best organizations have a clear view of what makes for success. Excellent organizations make sure that their critical success factors are understood by all employees.

But accurate identification is not easy and it is common to find survival confused with success. Without looking after its survival factors, a company could be left on the rocks. Without concentrating on its critical success factors, it will not *win*.

Reducing the myriad activities of your organization to a few essential operations is an excellent way to get to the heart of a company and find its driving force.

The activities that contribute to big profits or big losses point to critical success factors. All companies – whether large and complicated like oil companies or small and apparently simple like a grocer's shop – have a heart. Everything else is a sideshow.

For the Mobil Oil Company success depends on finding the right holes in the ground and owning them. Mobil's ability to refine the oil, though essential, is not critical to its success.

Critical success factors lie somewhere in what Michael Porter in *Competitive Advantage* defines as the 'value chain' – research/design, devel-opment, production, marketing/sales and distribution. Emphasis on success in one or more of these five areas enables a company to create and sustain an advantage over its competitors.

If big profits depend on consumer awareness, critical success lies in the marketing/sales section of the value chain. The quality of the product may determine survival, but for the manufacturer of cola drinks or lager, success depends on reaching the parts other advertisers haven't reached.

Successful companies keep in touch with the fundamentals of their business and concentrate on promoting and developing existing strengths. They diversify only when all other options have been exhausted.

Even with the emphasis still on the same section of the value chain, companies can run into trouble if they have failed to recognize their particular critical success factor.

When Quaker Oats extended its well-established sales and marketing strategy to include toys and restaurants as well as foods, their original products lost their market dominance.

The collapse of large companies can often be blamed on innovation that drains their life blood without regard for the heart of the business.

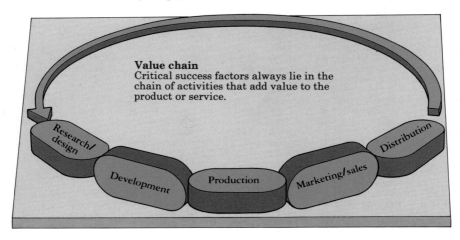

Value chain
Critical success factors always lie in the chain of activities that add value to the product or service.

Research/design

Development

Production

Marketing/sales

Distribution

From the mid-sixties through the late seventies, the car industry was largely in stasis. The technology was not moving, the markets unchanged. The race went to the organization that could make the product for the least money. During this period, the rise to prominence of the finance function at Ford Motor Company was the evidence of this critical success factor and gave rise to company sayings such as, 'We don't make cars, we make money.' But the game changed: fuel economy and pollution concerns have pushed manufacturers into computer management of the car's power unit, with a shift of success factors away from production cost into research. Ford is fit to face the major challenges of the nineties.

Sears, Roebuck and Co retained their critical success factor in the distribution section of the 'value chain' by adapting to changing circumstances. They did so with such resounding success that it took them right through two world wars and the Depression. Until the mid-1920s success was based on providing quality goods by mail order to the isolated American farmer. 'Satisfaction guaranteed or your money back' remained critical to success. But the change in markets brought about by the automobile made the company switch the emphasis from distribution by mail order to retail stores in cities. Thus, Sears served the motorized farmer as well as the city dweller with limited purchasing power.

SEARS, ROEBUCK AND CO.

In the five years up to 1990, THORN EMI grew profits by 203 per cent. Colin Southgate, the Chairman, attributes the success to adhering to a clear corporate strategy. The restructuring of THORN EMI that he initiated led to a focus on a limited number of businesses with the greatest international potential. This global strategy has expressed itself in a series of disposals of over 60 . companies that did not fit the new focus. The funds generated have led to the acquisition of 30 carefully selected businesses that complement the main activities. Significantly 90 per cent of this focused investment has been outside the United Kingdom.

In order for staff to maximize their potential, responsibility is devolved throughout the company giving people a sense of 'ownership' of their activities. Imagination, innovation and flexibility are all encouraged and the results are left to speak for themselves.

Adapting to survive

Your organization's critical success factor may be different next year and then again the year after. Markets and environments do not stand still, and critical success factors must work toward a future goal.

A company's ability to adapt to change is the key to its long-term success. Strength in the marketplace is of direct concern to someone who is looking to build a career in a particular organization.

If a company is to be consistently successful in adapting to new circumstances, its power structure has to be in tune with the realities of a changing marketplace, a changing world economy and shifts in society.

Is your organization recruiting high-calibre young people with leadership potential? Are those in charge of your organization harping on about outmoded themes or looking to the future?

Is your organization's future policy based on fashion, which starts in the centre, moves outward and dies? Or is it in tune with trends that start at grassroots level and grow?

Some organizations are flexible enough to respond quickly to new circumstances. Others are too short-sighted or too cumbersome to adapt to change.

The Minnesota Mining & Manufacturing Company makes 45,000 different products, among them the highly profitable Post-it note pads. The secret of success lies in 3M's ability to nurture creativity: change is an essential part of the company's corporate philosophy. National Cash Register left it almost too late to adapt to the electronic age. The once great British engineering company Alfred Herbert was unable to change and is now extinct.

Does your organization shrink from the prospect of change? Or does it embrace change as a means of gaining competitive advantage?

Signs of an organization heading for problems

● Diminishing market share
● Low profit margins together with low volume
● Ageing products
● Consistent dissatisfaction of customers
● Quality/reliability problems
● Consistently late deliveries
● Heavy dependence on one or two customers/suppliers
● Long-term fixed-price contracts
● Heavy borrowing requirement
● Production methods which are old-fashioned
● Poor industrial relations
● High turnover of employees
● Management out of tune with commercial realities
● Top-heavy organization
● Inflexible management
● Lack of communication between management and employees
● Inward-looking management

Signs of a forward-looking company

● Awareness of competition
● High investment in research and development
● Regular flow of new products
● Careful use of consumer research and test marketing
● Rapid response to complaints of customers
● The quality the customer wants
● Concern for customer service
● Pricing that is appropriate to the customer
● Enthusiastic employees
● Accessible management
● Flexible organization
● Decentralized decision-making
● Concentration on critical success factors
● Supportive financial controls

In 1950, Britain made 80 per cent of the world's motor cycles. Like other famous makes, Triumph was badly hit by inefficient and old-fashioned production methods, poor marketing and product development and, of course, Japanese competition. Britain's share of the world market for motor cycles has fallen below one per cent. But Triumph still exists and is even launching a new superbike, the Trophy 1200, in the early nineties. Success for the company will depend on many things, not least on creating an after-sales service to match their German and Japanese competitors.

Traditional shipbuilding industries in the developed countries of Europe and the USA have been squeezed out of business by world labour forces. The need for developing countries with largely unskilled labour forces to employ large numbers of people has led their governments to support such heavy industries by subsidizing them. The more forward-looking Western shipbuilders saw that a market remained for specialist ships and for sophisticated engineering components such as automated steering systems. Their ability to adapt to changing world trends ensured their survival.

No business is more competitive and more subject to change than the computer industry, and few companies have been quicker on their feet than Apple, whose founders spotted a new market and exploited it before anyone else. The Macintosh™ was a great success. Its user-friendliness posed a significant threat to IBM and in the early nineties, these intense commercial rivals agreed to cooperate in research – something which would have been unthinkable before. It was a strategic master stroke, a response to customer demand for their machines to be compatible.

Making the right choice

Choosing the organization that is right for you is never easy. To be sure what life inside any organization is like is impossible without actually being part of it for some time. Even if you get the answer right initially, situations can change. The loss of a major customer, a takeover, financial difficulties or the departure of your immediate boss can bring dramatic and often unexpected change.

Once inside and working hard there is still no guarantee that success is yours. The social maelstrom of business (often as complex and uncompromising as family relationships) can cause frustration and failure.

Factors which ought not, perhaps,

Its public image
● Are you comfortable with the face your organization presents to the world?
● Does the advertising and other literature give an accurate picture?
● Do you feel your organization earns its reputation? If not, can you see why?
● Is it reflecting where the organization is going?

Size and shape
● Does the size of your organization suit the point you are at in your career?
● Is it providing you with the right experience?
● Are you a big fish in a small pond? If so, is that the way you want to stay?
● Is it time to seek a different organization and another range of issues?
● Can you quantify clearly what you have learnt in this organization in the last 12 months?
● Are your particular talents being exploited?
● Is the organization run from the centre or do you have local autonomy for important decisions?
● Is it growing or in decline?
● Is it characterized by leanness, efficiency and profitability or is it bureaucratic and hampered by its own systems?

Culture
● Can you believe in what your company is doing or making?
● Is it positive or negative, backward-facing or forward-looking?
● What behaviour patterns are valued? Loyalty, respect for authority, conforming? Diligence, meeting deadlines, holding your budget? Getting results? Generating new ideas? Questioning the status quo? Seeking new directions?
● Is the culture appropriate to the market in which it operates?
● Is the culture one into which you can fit?
● Are your values in tune with those espoused by the organization?
● What is the reaction of your spouse/friends to your definition of this culture?

Power structure
● Do you know who has real power? Do the holders of power know you? If not, are they likely to do so in the foreseeable future?
● Can you point to those who have influence but may not have power?
● Do *all* the most senior figures actually have power?
● Could you draw the unofficial links (family, education, social, etc) on the organization chart?
● Do you have access to enough influence or power to do your job effectively?
● What are the backgrounds of the top management group?
● Do you respect them?
● Are the skills, knowledge and/or contacts of those in power relevant to today's business ... and how about tomorrow's?

to be a part of a respectable commercial organization are often, in reality, the essential factors in individual and corporate success and failure. Envy, spite, greed, bloody-mindedness, cunning may all have to be countered! Enthusiasm, energy, determination, skill, competence, conscientiousness will have to be generated.

And yet, once the cultural and tribal issues are recognized, when you sort out how to handle the rules, deal with power, concentrate on basic business transactions, management becomes much easier.

Getting to grips with these issues will involve your answering regularly the following types of questions:

Tribal features
● Can you recognize the tribes and their features (language, dress, rituals, etc) that exist in the organization?
● Which are the most powerful tribes in the organization at the moment?
● Which are the tribal features that make your department stand out?
● Do you have a clear view of your own department's contribution to the organization? Is it important to the core of the business, necessary or just nice?
● Is your department consulted first on new ideas? If not, should it be?

Rules
● Does your organization have a rule book? Is there any indication that it is a working document or merely a rarely consulted reference book?
● What are the unwritten rules and operating codes?
● Do you know what the important rules are and can you justify them in the light of the critical success factors of the business?
● To whom would you look for cover and support if you needed to break them?

Winners
● Can you identify the leaders of winning teams in your organization?
● Is yours a winning department, full of enthusiasts? Is their enthusiasm directed at profitable activities?
● Could they survive losing the person who leads them?
● Does it suit you to be one of the winning pack?
● If your team is less valued than others, how could it be improved?
● Would you know how to create a winning team if you were given a chance?

The heart
● Can you define what makes your organization tick?
● Do you know *what* makes its profit?
● Do you know *who* makes its profit?
● Can you describe your organization's critical success factors?
● If you don't know your organization's critical success factors, how can you find out? Is it possible that no attempt has been made to define them?
● Is there any opportunity for you to take the lead in getting them defined?

The future
● Is your organization responsive to change?
● Where do you fit into tomorrow's organization?
● What significant changes are on the horizon? Define them under 'environmental influences', 'legal changes', 'sociological conditions', 'political influences', 'technological advances'.
● Are the people your organization is recruiting now going to make chief executives in the 21st century?
● Have you prepared a list of those signs that may indicate that your organization is well equipped for the future? Or on its way into trouble?

What is a business?

The enterprise in which you operate as a manager is unique. Nevertheless, every corporation, foundation, government department, even a small business, has a number of common features.

An organization comes into being and continues to function as a result of internal and external influences.

It must have objectives, explicit or implicit. These can range from maximization of return on investment to provision of a service to the community.

There must be owners. These may range from shareholders to the electorate who vote in a government. The owners provide the initial funding for the organization, which can then attract or generate additional funding.

The owners always have the right to influence the organization's objectives and its direction. (Even a tax-payer has the right to vote for a change in the direction of a democratically elected government.)

To operate effectively, the organization also needs a management control structure, usually of hierarchical form. Even in the apparently equal partnerships of some financial institutions, there is usually a structure of command and a system of ranking hidden from public view. Organizations always contain people who lead and those who are led.

With funding and a management structure, the organization can operate and put its objectives into effect. Operations, whether the manufacture and production of goods and materials or the provision of services or financial resources, are usually carried out by a team of people. They are responsible through the management structure to the owners. The responsibility

	Corporation (public/private)	Public utility
Objective	To make profit or raise net assets by providing goods or services	To provide optimum service in a specific field within a pre-determined budget
Owners	Investors, share-holders, sole owners	Government, local or national
Control structure	Board of directors elected by franchised shareholders	Board of directors usually nominated by the appropriate government body
Operations	Chairman, managing director, executive directors, managers	Chairman, non-executive directors, executive directors, managers
Prime activities	Trading, manufacture and provision of services	Provision of service
Business emphasis	Maximization of profit or return	To increase the quality and range of the service provided

for the day-to-day operations is therefore nearly always delegated to the executive management.

The operations of any organization are influenced by two further common factors: the organization's prime activities and the stress placed on certain business functions (eg selling, quality assurance, recruitment, purchasing).

Prime activities are the achievement of the owners' objectives and are as varied as the organizations themselves. In every organization, however, these core activities form the mainstream of the business and the reason for being in business.

Although operational management may have some degree of flexibility in developing the growth and direction of these activities, they nevertheless remain the essential product of the organization until such time as the owners change their objectives.

The amount of stress placed on individual functions, however, can be influenced by the management structure. There are always a number of routes or strategies by which the objectives of the organization can be achieved. The ability to direct the way in which a business develops is one of the prime motivational factors for executive managers.

Where there are different degrees of success in achieving the organization's objectives, this can often be attributed to the abilities of the individuals within the management structure to direct the emphasis and thrust of the business to achieve the best results.

Within any organization, which is set up to control and manage a business, these elements are always apparent to a greater or lesser degree.

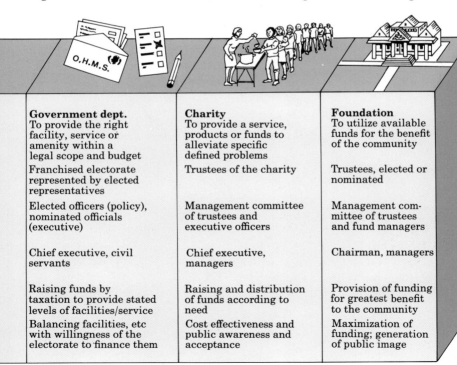

Government dept.	Charity	Foundation
To provide the right facility, service or amenity within a legal scope and budget	To provide a service, products or funds to alleviate specific defined problems	To utilize available funds for the benefit of the community
Franchised electorate represented by elected representatives	Trustees of the charity	Trustees, elected or nominated
Elected officers (policy), nominated officials (executive)	Management committee of trustees and executive officers	Management committee of trustees and fund managers
Chief executive, civil servants	Chief executive, managers	Chairman, managers
Raising funds by taxation to provide stated levels of facilities/service	Raising and distribution of funds according to need	Provision of funding for greatest benefit to the community
Balancing facilities, etc with willingness of the electorate to finance them	Cost effectiveness and public awareness and acceptance	Maximization of funding; generation of public image

The anatomy of a company

A business is an enterprise created for the purpose of trading for profit and other assets it generates. Essentially it consists of groups of people joining together for the common purpose of achieving a reward in return for the injection of resources into the enterprise.

The groups of people are owners and employees. Trading activity consists of three core functions:

● Buying: the acquisition of materials and resources for use in the business

● Making : changing the state of the materials and resources (ie adding value)

● Selling: the disposal of the materials and enhanced resources.

Subsidiary activities within the business include:

● Management, which provides direction for the business and its parts

● Control, including planning, scheduling, monitoring measurement and reporting

● Administration, which provides the functions and systems supporting the organization and all communications between the constituent parts.

The success of the enterprise is defined by the profit it generates (or sales income less the cost of achieving it). The quality of success is measured by comparing the ability of the enterprise to generate profit with the performance of other enterprises in similar industries.

The markets

Each business coexists with its competitors in four marketplaces:

● The customer market in which customers and potential customers exist.

● The ownership market, in which the ownership of companies may be traded. (The trading of ownership is a business in its own right: the increased value of the company through its enhanced performance, or the perceived probability of its enhanced performances relative to other businesses.)

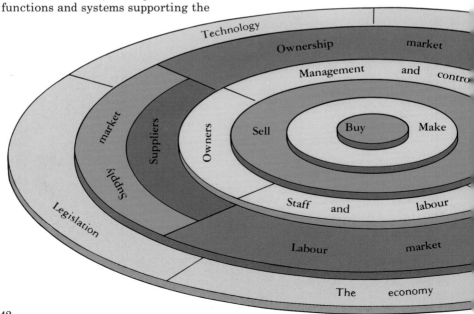

● The supply market, where physical assets may be obtained including loan capital, fixed assets, supplies and consumables.

● The labour market, which resembles the supply market except that it relates to the acquisition of persons.

The environment

The markets exist within an environment which contains other organizations that have no direct impact on the business's trading. Some of the organizations (eg governments) have direct but not trading relationships with the business. Most do not. However, they will have an indirect impact on the business through perceived changes in:

● The economy
● Legislation
● Technology
● Ecology/pollution
● Social attitudes

The business organism

A business is a living entity. Its anatomy and physiology can be described in terms of:

● The heart: buying, making and selling are the heart of a business. Heart failure, arising from lack of management blood or the collapse of individual functions, causes death.

● Blood supply: management is the life blood of a business, carrying life-giving oxygen (ideas of direction).

● The skeleton: businesses are vertebrates. Their structure is defined by organization. As the business grows, its skeleton should change in shape as well as in size.

● The nervous system: communication is carried out by the nervous system. The brain issues instructions, plans all schedules. The nerves detect variations of behaviour, measuring them and reporting back to the brain, which analyses the signals, modifies them and issues revised instructions.

● Behaviour: businesses are social animals whose behaviour ranges from contributory to predatory.

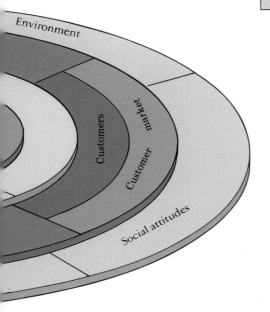

Businesses exist in a complex of markets consisting of the people/organizations with whom the business interacts, within an environment (*outer ring*) containing organizations, factors and attitudes which affect the markets.

The structure of a business

In order to achieve its objectives, every organization must continually keep in balance the external and internal forces which affect it.

Most organizations carry out this balancing process by means of some form of management committee, or board of directors, coordinated by a chief executive.

Depending on the type of organization, the board may be two tiered, ie having a non-executive, policy-making body that has been elected by shareholders with a second operating executive committee; or it may be a combination of both.

This combination of non-executive and executive officers provides the mechanism by which the external and internal forces are balanced at the highest level within the organization.

The board or committee then provides the policy guidance and directional control for the organization's operating management.

The operating management is responsible for the day-to-day running of the business, usually through a hierarchical structure of subordinate managers down to foremen and supervisors.

These managers are then organized divisionally and by departmental disciplines but cannot function independently in a vacuum.

In consequence, in almost every organization there are also a number of key sub-committees which, collectively, are responsible for the overall coordination of medium and short-term strategies.

The ever-constant interplay between the separate functions, particularly in the transfer of data and information, allows the organization to function cohesively.

Although no two organizations are identical and their objectives and business emphasis may widely differ, each will nevertheless function in this same way.

The functions of a typical organization

The central framework of a typical business (*right*) is affected by external and internal forces.

External forces include:
Owners: private individuals purchase a share of business equity with the expectation of a share of distributed profits.

Financial institutions invest funds in the business to create more wealth.

Banks: these provide cash funding for the operation of the business, based on agreed security, to generate wealth from interest levied.

Legislation: including company and trade union law, environmental and other national statutory legislation. It dictates the framework in which the operations of the organization can be conducted.

Auditors: independent accountants elected by the shareholders to verify the accuracy of corporate financial information and performance and compliance with statutory or regulatory financial requirements.

Internal forces include:
Operating committees: comprising nominees from the board of directors and senior management. Responsible for formulation of policy and directional control for activities such as:
● Product policy
● Finance and treasury
● Corporate strategy
● Human resources
● Quality

Departmental directors: heads of departments responsible for direction and performance against objectives and budgets for areas such as:
● Finance
● Sales
● Production
● Product development
● Information systems

Managers: executives contracted by the organization to coordinate, manage or provide specialist skills. Operate within specific parameters laid down by the board and departmental directors. Control day-to-day operations and management of staff and labour.

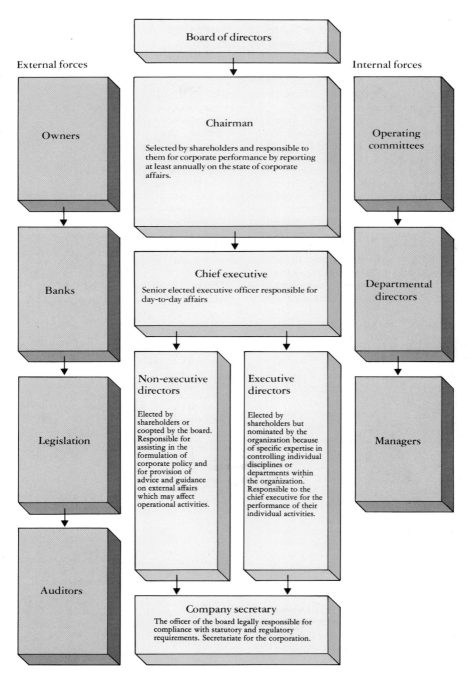

Board of directors

External forces

Chairman

Selected by shareholders and responsible to them for corporate performance by reporting at least annually on the state of corporate affairs.

Internal forces

Owners

Operating committees

Chief executive

Senior elected executive officer responsible for day-to-day affairs

Banks

Departmental directors

Non-executive directors

Elected by shareholders or coopted by the board. Responsible for assisting in the formulation of corporate policy and for provision of advice and guidance on external affairs which may affect operational activities.

Executive directors

Elected by shareholders but nominated by the organization because of specific expertise in controlling individual disciplines or departments within the organization. Responsible to the chief executive for the performance of their individual activities.

Legislation

Managers

Auditors

Company secretary

The officer of the board legally responsible for compliance with statutory and regulatory requirements. Secretariate for the corporation.

Planning future directions

Strategy was originally a term applied to warfare; it was defined as 'the art of planning and directing larger military movements and the operations of war'. In business, strategic management is now accepted as the discipline of managing any organization's resources to achieve long-term objectives.

The origins of strategic business management are to be found in the long-range planning used in the fifties and sixties when markets were expanding and company policy was based on a belief in growth.

The stagnation of the early seventies highlighted the growing awareness that the then available planning techniques were inadequate to deal with business problems.

The new concept was that the fundamental strength of a company could be related to the development of strategic success potentials.

Strategic phases

The strategy of an organization has a life cycle: a dormant phase and a development phase. Because strategic issues are not considered or minor adjustments are made to strategy through a process of periodic review, organizations spend most of their time in the dormant phase.

From time to time, however, organizations recognize that they have a need for a fundamental appraisal of where the business is going. Upon recognizing the need for fundamental change, management embarks on the development of a strategic success position (SSP).

Strategic success potentials

A company's potential for strategic success may be defined as those company activities which result in above average long-term profits. They are generally related to products and mar-

Typical approach

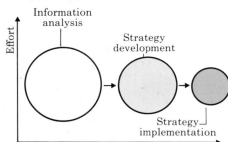

Too often, resources are misallocated in a strategy process. So much effort goes into information analysis that strategy development and implementation receive less overall effort. This inevitably results in less effective strategies and incomplete implementation. It is estimated that 95 per cent of the strategic plans developed in the last two decades were not fully implemented.

Better approach

Increasing the level of effort devoted to strategy development and implementation, and merging the phases by emphasizing improvements that can be implemented without waiting for the completion of the entire process, offers a better chance of sucessful implementation.

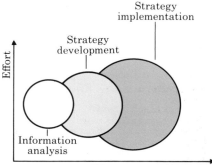

kets and are commonly perceived as high-quality/service standards, public image, low production costs or distribution advantages.

Traditionally, success potentials are identified from analysis of
● The company's characteristics in the context of its competition
● The environment and the potential for success that it offers.

More recently, it has become accepted that there are two further key attributes:
● Flexibility, or the potential for altering strategy at short notice in a rapidly changing environment
● Implementability, or the ability of an organization to accept a strategy in view of its culture.

Strategic planning
Commonly not a conscious process, strategic planning should include:
● Setting objectives, or redefining what 'success' should mean to the organization
● Information analysis or reviewing the characteristics of the organization and the environment to link internal strengths to external opportunities
● Strategic choice, or taking decisions on the direction of the company and formulating a plan.

Implementation of strategy
The most important aspect of strategic management is the organization and control of implementing the business plan. The 'best' technical plan will not succeed unless it is appropriate to the culture of the organization. Failure to communicate the strategy will mean that there is little chance of operational managers recognizing the direction of the company and taking appropriate decisions. The priorities of the company should be demonstrated to operational managers.

The strategic cycle

Developing a strategy
Business plan annual update
Implementation of strategy
Information analysis
Business plan annual update

Performance deterioration

Business plan

Strategic planning

Environment change
Management/owner change

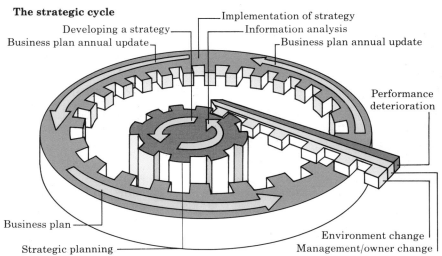

The strategic changes normally occur because:
1 The aspirations and requirements of the owners and/or managers have changed (or the individuals themselves have changed).
2 The environment has changed:
● Market opportunity has increased/decreased.
● Technology offers increased opportunities/threats.
● Economy has improved/declined or led to a modified distribution of wealth.
● The social and/or legislative background has altered.
3 The present plan is failing to meet its perceived objectives because of competitive activity or poor performance.

Analysing your position

Strategic analysis means measuring the organization's strengths and weaknesses and the opportunities and threats presented by the environment.

It is best carried out by the organization's own management in conjunction with external consultants. Management must be involved if it is to believe the output of the analysis and provide detailed knowledge of the organization.

Consultants provide the specialist analytical skills and an independent view to ensure management does not believe its own propaganda.

SWOT

SWOT is an acronym for Strengths, Weaknesses, Opportunities and Threats.

Strengths and weaknesses are internal characteristics of all organizations. The most common technique for identifying them is brainstorming by groups of 10 to 12 senior managers. Once the key factors have been subjectively identified, detailed objective analysis is required.

External circumstance is regarded as an opportunity or a threat depending on the organization's ability to exploit it. A progressive company welcomes technological change; a conservative company, however, feels at risk from it.

Base potential

Organizations tend to be either too optimistic or pessimistic and this is usually reflected in managers' perceptions of their own companies. Some companies have a tendency to believe their own (positive) propaganda, whereas others often see only their own faults.

The SWOT analysis must therefore be vigorously tested. Base potential analysis looks in detail at the internal parts of the analysis using five main headings:

Existing resource: what financial facilities are available; how adequate are the current physical assets and labour force as a base for the future? How strong are existing products?

Experience: how experienced is the organization at managing change; product development; operating in existing and new markets?

Control: how good are the information systems; does the organization adequately plan/budget; who makes the decisions?

Leadership: how involved are the owners; what are their personal ambitions/objectives; what is the organization's preferred management style?

Ideas: how active is the organization in research and development; are good ideas encouraged/developed/promoted?

Objective analysis of this nature will help identify true strengths and weaknesses. Often external consultants are used to facilitate the process and to provide independent objectivity.

The consultant's role

Consultants can help management identify and gather the information needed for successful strategic analysis. Their objective views are particularly helpful when attempting to interpret it as the basis for longer term direction setting. You should work closely with them on:

- Validation of findings
- Description of internal processes and capacities
- Review of operative and junior management skills
- Review of middle management skills
- Quantitative market research
- Competition analysis
- Review of all technological innovation
- Organization review
- Survey of customer opinions and attitudes
- Validation of all management claims
- Preparing comparative reports.

SWOT, the acronym of strengths, weaknesses, opportunities and threats, is a summing up of the factors affecting strategic analysis.

Strengths represent the basis on which success can be built.

Analysis may reveal weaknesses, such as obsolescent machinery, which can be remedied if financial resources are strong.

Opportunities should be sought, recognized and grasped as they arise.

Threats must be acknowledged and steps taken to deal with them.

SWOT

Internal – strengths and weaknesses

People	– skills, training, attitude
Organization	– structure and relationships
Systems/ Communications	– formal/informal, manual, computer – and telecommunication
Products	– quality, life, cost
Production	– nature, capacity, quality
Finance	– balance sheet, profit and loss account, cash flow
Credentials	– reputation, track record, customer perception
Knowledge	– technical, market, competition

External – opportunities and threats

Market	– growth, decline, movement, fashion
Technology	– product development, substitution, production technology
Economy	– export/import, sterling strength
Society	– sales practice, employment practice, trade union practice
Legislation	– consumer protection, product liability
Ecology	– energy, raw materials, recycling, environmental protection, pollution control

Base potential

Existing resource	Experience	Control	Leadership	Ideas
Liquidity and availability of finance	Age of company	Adequacy of information and control systems	Ownership and involvement of owners	Research and development – if any
Technology	Experience of:		Age of owners	
Physical assets	– borrowing	Degree of professionalism and responsibility of management team	Professional occupational base of key directors	Number of ideas currently being seriously considered
Labour quality, skills, age, attitude, flexibility	– product development – different markets		Personal objectives and degree of ambition	Degree of development and/or testing of these ideas
Product range and life	– external agents	Adequacy of planning and budgeting	Education and/or training background	Degree of market planning of these ideas
Managerial resources	– moving location	Degree of delegation to the team	Personal capabilities	
Customer base and loyalty	– managing growth		Management style	
			Personal attitude to change	
			Degree of strategic awareness and understanding of environment	

Writing a strategic plan

The objective of strategic planning is to change the behaviour of everyone from the top down. Awareness of and commitment to the same direction should result in actual movement in the same direction.

The strategic plan is the document which encapsulates the thinking which has gone into setting this direction. It need not be bulky, but it should provide a clear framework or map against which more detailed annual business and functional plans can be developed and reviewed.

A strategic planning framework

Many strategic plans are too complicated. The best strategies have a simplicity which readily conveys the linkages between the various steps in the process. Key elements include:

● **Mission (or vision) statement** The long term aim, the *raison d'être*. It is often the most difficult stage to agree, perhaps because it is more visible than the rest of the plan. The statement should be easily understood and should define the business the company wants to be in, be measurable, differentiate the company from competition, be relevant to everyone, and be stimulating and exciting. The mission is an important statement, a key means of communicating the strategy to the work force.

● **Goals** Elaborate the key elements of the mission. As such they will often be agreed upon before the mission statement is settled. Goals are usually considered in these categories:

1 **Distinctive capabilities** Form the basis of the company's competitive strategy. What can the company do which sets it apart? What differentiates it from its competitors?

2 **Products/market** Cover the various sectors of the business and define the range of activities the company wishes to be occupied in. Geographical boundaries ('in the UK', 'in Europe') will also be considered.

3 **Position** What the company wishes to achieve related to market share and physical size.

4 **Profitability** The expectations of the key stakeholders (owners) will be reflected, as will the company's wishes to provide funds for future investment.

5 **Values** An expression of the shared values and beliefs toward which managers and employees will direct their policies and actions.

● **Measures of performance** The milestones by which the organization can assess its progress in attaining its declared goals over time. They recognize that the goals cannot be achieved overnight and set standards of achievement/targets to be reached along the way. Milestones need to be reviewed, and possibly amended, as activities progress against the plan.

● **Functional strategies** The principal actions which will allow the milestones to be reached and therefore the goals to be achieved. They set the objectives for each department across the organization and are therefore a prime input to the detailed business plans and budgets.

Making the plan work

Preparation of a strategic plan alone will not make things happen. Chances of success are enhanced if:

● Management is committed to implementing the plan and their actions match their words.

● An appropriate organizational structure is established. An inappropriate structure can be a stumbling block. Companies often find that they have some wrong people in wrong jobs – even at the very top.

● The plan is communicated to all staff. Everybody doesn't need all of the detail, but everyone needs to know the essence so that they can play their part in its implementation.

● Management information reflects what is trying to be achieved. This may require systems development.

● Progress is reviewed regularly.

Essential features

Management organization

Growth and development
Every enterprise is unique. It comprises individuals directed toward survival and success in a given market or environment, within defined locations and resource constraints, and growing from a variety of origins.

However, there are typical organizational traits in all enterprises. These are expressed singly or in combination.

The elements influencing organization growth and structure affect authority patterns and styles of operation.

Origin and foundation
A partnership established by two or more individuals requires collective decision-making. This is typical of, say, professional firms of lawyers, accountants and architects. Rapid decision-making on commercial issues may not be easy to achieve.

In a company established and developed by one strong individual, as in a family firm, his/her influence is likely to remain pre-eminent. The key to understanding the company is to analyse the links within management.

An enterprise founded as a trust or by a benefactor reflects the original intent for which it was established. It might be paternalistic toward its employees and make some decisions on a basis other than a commercial one.

Growth pattern
In theory a company's growth may be classified as organic or acquisitive. In practice, companies exhibit features of both.

Organic structures are those which, having originated as a single company based on one or a range of products and services, have grown through internal expansion, new products and the establishment of new operations integral to the existing business.

Acquisitive or conglomerate structures are those which started out as single product enterprises but which have expanded by acquisition and absorption, either of related businesses or as part of diversification of different operations.

These organizations may encounter greater difficulties in the control and integration of a variety of management styles and company cultures. They tend toward decentralized control from a central point.

Stage of development
As in human life, an enterprise has several 'ages', although with clever management it might more closely approximate immortality. The stage of a company's evolution is reflected in its organization. Within large conglomerates with decentralized control several subsidiary operations may coexist at different levels of development. The main stages are start-up, growth and consolidation, followed by expansion or standstill.

Physical location
A company with dispersed manufacturing, sales or distribution activities will tend to decentralize control over operations. It may retain centralized control over product policy, standards, credit and finance, especially if it has grown organically.

Markets
The structure, size and nature of markets require particular organizational responses from a company, such as a split of organization between domestic and international, or major and minor customers.

Products/services
A company may organize along logical product lines such as automobiles and trucks, or may centralize certain product aspects such as engines.

The nature of the product and the process by which it is manufactured influence the shape of the structure.

Social environment
The social values within the company's operating environment influence its structure. For instance, local employment customs or laws create requirements in terms of manning and therefore management.

The successful management of any large enterprise, be it the construction of the pyramids or the running of one of today's giant multinational conglomerates, depends on the development of a soundly based structure and the application of clear organizational principles.

Business management has become increasingly complex with a bewildering choice of products, some highly specialized production processes and sophisticated marketing practices. Facilities and operations are progressively more capital intensive, financial structures and funding more involved, and government interference more extensive.

The pressure on the workforce has increased as business has become more exacting. Organizations of all types are now effectively part of a global market with its attendant currency and trading complications.

In today's commercial environment, organization, and its related principles, is therefore more important than ever.

While most business managers accept that effective organization is crucial to business success, opinions differ as to the exact nature and significance of organization.

Obviously, a basic objective of most business enterprises is to survive in a competitive market. The ability to do so can be measured in terms of profit growth and return on capital.

Individual companies have their own particular targets concerning the types of goods or services produced, the degree of diversification of products and the market sector in which to operate; but all are directed toward the same goal.

Attaining this objective depends on the coordination of the main elements of a business operation: people, capital, facilities and information.

In addition, an organization structure fulfils secondary but important requirements: it must be low cost and economical; it should be as simple as possible; and it should permit the development and testing of key future management.

The essential features of a structured organization

In every complex environment, good organization:
● Forms a 'route map' through which the affairs of the enterprise can be planned, directed and controlled.
● Highlights and isolates key activities which need resources and control.
● Provides for definition, orderliness and objectivity in human affairs, which otherwise would almost certainly become confused.
● Enables each member of the organization to understand his/her role, duties and relationships.
● Helps to identify and thus eliminate both duplication of effort and unnecessary activity.

● Provides a practical means for the allocation and control of costs, budgets and human resources.
● Permits the objective measurement of results in terms of achievement against tasks, profit, savings standards and other agreed criteria.
● Facilitates the communication of data and instructions to the people required to effect action.
● Provides identity and a sense of belonging to a group which has a common objective, and thus supports the members' morale.
● Speeds up the response of the business to external events or pressures in its environment, such as new competitive products, price changes or labour shortages.

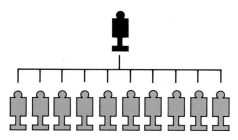

Span of management

It is generally accepted that the maximum numbers of subordinates who can be adequately supervised by one manager is in the region of 8 to 10. The number of direct relationships and subrelationships created by numbers beyond this level means that it is usually necessary to create additional layers of management to control them effectively. The Roman army recognized this need by organizing itself into cohorts (ten soldiers) and such principles are still valid in modern business.

The number of functions or departments which can be controlled effectively by one manager is also limited. Working groups should be manageable, economic and of optimum size.

As the number of subordinates supervised increases, so the number of relationships between them and their supervisor also increases. The increasing complexity of relationships should be taken into account when determining the optimum span of management, as should the following factors:
● Degree of interaction between the units or personnel being supervised
● Extent to which the manager or supervisor carries out non-managerial work
● Similarity or dissimilarity of the activities being controlled
● Degree of delegation which is possible depending on the abilities of those being managed and on the complexity of the work
● Incidence of new problems
● Extent of standardized procedures
● Degree of physical dispersion of the activities to be controlled

The application of organizational principles

An organization's leaders should seek and communicate clarity and simplicity. In doing so, the following key principles are important.
1 The grouping of activities
● Separate organizational components should be established only when they comprise logically separable functions.
● Separate functions should as far as possible be related to a common objective or leading function.
● The optimum span of management should be determined.
2 Authority and responsibility
● Responsibility should be defined clearly and assigned to one person.
● Responsibility should be matched with the appropriate authority.
● The number of levels of authority should be kept as low as possible.
● Clear lines of authority and accountability must run from the highest to the lowest levels.
3 Working relationships
● Working relationships must be clear and practicable.
● Reporting relationships should be consistent with the nature of the responsibilities exercised.
● Higher authority must be held fully accountable for the acts and duties of its subordinates and be responsible for their development.
● An organization should provide for the development of leaders.

Choosing a structure

When considering the optimum structure for itself, a business will ensure:
● Consistency of quality of service/product
● Adherence to agreed corporate directions and standards
● Cost effective methods of administering itself.

In order to achieve these it needs to:
● Avoid duplication or conflict of effort
● Exercise control to ensure that various parts of the organization stay within agreed boundaries (budgets, regions, product ranges etc) or seek approval before going outside
● Establish good information flow on customer satisfaction, local market conditions and competitor activities.

The business, therefore, usually has to ask itself how much control a few senior people should have.

Consciously or otherwise, all businesses consider the question of centralization versus decentralization.

This question will concern the division of power between head office and branches. At another level it will involve how much autonomy the production department should have to decide its own buying patterns, quality control procedures etc.

At an even lower level it will be a question of whether or not a purchasing supervisor should make decisions about, say, buying in greater bulk to get a higher discount.

Many organizations never come to terms with the natural tension between the centre and the periphery and alternate between centralized and decentralized approaches. They will usually need a mixture of both.

With the increasing rate of change, greater competition from unexpected sources (banks providing mortgages, food supermarkets selling clothes), increasing demands and rising expectations, the question of organizational structure can have a significant impact on a business's profitability.

Organizational patterns

There are a number of different issues to consider when establishing an organizational structure, such as: top management's desire to exercise close control; size of operation; diversity of product range; quality of middle management; and geographic spread. The more common organizational patterns include:

Centralized organization
Authority is concentrated in one central point or position. Major decisions are made by one controlling body. Delegation generally operates through formalized procedures and authority levels, or by recognized custom and practice.

Decentralized organization
Decision-making is dispersed into small units. Decentralization may be necessitated by geography, product mix or market.

Functional organization
Resources and authority are structured on the basis of recognized industrial or professional skills, such as marketing, finance, production, sales and personnel. The heads of these functions are responsible for control of their specialist resources, professional standards and liaison/communication across functions.

Matrix organization
Project-oriented authority is superimposed on functional skills. Thus a researcher or project leader can call on, use and direct resources from another part of the organization to achieve the project's goals.

Line and staff organization
Essentially, line management has direct control over a line process which can contain staff of many disciplines: a production, sales or research team.

Staff functions are essentially the advisors, providers of recommendations to senior managers, reviewers and analysers of policy. Managers in staff functions have line control only for their own personnel.

How a company evolves

Start-up
● Limited number of people with individual roles
● May be unstructured or project orientated
● Requires strong leadership and flexible staff to survive
● Many enterprises do not get past this stage

Development
● May have to survive a crisis of autonomy
● Rapid growth and change
● Begins to define structure, customs and role of employees
● Forms the culture of the company
● Emphasis on product development to support growth plans

Consolidation
● The period needs strong direction
● Consolidation of present position
● Takes time to consider gains and losses

● Time to plan for new products, future growth and/or acquisition
● May suffer a crisis of control
● Potential to reach a plateau, expand or decline

Plateau
● Little or no change made to profile and products
● Several possible reasons:
  1 No new ideas are generated
  2 Skills are not available
  3 Rest on success of current projects
● May continue for long periods
● Eventually will decline or expand

Expansion will happen through
● The development and introduction of new products or services, or
● Acquisition

Decline happens because
● Either a more expansive company will buy it, or
● Rising costs and uncompetitive products will force it out of business.

Advantages of centralization

● Broad overview of business is easier to achieve. Strategic direction setting may be easier.
● Gives absolute and clear control.
● Makes administration easier.
● Common standards can be monitored.
● Provides certain service or expert functions cost effectively.
● Inconsistent, maybe conflicting, decisions are easier to avoid.
● Can eliminate possible competition which may be undesirable, eg a similar product being sold at different prices by two parts of the same organization.
● Allows an overview of the business because it avoids, for example, differing priorities and information systems.
● Economies of scale (eg bulk buying) can be achieved.

Advantages of decentralization

● Local management can react to changing local conditions so that the business is 'light on its feet'.
● Decision-making is quicker, clearer and based on more precise understanding of local conditions.
● Local responsibility and authority develop more managers of quality.
● Higher involvement and motivation can lead to greater productivity and increased profits.
● The greater likelihood of innovation, creativity and non-acceptance of a status quo will make for a healthier business.
● Administration and paperwork are minimized.
● Functional departments (personnel, legal etc) are more in touch and leaner. It is easier to control their operations.

Equity and long-term debt

Business needs cash to get going. Premises need to be rented or purchased, plant and machinery have to be leased or bought, raw materials must be purchased, and the workforce has to be paid from the day the business starts.

Few entrepreneurs can afford to start up using only their own savings. They need to know where to go for other capital and what costs and benefits may result.

The capital of the owners is equity. This is the most exposed form of finance because the owners receive a return on investment only after all others – employees, creditors, bankers and other lenders – have received their legal entitlement.

Should the business face liquidation, equity will be repaid only after everyone else has received what is owing.

Should the business prosper, however, the owners can claim all of the profit after the fixed interest charges on the debt capital have been met.

A company need not limit its equity capital to the cash contributed by the entrepreneurs: venture capital, the USM and the Stock Exchange provide more equity finance.

Other forms of capital are long-term debts, which can vary in amount, purpose and legal entitlement.

Providers of long-term debt usually seek to secure their debt over the existing fixed assets of the business. This is precisely what happens in the domestic mortgage market where the building society or bank lends on the title deeds of the property for which the loan is required.

Long-term debt must be repaid at the end of the stated term unless both sides are willing to renegotiate terms for another period.

Lenders must be paid interest each year at a rate which is normally linked to bank base rate. When the profits of the business fall, this interest commitment can become a burden.

Equity

The owners' equity in a company is a residual interest, a claim on the assets not required to meet the claims of lenders and creditors.

Equity comprises the amounts originally contributed by the owners, together with profits from previous years not distributed by way of dividend.

Equity is represented by the net assets of the firm which it has helped fund.

Long-term financing

Where a business needs capital for, say, longer than ten years, it may approach one or more of the following providers:
- Clearing banks
- Merchant banks
- Pension funds

Two forms of long-term financing are popular:

1 Debentures or loan stock tend to be issued by well-established companies seeking additional capital. A debenture is a loan secured on specific fixed assets or through a 'floating charge' on the business as a whole. If the business gets into difficulties, the proceeds of certain assets are used to repay the debentures.

Loan stock is often issued with a convertible option attached to it; at the end of a stated period, the lender may convert it into ordinary shares.

2 Sale and leaseback: a business can sell a valuable asset, usually a building or piece of land, to a finance house for a capital sum and then lease back the asset for an annual rental.

A badly constructed financial package can seriously damage the health of the company. Take professional advice before commitment to any form of finance.

Gearing is the relationship between equity capital and long-term debt. Companies should keep a reasonable balance between the two. Generally, lenders will not provide more money than the owners have provided.

Gearing has an impact on the owners' return. In general, a company with a low gearing ratio will weather an economic storm better than one that is highly geared.

(Figures in pounds sterling)	Highly geared Company	Lowly geared Company
Equity	40,000	80,000
10% Long-term debt	60,000	20,000
	100,000	100,000
Gearing	60%	20%

	Year 1	Year 2	Year 3	Year 4
Profits before interest	15,000	10,000	7,500	6,000
Highly geared Company				
Interest	6,000	6,000	6,000	6,000
Available to equity	9,000	4,000	1,500	0
	15,000	10,000	7,500	6,000
Lowly geared company				
Interest	2,000	2,000	2,000	2,000
Available to equity	13,000	8,000	5,500	4,000
	15,000	10,000	7,500	6,000
Return on equity				
High	22.5%	10%	3.75%	
Low	16.25%	10%	6.88%	5%

The fall in owners' earnings is less dramatic (16.25% to 5%) with low gearing than with high gearing (22.5% to nil). But if corporate profits were rising, the highly geared owners would enjoy a much steeper climb in their return.

More equity finance?

Each of the three main sources of fresh equity finance has advantages, depending on the growth profile of the company and on the motives of the existing owners.

1 Venture capital is supplied by venture firms specifically set up by investment trusts, banks, even government agencies, to provide equity for companies showing potential for high growth. Because of the high risks involved, these firms tend to look for high returns. They expect to realize their investment when the company grows. They leave operational control to existing management, but expect to be involved in major decisions.

2 Entry into the unlisted securities market (USM) is a natural stage in the development of a successful company from a relatively small, privately owned business into a mature public company. The USM allows companies to raise money from outside investors and entrepreneurs and so unlock some of the capital tied up in the business. Although the company's capital base expands with the influx of new investors, the owners retain management and voting control. At least 10 per cent of the equity must be in public hands.

3 The Stock Exchange option is available only to relatively large companies with, for example, a minimum market capitalization of £700,000 at the outset. At least 25 per cent of the equity must be in public hands. Initially, the Stock Exchange does not present possibilities to raise capital, only to provide a public market to buy and sell existing shares in the company. Only when the company has built up a solid reputation in terms of products, profits and prospects will it be able to expand its equity base by issuing fresh shares.

Working capital management

A business will collapse without funds generated from within. Sooner rather than later a company must generate sufficient funds from normal trading operations to maintain the existing level of business and to provide the backbone of future expansion.

Profit must be the starting point for internally generated funds. Profit is the surplus left when the costs of producing and selling have been deducted from the revenue derived from sales. But a company does not keep all of its profit. Taxation takes a percentage and shareholders want a return on their investment. Skilful managers attempt to minimize taxation wherever possible and to create a balance between amounts paid out to shareholders and amounts retained in the company.

Shareholders receive a modest return on their capital, enough to stop them seeking other investment opportunities. By and large, they appreciate that profits retained in the business are used to sustain and expand the company's operating capability.

With an underlying trend of internally generated retained profits, the company has a future.

But beware! Profit is not cash. Profit is measured by using a number of accounting conventions, some of which have no bearing on cash flow. For example, depreciation, a non-cash item for the business, is charged on the property and plant and thus reduces profit.

Managers tend to be more concerned with cash, or liquidity, than with profits. Wages, dividends, taxes, the heating bill are all cash leakages, not profits. So-called profitable companies have gone out of business because they ran out of cash.

Managers should be able to understand how cash is pumped around the business, where the pressure points are for more cash and where surplus cash can be drained off.

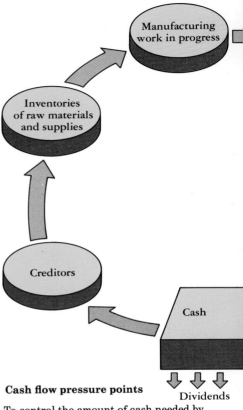

Cash flow pressure points

To control the amount of cash needed by normal operations of the business, astute managers make sure the flow is as fast as possible. They keep tabs on three pressure points:

Creditors: raw materials and supplies are needed for manufacturing operations. Every attempt should be made to use suppliers who allow a generous credit period before requiring cash payment. Often a company is better off to forgo a discount for quick payment so that it can hold on to its cash. But it is seldom worth keeping important suppliers waiting – they could suspend supplies or even go out of business and leave you without a source of supply.

Inventories and manufacturing work-in-progress: stocks of raw materials are held to prevent disruptions in production or to avoid an imminent price rise. The

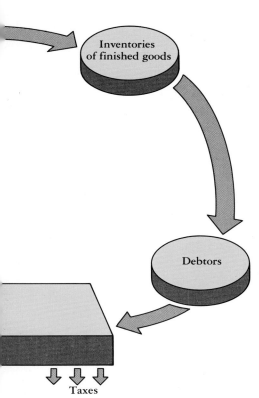

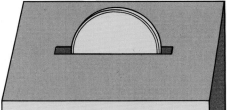

The treasury function: the big company's answer to cash management

A company involved in international trading increases its problems. Treasury departments within international companies concern themselves with the complete range of issues surrounding cash movements and holdings. Ask:
● Does the company have any bank accounts with credit balances? Idle balances on current account with banks earn no interest. Efficient treasury systems arrange to use cash as it becomes available.
● Has the company optimized its collection system to obtain the same value as its customers?
● Does the company know the bank charges associated with each aspect of the business? Is it using the bank best equipped to handle each aspect of the business?
● Is the company familiar with the full range of borrowing and deposit instruments available? Do any opportunities exist for refinancing on more favourable terms?
● Does the company monitor its currency exposure to keep the risk within acceptable limits? Is it covering the risk at the lowest cost? The volatility of foreign exchange markets can put at risk even the most advantageous of overseas markets.
● Does the company have a system which effectively controls investment in working capital at operating levels?

Taxes

levels of work-in-progress and finished goods are determined by the volume of production required to meet future sales. Inventories avoid stock-outs which are disruptive, expensive and damaging to customer goodwill. But inventories are costly. Managers must ensure that the minimum levels are carried in order to minimize the cash outlay. In a recession, one of the first actions a manager takes is to de-stock so that cash can be squeezed out of the system for critical use.

Debtors: unless you operate in the retail sector where cash sales are a significant part of operations, credit sales are unavoidable. If your competitors offer credit terms then so must you. The more generous the terms, the more expense for the seller. You must strive for a balance between giving good terms, which attract customers, and having a strict collection policy, which minimizes cash outlay but could alienate customers.

Cash forecasting

An essential component of working capital management is negotiating borrowing facilities with the company's bankers. Most banks insist on a cash flow forecast for at least the next 12 months, but this laborious procedure can be simplified by the use of a microcomputer spreadsheet.

Sample cash flow forecast

Three graduates in computer science are planning to form a company from January to design, manufacture and sell floppy disks for microcomputers.
● Each graduate will introduce £15,000 in cash. The bank they have approached for a borrowing facility of £30,000 requires an initial cash forecast for the first six months' trading.

● A factory has been located costing £24,000 but the local development corporation is prepared to accept £12,000 immediately and offer a mortgage on the balance with interest payable at 10 per cent per annum on the last day of each month. Capital repayment on the loan will begin in July.
● Equipment, plant and vehicles costing £30,000 must be acquired and paid for within the first month of trading. It is anticipated that one of the vehicles will be sold during June for £500.
● Selling price will be £6, and expected sales are as follows, in units: January nil; February 2,000; March 2,500, and for each month thereafter, 3,000; 10 per cent of sales will be for

CASH FORECAST for period January to June

(Figures in pounds sterling)

	January	February	March	April
OPENING CASH BALANCE	0	−8,600	−25,200	−30,100
Capital introduction	45,000			
1 Cash sales		1,200	1,500	1,800
Cash from credit sales			10,800	13,500
Asset sales				
RECEIPTS	45,000	1,200	12,300	15,300
Wages	6,000	6,000	6,000	6,000
2 Raw materials		4,200	3,000	3,000
Production overhead		1,800	1,800	1,800
Administration overhead		1,700	1,700	1,700
Selling & distribution			600	700
Advertising	2,500	1,000	1,000	1,000
Factory	12,000			
Equipment, plant, vehicles	30,000			
Interest on mortgage	100	100	100	100
Drawings	3,000	3,000	3,000	3,000
PAYMENTS	53,600	17,800	17,200	17,300
MOVEMENT IN CASH	−8,600	−16,600	−4,900	−2,000
3 **CLOSING CASH BALANCE**	−8,600	−25,200	−30,100	−32,100
FACILITY	30,000	30,000	30,000	30,000
4 ADDITIONAL NEEDS	—	—	100	2,100

cash. The balance will be sold on credit for settlement in the month following delivery (see note 1).

● At the projected maximum level of production of 3,000 disks per month, wages will be £6,000 per month.

● Each disk made will cost £1 for materials (see note 2).

● Materials, production and administration overheads will be paid in the month following that of supply of the goods or services. Production overheads are likely to be £1,800 per month and administrative overheads £1,700 per month. All other expenses are paid in the month in which they are incurred.

● Sufficient materials will be purchased in January both to manufacture the disks to be sold in February and to maintain a raw material inventory of 1,200. The inventory of finished goods will be maintained at 1,500 disks, built up during January and February, and the production level for any month will then be that of the next month's sales (see note 2).

● Advertising: £2,500 in January, £1,000 in February, March and April, and £500 per month thereafter.

● Selling and distribution costs are to be paid: £600 in March, £700 in both April and May, and £800 in June.

● Each of the graduates proposes to withdraw £1,000 per month.

● For ease of calculation timing differences relating to VAT have been omitted.

1 Sales @ £6 each	Jan	Feb	Mar	April	May	June
Invoiced sales	–	£12,000	£15,000	£18,000	£18,000	£18,000
Cash received						
Cash sales 10% this month	–	£1,200	£1,500	£1,800	£1,800	£1,800
Debtors 90% next month	–	–	£10,800	£13,500	£16,200	£16,200

	May	June	Total
	– 32,100	– 30,900	0
			45,000
	1,800	1,800	8,100
	16,200	16,200	56,700
			500
	18,000	18,500	110,300
	6,000	6,000	36,000
	3,000	3,000	16,200
	1,800	1,800	9,000
	1,700	1,700	8,500
	700	800	2,800
	500	500	6,500
			12,000
			30,000
	100	100	600
	3,000	3,000	18,000
	16,800	16,900	139,600
	1,200	1,600	– 29,300
	– 30,900	– 29,300	– 29,300
	30,000	30,000	
	900	—	

2 Raw materials paid in month following supply:

January purchases:

for finished goods inventory	1,000
for February sale	2,000
	3,000
for raw materials inventory	1,200
paid in February	4,200
@ £1	£4,200

February purchases:

for finished goods inventory	500
for March sale	2,500
paid in March	3,000
@ £1	£3,000

March purchases:

for April sales	
paid in April	3,000
@ £1	£3,000

and so on

3 This set of cash outflows is typical of a start-up situation when substantial sums are spent in advance of sales. Provided the company is selling a profitable and needed product, this outflow will be reversed before long.

4 The graduates will need to renegotiate their facility in the first six months; they need at least £32,100. Provided subsequent months indicate an on-going cash recovery, most banks would agree to a top-up such as this. Every effort should be made to ensure that the finance requirements are adequately identified. Projections that are overly optimistic will not be accepted by an experienced lender and will detract from the credibility of the proposal.

The profit and loss account

Companies are obliged by law to prepare a set of financial statements each year. The law spells out what items must be included and, to a lesser extent, how they must be presented.

Many parties are interested in these statements: investors, employees, creditors, bankers, tax authorities and consumer groups. It is essential for managers to know how they are prepared and what they disclose.

The three principal financial statements are: the profit and loss account, the balance sheet, and the cash flow statement. The examples on these pages are taken from the accounts of Retail Stores PLC, a retail group of companies.

The profit and loss account is a measure of the operating performance of a business over a given period of time.

Companies do not necessarily use the calendar year as their reporting year; they prefer to use the natural business year in an attempt to measure performance at a time when most earnings activities have been concluded. But business is a continuum; it is not easily cut up into annual pieces.

The profit and loss account measures the normal operating activities of the business; specifically, it compares revenue for the year against the cost of goods sold and other expenses. It discloses revenues arising, or costs resulting, from non-operating activities, say the profit from selling a piece of land.

These 'extraordinary items' must be kept separate from the ongoing operating results to provide a true impression of the underlying trend in operating profitability.

After provision has been made for the tax due, the profit and loss account discloses how the profit will be used: as dividends to the shareholders and the balance to expand the company's future operations.

Accountants: a cautious breed

Accountants do not take the risk of reporting profit before they are reasonably certain the company will indeed earn it. Revenue and profits are not anticipated, but are recognized only when realized in the form of cash or other assets, the ultimate cash realization of which can be assessed with reasonable certainty.

On the other hand, provision is made for all known liabilities whether the amount is known with certainty or is a best estimate.

Companies must be consistent in the way they account for their transactions. They must not keep changing, say, the way in which they depreciate their assets, or methods they use to translate their dealings in foreign currencies. They are obliged to state their accounting policies in the annual report.

Assessing the profit and loss account

The accruals basis of accounting (as opposed to the cash basis) reports costs incurred as expenses in the year when the revenues to which they relate are recognized. Items in annual accounts have not necessarily been received or paid in cash by the end of the financial year. For example, a company pays £6,000 annual factory rent, in advance, halfway through the year. The profit and loss account would include £3,000 cost this year and £3,000 next year. Similarly, the turnover figure includes sales which have not been paid for at the year-end.

Profit before taxation is the best indicator of corporate performance and managerial efficiency. Below this level, the figures are affected by the tax payable which, because of the fiscal rules applying to UK companies, may be little influenced by the ordinary profit of the company.

Notes to the accounts are detailed, and sometimes complex, interpretations of the principal figures. Ask an accountant to explain them if you want to understand how the figures are made up.

Interpreting the profit and loss account

1 The cost of sales figure includes cost of goods purchased for resale, wages of shop assistants, and depreciation of shop fittings and equipment. A manufacturing company's costs would include raw materials, direct labour and manufacturing overheads.

2 Distribution costs and administration expenses include salaries and costs not included in cost of sales: rent, rates, energy and security costs, auditors' remuneration, depreciation on fixed assets, repairs categorized by the purpose for which they were incurred.

3 This group profit and loss account indicates that the results are those of a group of companies (parent company and subsidiaries). The shares in the subsidiaries not owned by the parent company (minority interest) are allocated their fair share of total group profits.

4 Earnings per share is calculated by dividing profit for the year after tax and minority interest by the number of issued shares. It is probably more significant than 'dividends per share' because it indicates the total earnings – dividends plus amounts retained for expansion – which each share has generated during the year. This figure tends to influence the market value of the shares. Companies strive to increase earnings per share each year.

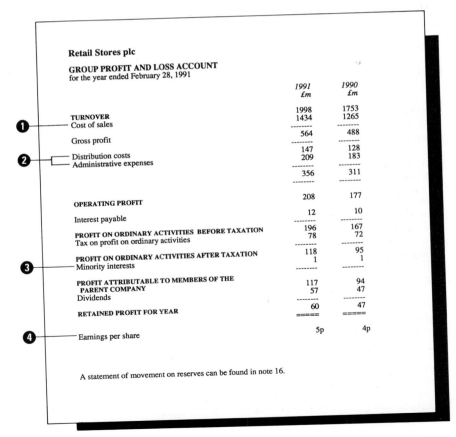

Retail Stores plc

GROUP PROFIT AND LOSS ACCOUNT
for the year ended February 28, 1991

	1991 £m	1990 £m
TURNOVER	1998	1753
Cost of sales	1434	1265
Gross profit	564	488
Distribution costs	147	128
Administrative expenses	209	183
	356	311
OPERATING PROFIT	208	177
Interest payable	12	10
PROFIT ON ORDINARY ACTIVITIES BEFORE TAXATION	196	167
Tax on profit on ordinary activities	78	72
PROFIT ON ORDINARY ACTIVITIES AFTER TAXATION	118	95
Minority interests	1	1
PROFIT ATTRIBUTABLE TO MEMBERS OF THE PARENT COMPANY	117	94
Dividends	57	47
RETAINED PROFIT FOR YEAR	60	47
Earnings per share	5p	4p

A statement of movement on reserves can be found in note 16.

The balance sheet

The balance sheet of a company is a statement of what it owns (assets) and what it owes (liabilities) at a particular time, usually the last day of the company's financial year. It is composed of three major classes of item: assets, liabilities and owners' equity.

Assets are resources of the company that have the potential for providing it with future economic services or benefits. Assets must be split into fixed assets (such as land, buildings, plant vehicles and intangible assets such as goodwill) and current assets (such as stocks of raw materials, work-in-progress and finished goods, debtors, short-term investments, prepaid expenses and cash).

Fixed assets are stated at acquisition cost or valuation. They must be depreciated (written off) over their useful lives.

Current assets are shown at their cash equivalent value. If it appears that one of the company's debtors is not going to pay, the asset 'debtors' must be reduced by this amount. Similarly, stock must be valued at the lower of cost or net realizable value.

Liabilities include obligations of a company to make payment in the foreseeable future for goods or services already received. Statute requires a company to distinguish between creditors who require payment within one year and those due after more than one year. Other liabilities include long-term debt, comprising loans and obligations under long-term leases, and deferred tax (provisions for tax payable or recoverable in future where the tax effect of a transaction is recognized in a different period to the accounting effect.

Owners' equity is a residual interest: it comprises the original capital that was contributed together with any profits which have not been distributed by way of dividend. The owners' equity is represented by the net assets of the company.

The basic balance sheet equation

Assets = liabilities + owners' equity.

Start-up Ltd was incorporated on 1 January with an issued share capital of £1,000, paid for in cash by the two founding directors. The first day balance sheet would be expressed:

Start-up Ltd		£
Assets	Cash-in-hand	1,000
Capital	Ordinary shares	1,000

During the first week of trading the company bought raw materials for £600, half of which were supplied on credit, and some machinery for £300. At the end of the first week, the balance sheet would look like this:

Start-up Ltd		£
Fixed assets	Machinery	30(
Current assets	Raw materials	600
	Cash-in-hand	400
		1,300
Capital		
Ordinary shares		1,000
Current liabilities		
Creditors		300
		1,300

An alternative presentation, adopted by Retail Stores PLC, would be shown in a columnar form:

Start-up Ltd	£	£
Fixed assets		
Machinery		300
Current assets		
Raw materials	600	
Cash-in-hand	400	
	1,000	
Current liabilities		
Creditors	300	
Net current assets		700
Net assets		1,000
Capital		
Ordinary shares		1,000

Balance sheet analysis

1 The value of stocks of unsold merchandise is hard to determine. Statutes require that stocks be valued at the lower of cost or net realizable value. Reported profit is affected by the valuation a company places on its closing stocks; a high value produces a high profit because more of the current year's costs are deferred. Auditors pay particular attention to client's procedures for counting and valuing stocks.

2 When a company issues shares, it must decide on their nominal (or face) value and the price at which they will be offered to the public. If the company offers shares of £1 nominal value for £1.25, the 25 pence is the share premium and is kept separate in the accounts. During 1990/91 Retail Stores PLC has issued some shares at a premium under an Employee Share Scheme.

3 In an attempt to overcome the unreality of historical costs, the company has revalued its fixed assets periodically in the past. The increases in the fixed assets have two effects: more depreciation is charged in the

profit and loss account; and the shareholders' equity increases automatically because of the effect of the balance sheet equation.

4 A company may retain some profits each year to fund future growth and expansion. This figure indicates the cumulative build-up in these retained profits.

Retail Stores plc

GROUP BALANCE SHEET
at February 28, 1991

	1991 £m	1990 £m
FIXED ASSETS Tangible assets	970	876
CURRENT ASSETS		
❶ Stocks	135	114
Debtors	34	40
Investments	43	76
Cash at bank and in hand	52	44
	264	274
CREDITORS: amounts falling due within one year	316	303
NET CURRENT LIABILITIES	(52)	(29)
TOTAL ASSETS LESS CURRENT LIABILITIES	918	847
CREDITORS: amounts falling due after more than one year	38	37
PROVISION FOR LIABILITIES AND CHARGES Deferred taxation	17	12
	55	49
	863	798
MINORITY INTERESTS	5	4
	858	794
CAPITAL AND RESERVES		
Called up share capital	231	230
❷ Share premium account	11	10
❸ Revaluation reserve	274	272
Profit and loss account ❹	342	282
	858	794

What a balance sheet is not

The net assets figure in the balance sheet does not represent their market value.

The figures in the accounts are based on the acquisition cost of the assets.

With land and buildings, unless there has been a revaluation, the acquisition may have happened years ago and bear little resemblance to the amounts the company would realize if it sold any or all of them: the balance sheet is not a statement of market values.

MEASURING THE BUSINESS
Cash flow statements

The cash flow statement has recently replaced the source and application of funds statement as a primary financial statement. It attempts to show information on the liquidity and viability of the reporting company which may not be evident from the company's balance sheet or profit and loss account. The cash flow statement tries to answer the following questions:
- Where have the profits gone?
- Are normal company operations generating sufficient cash to enable it to continue paying dividends?
- Where did the money for new assets come from? From operations or from borrowing?
- Is the company solvent, that is, has it sufficient liquid assets to meet its short-term obligations?
- How can the company be earning profits but still be short of cash?

A company's main source of cash must be its operations. If it cannot generate sufficient internal resources it will go out of business. To arrive at the figure for the net cash inflow from operations, the operating profit as disclosed in the profit and loss account must be adjusted for non-cash items, such as depreciation, and changes in balance sheet figures which have not yet generated a cash movement, such as an increase in debtors.

Cash generated from operations is usually used for investment activities, such as the purchase of fixed assets, or paying for finance (interest) and taxation. Other sources of cash include issues of new shares or the sale of fixed assets. The difference between cash inflows and cash outflows is reflected in either an increase or a decrease in cash and cash equivalents. Cash equivalents are included because cash in excess of immediate needs is often invested in short-term investments. These investments are seen as equivalent to cash as they are highly liquid and convertible into known amounts of cash without notice.

The audit

Shareholders, not management, appoint an independent firm of accountants to report each year on their examination of the accounts of the parent company and the group. The report states whether, in the auditors' opinion, the accounts give a true and fair view of the profit (or loss) and the cash flows for the year, and of the financial position at the year end. It also states whether in their opinion the accounts have been properly prepared in accordance with the provisions of the Companies Act.

The scope and extent of the auditors' work in the UK is governed by Auditing Standards laid down by the accountancy profession. In applying these standards, auditors take account of the characteristics of the business concerned and aim to ensure that the accounts comply with the relevant Companies Act provisions and accounting standards.

Auditors plan their work to discover any material misstatement of figures in the accounts. It is impracticable to check everything; there must be a balance between benefits and costs of an audit. Consequently auditors may not discover insignificant errors in the figures, or events such as fraud. Management must ensure that accounts are prepared and assets safeguarded. Books, records and internal controls may be used by auditors in their work but the audit report will only address errors or weaknesses in these if they cause material misstatements or uncertainty in the figures.

The audit report of Retail Stores PLC contains no reservations of opinion. If the auditors were doubtful about any important item included (or not included) in the accounts, they would have to give a 'qualified' opinion stating the specific reason and extent to which they were not satisfied.

66

What is happening at Retail Stores PLC?

The group had a net cash outflow during the year of £32 million before raising £2 million of capital via a share issue. The major outflows were fixed asset purchases, and dividend and tax payments. Cash inflows were insufficient to cover these outflows. Cash inflows were reduced by the marked increase in stocks and reduction in creditors. The net outflow of £30 million was financed by the sale of short-term investments and an increase in the bank overdraft, offset by an increase in the cash balance.

1 The figure of £49 million is made up from last year's final dividend of £30 million, paid in the current year, along with the current year's interim dividend of £19 million.

2 Cash and cash equivalents include cash in the bank, bank overdrafts and short-term investments.

3 Build-up in stocks from the beginning of the year (£114 million) to the end of the year (£135 million) equals a £21 million increase during the year. Stock locks up cash which could be used for more critical purposes but reflects management's view of higher prospective sales.

4 Cash flow statements are reconciled to the figures in the balance sheet for financing items (as shown) and cash and cash equivalents in the notes to the primary financial statements.

Retail Stores plc
GROUP CASH FLOW STATEMENT
for the year ended February 28 1991

	£m	£m
Net cash inflow from operating activities		202
Returns on investments and servicing of finance		
Interest paid	(12)	
Dividends paid ❶	(49)	(61)
		(50)
Taxation paid		
Investing activities		
Sale of fixed assets	3	
Purchase of new fixed assets	(126)	(123)
		(32)
Net cash outflow before financing		
Financing		
Issue of ordinary share capital	(2)	
Net cash inflow from financing		(2)
Decrease in cash and cash equivalents ❷		(30)
		(32)

	£m	£m
Reconciliation of operating profit to net cash from operating activities		208
Operating profit	28	
Depreciation	3	
Loss on disposal of fixed assets	6	
Decrease in debtors	(21)	
Increase in stocks ❸	(22)	
Decrease in creditors		(6)
		202
Net cash inflow from operating activities		

	£m
Analysis of changes in financing during the year ❹	
Share capital and share premium	
Balance at 1 March 1990	240
Net cash inflow from financing	2
Balance at 28 February 1991	242

Report of the auditors to the members of Retail Stores PLC

We have audited the accounts in accordance with Auditing Standards.

In our opinion the accounts give a true and fair view of the state of affairs of the group at 28 February 1991 and of the profit and cash flows of the group for the year then ended and have been properly prepared in accordance with the Companies Act 1985.

Ernst & Young
Chartered Accountants

London, 25 June 1991

Valuing a company

Value, like beauty, lies in the eye of the beholder. Companies are valued for takeover, merger, stock market flotation, and for capital taxes.

Since two parties – the owners of the shares and the outsiders – are always involved, valuation is part technical calculation, part negotiation.

Negotiations are affected by the perceived strengths and weaknesses of the parties concerned, and their relative size is not the only factor.

The valuation will be influenced by the needs of the buyer and seller, and also by the size of the holding.

Size of shareholding

A large shareholding can give the shareholders power to influence the management of the company and thus an element of control over its decisions and resources.

Control over investment decisions and dividend policy will have a greater cost than the technical valuation placed on the shares.

Potential buyers of such a shareholding will look further than the company's accounts. They will be interested in issues such as management strength/style, customer base, key locations, products, patents, market penetration, image and potential growth.

A smaller shareholding may be easier to value – and cheaper to buy. The technical valuations may be enough to answer questions regarding the investor's preference for income or capital growth.

The needs of the buyers and sellers

As well as deciding how well the acquired investment will complement their existing holdings or how well the acquired business will complement their existing activities, buyers may also be considering how saleable the acquisition will be in the future.

Here, buyers will consider both the company's assets and the shares themselves.

The price which buyers are willing to pay for a business will reflect their

---

Technical valuation of shares

Technical calculation is based on:
1 Balance sheet valuation Retail Stores PLC has £858 million of net assets in the balance sheet. Its share capital comprises around 2,310 million ordinary 10p shares. Each one is therefore worth £0.37 in terms of net assets. But two significant features cause an analyst to be wary of this assets per share: the assets are valued at cost in the balance sheet and are in fact worth considerably more in current value terms; and good management make their assets work for the business – dynamic earnings potential is favoured more than static asset values.
2 Market valuation If the company has a Stock Exchange quotation (Retail Stores PLC's is 74 pence), it is simple to value relatively small blocks of shares. However, if a sizeable block of shares, say

---

desire to acquire it. The difference between the technical valuation and any higher purchase price could reflect, among other things, the strength of the buyers' desire or their view of the business's potential. This difference is known as goodwill.

Buyers may pay more than the technical value to protect markets or supply lines or improve margins.

The sellers' primary concern could be the original cost of their investment, and thus a desire to maximize a profit or minimize a loss on it.

But sellers could equally need cash in order to take advantage of another investment opportunity or to meet cash flow problems. Speed of sale may take precedence over their own technical valuation. If such pressures do not exist, the process of valuing the company will be approached in a similar way to the buyers'.

that held by a pension fund, is sold (or purchased) this action alone will disturb the equilibrium between supply and demand and the price will fall or rise. The market capitalization valuation is the current market value per share multiplied by the number of issued shares: 2,310 million shares × 74 pence = £1,709 million.

3 Earnings valuation A company's stock market value is based on a combination of factors but probably the major factor is the earnings potential of the company. This is assessed taking into account future growth in new products and markets, known cost reduction programmes, and quality of management. Potential earnings are then multiplied by the company's Price Earnings ratio (PE). The PE ratio expresses the number of years' earnings represented by the current market price.

PE of Retail Stores PLC

$$= \frac{\text{Market value}}{\text{Earnings per share}}$$

$$= \frac{74}{5} = 14.8 \text{ (say 15)}$$

Current earnings of Retail Stores PLC = £117 million

Earnings per share is therefore 5p (117 ÷ 2,310)

Potential earnings next year +30% = £152 million

Earnings valuation = £152 million × 15 = £2,280 million or £0.99 per share.

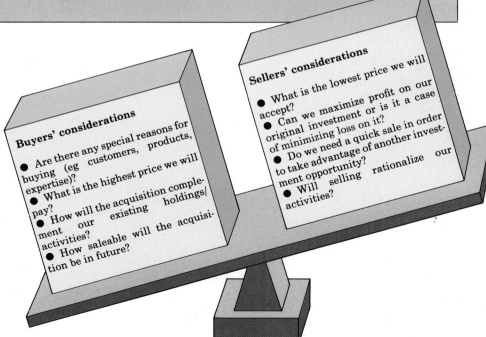

Buyers' considerations

● Are there any special reasons for buying (eg customers, products, expertise)?
● What is the highest price we will pay?
● How will the acquisition complement our existing holdings/activities?
● How saleable will the acquisition be in future?

Sellers' considerations

● What is the lowest price we will accept?
● Can we maximize profit on our original investment or is it a case of minimizing loss on it?
● Do we need a quick sale in order to take advantage of another investment opportunity?
● Will selling rationalize our activities?

Ratio analysis

Once you understand how a set of accounts is constructed, you need to be able to analyse them to find out what they really disclose. Interpreting and analysing financial statements and related information will enable you, as a manager, to compare the performance of your company this year with last year, to compare your company with its competitors, and to detect weaknesses you can improve.

Absolute figures in financial statements do not tell you much. For example, to be told that Retail Stores PLC made £196 million profits before tax is not particularly useful unless it is related to, say, the turnover which produced the profit or to the capital employed in the group.

For ratios to be meaningful, they

Liquidity

Your first concern as a manager is to ensure the short-run survival of the company. The current ratio is a generally accepted measure of short-term solvency. It indicates the extent to which the claims of short-term creditors are covered by current assets:

Current ratio
$$= \frac{\text{Current assets}}{\text{Current liabilities}}$$
$$= \frac{264}{316} = 0.84 \text{ times}$$

The quick ratio is based on the assumption that stocks will not be converted to cash quickly enough to meet the timescale for payment of creditors. To provide a more rigorous test of the company's ability to meet its short-term obligations, this item is removed from the calculation.

Quick ratio
$$= \frac{\text{Current assets} - \text{Stocks}}{\text{Current liabilities}}$$
$$= \frac{264 - 135}{316} = 0.41 \text{ times}$$

Managers should aim to extend the period of credit taken to pay suppliers. Too long a period, however, will lead to poor trade relations with suppliers, and may even be an indication of cash flow problems.

Capital structure

The net assets of a company can be financed by a mixture of owners' equity and long-term debt. Gearing ratios analyse this by measuring the contributions of shareholders against the funds provided by the lenders of loan capital. Retail Stores PLC has no long-term debt; but the significant ratio is:

$$= \frac{\text{Long-term debt}}{\text{Capital employed}} \times 100$$

The profit and loss account provides another useful angle on the capital structure. Is there a healthy margin of safety in the profits to meet the fixed interest payments on long-term debt? An overgeared company may show signs of running out of profit to pay this fixed burden. A commonly used measure is whether profit before interest and tax covers interest charges at least twice over.

Interest cover
$$= \frac{\text{Profit before interest} + \text{taxes}}{\text{Interest charges}}$$

To be sure that their dividend is safe, shareholders will want profits compared with the dividend payable:

Dividend cover
$$= \frac{\text{Profit for the financial year}}{\text{Dividend payable}}$$
$$= \frac{117}{57} = 2.05$$

must be compared with equivalent ratios for previous years and with those of the industry in which the company operates. Industrial ratios are produced by a variety of clearing houses for industrial statistics.

Ratios reduce the amount of data contained in the financial statements to workable form. Ratio analysis can also be applied to relate financial per-formance to non-financial data. These aims are defeated if too many are calculated. It is essential that you identify the ratios, both financial and non-financial, which will enable you to monitor the performance of your company effectively.

Ratios lead you to ask the right questions; however, they seldom pro-vide conclusive answers.

Activity and efficiency

Ratios which relate to non-financial information can be vital in assessing the performance of a company. For example:

Retail sector – measure turnover in relation to selling area.

Airlines – the load factor, that is, the number of passengers on each plane is essential to success.

The ratios showing stock turnover and average collection period help managers and outsiders to judge how effectively a company manages its assets. Rapid stock turnover is typical of the retail sector. Manufac-turing companies tend to show a much slower turnover.

$$\frac{Stock}{turnover} = \frac{Sales}{Stock}$$

$$= \frac{1998}{135} = 14.8 \text{ times}$$

A rapid collection period is typical of the retail sector which tends to avoid substantial credit sales. Manufacturing companies' collec-tion periods can often creep up to 60 days and more.

$$\frac{Average}{collection} = \frac{Debtors}{Sales \, per \, day}$$
$$period$$

$$\frac{34}{1998 \div 365} = 6 \text{ days}$$

Profitability

Gross margin is the gap between sales and variable costs, those costs directly affected by the volume of trade. Corrective action must be taken if margins fall too low, since gross margin represents the real income of the business.

$$\frac{Gross}{margin} = \frac{Sales - variable \, costs}{Sales}$$

Net profit margin shows manage-ment's overall use of resources under its control.

$$\frac{Net \, profit}{margin} = \frac{Profit \, before \, taxes}{Sales} \times 100$$

$$= \frac{196}{1998} \times 100 = 9.8\%$$

Return on capital employed is a prime yardstick in assessing a com-pany's profitability. It indicates how well a company is utilizing its assets.

$$\frac{Return}{on \, capital} = \frac{Profit \, before \, taxes}{Capital \, employed} \times 100$$
$$employed$$

$$= \frac{196}{858} \times 100 = 22.8\%$$

If a quoted company fails to earn a decent return, the share price will fall and prejudice chances of secur-ing additional capital or long-term debt on beneficial terms.

Management accounting

Money is the common denominator used to evaluate business decisions and to measure a company's performance. Most business transactions are recorded, analysed and presented in financial terms; they are almost always coordinated within the finance function.

Finance provides an important service to the operating activities in managing their resources. It is not, however, an unlimited source of management information. The same information can be analysed and presented in many different ways. It is up to you as a manager to ensure the system is providing you with the information you need.

The structure of the finance function varies from company to company. The typical structure in large organizations is shown below. The role of the financial accounting and treasury departments, collectively responsible for external reporting and cash management, is described on the opposite page.

Management accounting is the department to which you will have most exposure as a manager. Financial information should be analysed here and disseminated in 'user friendly' form as the basis for decision-making. The department also provides an early warning system for planning and controlling the business.

The role of management accounting is essentially to do three things:

The finance function

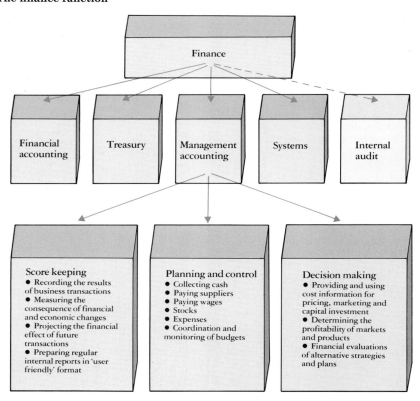

Finance

Financial accounting | Treasury | Management accounting | Systems | Internal audit

Score keeping
- Recording the results of business transactions
- Measuring the consequence of financial and economic changes
- Projecting the financial effect of future transactions
- Preparing regular internal reports in 'user friendly' format

Planning and control
- Collecting cash
- Paying suppliers
- Paying wages
- Stocks
- Expenses
- Coordination and monitoring of budgets

Decision making
- Providing and using cost information for pricing, marketing and capital investment
- Determining the profitability of markets and products
- Financial evaluations of alternative strategies and plans

● Score keeping: keeping track of transactions and the subsequent impact on the wealth of the business.
● Planning and control of essential functions, including the overall framework of planning, budgeting and tracking actual performance to plan.
● Decision-making: providing sufficient information for managers to determine future activities.

Management accounting information is provided on a regular basis, usually monthly or quarterly. At the higher level, this will be in the form of a profit and loss account and balance sheet for the period, and at the lower level in the form of departmental performance against prior targets. Many companies include projected results for the full year period, updated with the same regularity.

In most cases the information is classified and summarized along the lines of responsibility that reflect the organizational structure. In reality, information systems that do not accurately reflect an organization's informal lines of responsibility and working methods tend to be discredited or bypassed by other informal reporting systems.

If you devote considerable resources to producing information for specific purposes, assess whether it could be produced more efficiently from other systems. The information provided should be geared to your requirements.

1 Financial accounting
● Recording business transactions
● Collecting income/paying debts
● Preparing statutory financial statements

2 Treasury
● Ensuring the business receives the best return on cash not presently in use
● Providing enough cash to pay debts
● Foreign exchange transactions
● Providing information on cash flow for reporting and budgeting

3 Management accounting
Recording, interpreting and analysing financial information for internal planning, control and decision making

4 Systems
● Planning computer strategy
● Reducing complexities in the availability and flow of information
● Providing database financial and non-financial information
● Selecting computer equipment
● Implementing computer systems

5 Internal audit
To preserve its objectivity, IA often reports directly to the chief executive or similar.
● Examining and reporting on the effectiveness of policies, procedures and programmes
● Advising on new control procedures
● Examining areas of the business for improved value for money

Working with the accounting function

The success of the accounting function depends on its relationship with user areas. Both the accountant and the user need to understand what is being produced and why.
● Be careful of jargon. Most of the terms used by accountants (eg 'profit', 'loss', 'value', 'cost') do not have common, widely accepted definitions. It is a good idea to ask your accountant to explain to you the accounting techniques and concepts in your organization.
● Test and question the assumptions the accountants are making. Different financial measures produce different outcomes.
● If you require *ad hoc* information from accounting, state your requirements. Don't merely ask for a figure but be precise and explain exactly what you are trying to do. The accountant will then be able to provide the data most relevant to your particular needs.

Budgetary control

Budgets help to make an organization run more smoothly and profitably. The overall budget is the master budget, made up of departmental budgets. Anyone who influences cost should be given a budget against which to measure actual expense. Budget holders must exist within a well-defined structure to avoid overlap of responsibilities.

Targets for individual budget holders can be dictated by senior management or negotiated so that they challenge rather than constrain.

Budgeting methods vary depending on the organization, department and type of expense, and include standard costs, revised annually for production costs; prior year level, adjusted for administration costs or selling expenses; and zero-based budgeting for research and development, which assumes that expenditure is nil, so that each cost element has to be justified separately.

Where budgets are always based solely on prior year expenditure, inefficiencies and overspending may be carried forward from one year to the next: a zero based budget produced every few years is a useful method of budget checking.

Costs, the prime ingredients of budgets, can be classified as variable or fixed. Variable costs vary directly with the level of output. For example, the cost of sheet metal for car body panels increases with the number of panels produced. Fixed costs, eg depreciation and rents, are independent of volume level and tend to change with time.

Flexed budgeting allows for changes in the activity level of a business. It assumes that additional sales mean more profit and managers should not be penalized for the normal cost of producing the extra units.

Budgets are flexed by adjusting the allowance by an amount equal to the variable cost of the incremental or decremental volume.

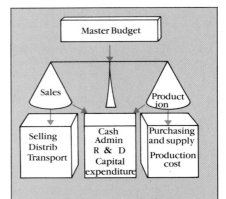

Budget coordination

If one aspect constrains the activity of the organization as a whole, it must be budgeted first. Budget coordination is normally undertaken by the senior accountant or through a budget committee.

All subsidiary budgets should be balanced to adjust targets for limiting factors imposed by one function on another. The principal limiting factor is usually the level of sales.

The budgeting process

Budget preparation begins with forecast sales and information on external factors, such as inflation. Departmental targets are set or negotiated.

Departmental budgets are consolidated to eliminate inconsistencies between them and the company's overall profit objectives.

When budgets have been accepted by senior management, the flow of costs, revenues and capital expenditure is scheduled. Each budget holder receives a monthly target against which to measure expenditure.

Variance (the difference between budget and actual expense) is analysed. If necessary, corrective action is taken which is fed into the overall planning process and ensures the company stays on course to achieve its financial targets. It is always crucial to understand the nature of variances so that corrective action is not superficial or short-term.

Good managers understand the contribution their teams' budgets make to the company's overall budget.

Controlling the budgeting process

Successful budgeting is essentially people-oriented and depends on:
● Cooperation and communication between budget holders.
● Targets that are perceived to be realistic and achievable.
● Managers' individual objectives being consistent with the overall objectives in the master budget.

Feedback should be constructive, not punitive. Reports for individual budget holders should highlight significant variances.

Budget reports should also be:
● Designed for each user in a format that is easily understood.
● Produced on a timely basis so that the user can relate the information to recent events.
● Accurate, to maintain the budget holder's confidence in the system.
● Increasingly detailed through lower levels of the organization.
● Supported by regular meetings between managers and their subordinates to review progress.

Advantages of budgets

Budgets can be time consuming to prepare and review and, if imposed from above, they may constrain individuals. However, budgets do have significant advantages.
● The organization's objectives are clearly defined in financial terms.
● Key actions which the organization may need to take are highlighted.
● Responsibilities and yardsticks against which to measure performance are defined.
● An overview of the organization's entire activities is contructed and decisions about trade-off of resources and priorities can be made at a high level.
● Inter-departmental conflict is reduced.
● Early warning of problems is given so that corrective action may be initiated.
● Correctly performed, the budgeting process can be a positive motivating stimulus.

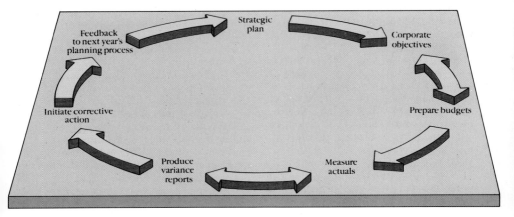

Strategic plan → Corporate objectives → Prepare budgets → Measure actuals → Produce variance reports → Initiate corrective action → Feedback to next year's planning process

Costs and pricing

Your organization will have costing systems which collect and classify costs into different categories, at different times and, in some cases, in different currencies. You, as a manager, must understand the cost structure of your business well enough to know the financial implications of the decisions you are making.

Some costs such as labour and materials, can be charged as direct costs to a particular product or process. Other costs, such as heating, lighting, maintenance and depreciation, have to be apportioned as indirect costs.

The basis for apportioning costs varies by cost category and type of business. Different methods present different product costs and therefore affect decision-making. Your accounting department will tell you which basis of cost apportionment it uses.

All decision-making requires cost information to evaluate choices. If, say, you visited a car showroom you would want to know how much each car cost before deciding to buy.

Cost information is referred to when pricing products. Pricing decisions are based on the perceived value to the customer, or 'what the market will bear'. They depend on awareness of the customer, the structure of the market and the price and the quality of competitors' products. Price setting is a major determinant of a firm's short-term profitability and a product's long-term success.

If the price is too high, sales will be reduced according to the degree of responsiveness, or elasticity, of demand to changes in price. High prices that generate high profits attract other firms to make close substitutes. But if the price is too low, the firm may not recover its costs.

Cost based pricing

In cost based or cost plus pricing, a profit mark-up is applied to the total unit cost of the product. The amount

---

Costing systems

Costing systems are used to determine the cost of a unit of output. The most popular systems are process costing, job costing and operation costing.

Process costing is used where large volumes of identical products pass through continuous production operations. The total cost of each operation is calculated for a given period, then divided by the number of units produced to give an average cost per unit.

Job costing is used in industries which produce to order. Costs can be identified against the job for every stage of the production cycle, separately for direct and indirect expenses.

Operation costing is used to develop the cost per unit of service rendered.

---

of profit mark-up varies. For example, a product may be premium priced because it is technologically advanced or because it has a reputation for quality and reliability.

Alternatively, the profit mark-up may be set to achieve a target rate of return on capital employed, for a forecast level of sales. This is common with component suppliers whose prices are influenced by their dependence on a single manufacturer.

Market based pricing

Costs may be of secondary importance in determining how low prices can be set. In the oil and motor industries, for example, prices are based on that of the market leader, adjusted for product feature differences.

Variants of market based pricing include price discrimination in which the same product is offered to different customers at different prices, and competitive tendering which is based on the assumed pricing strategies of competitors.

Costs are a fundamental tool for decision-making but, like profits, can be expressed in many different ways.

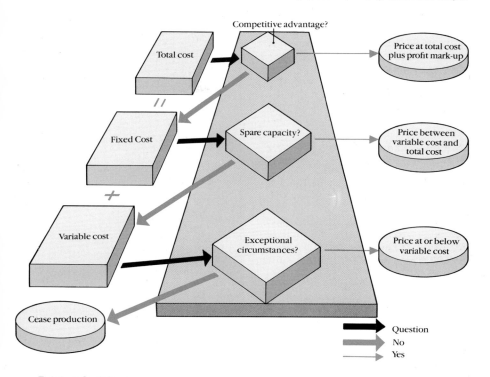

Pricing decisions

1 Competitive advantage: the first question you should ask is, does the product have a competitive advantage? It may be technically advanced or innovative, or your organization might be the market leader with an established brand image.

If the answer is yes, you can use cost plus pricing to develop the selling price. The mark-up will depend on the market and on the product's level of competitive advantage. Pricing at cost enables an organization to break even. The ability to pursue cost plus pricing should ensure an organization's long-term profitability.

If the answer is no . . .

2 Look at spare capacity: do you have enough to produce the product without incurring additional fixed costs, eg additional machinery, extra staff or more warehousing facilities? This question might arise in a competitive tendering situation where the objective is to price as low as possible yet make some contribution to fixed costs already incurred.

If spare capacity is available, you can afford to price the product at variable costs, plus some mark-up respresenting a contribution to fixed costs.

If the answer is no . . .

3 Exceptional circumstances: you are really now taking pricing decisions at the margin. If you don't recover your variable costs, you are not even getting back the additional costs you will incur in producing these units.

There are exceptional circumstances that might make this avenue viable. Such exceptions depend on the other objectives of the firm, against which profitability can be traded off. For example, the firm may wish to establish a brand image, or to attract sales of other highly profitable products in the range, or to generate high profits in the after sales market through service and supply.

If there are no exceptional circumstances, then you should immediately cease production, since that product will never be profitable.

77

Long-term planning

Cost information is used not only to make decisions about the day-to-day running of the business, but also to assist long-term plans. Managers need cost information to compare revenue or profits generated in the future with costs incurred today.

As part of the strategic and business planning process, accountants will help to:
● Evaluate future alternatives and measure the profitability of projects spanning a number of years
● Project the firm's profit and loss account and the balance sheet over the next five or ten years.

Areas where sound financial planning plays an important role include:
● The launching of new products
● The replacement of existing equipment or buildings
● Whether to make or buy a particular component
● Where and when to locate new production facilities.
● Whether to lease or to buy equipment.

But no one knows with certainty what will happen in the future. Assumptions have to be made so that costs and benefits, not easily expressed in cash terms, can be measured. How would you measure, say, the benefits of an improvement in your firm's market image, or in employee morale?

You are the best person to predict the outcome of decisions affecting your department. So, while you should trust your accountants' skill and expertise, you should not rely solely on their judgements. Make sure that they take into account all the non-financial benefits you expect to accrue from a particular project.

Decisions should not be based on financial criteria alone. Financial evaluation is one aspect of the decision-making process, along with other factors, such as the validity of the assumptions and the sensitivity of the costs to change.

Financial evaluation techniques

	Original investment	1st year
Cash flows	−1000	300
Cumulative (net) discounted cash flows	−1000	−700
		└─── Payback ───
Discounted cash flow (DCF) 10% rate	−1000	273
Cumulative (net) discounted cash flows	−1000	−727
Discounted cash flow (DCF) 25% rate	−1000	240
Cumulative (net) discounted cash flows	−1000	−760

Capital investment budgeting involves decisions about how to invest money in projects now to maximize cash returns. Is the project profitable in its own right? Will it generate a rate of return at least equivalent to investing the money elsewhere at the same risk?

Imagine your company is considering whether to invest £1 million in a new production line (*see above*). How should the company decide whether to go ahead?

If, by making certain assumptions about future cash flows, your accountants measure the profitability of the project, on what basis would they make their decision? There are three common approaches:
● The straightforward payback method asks: How quickly will the initial investment be repaid? In this example, it

(Figures in units of one thousand pounds sterling)					
2nd year	3rd year	4th year	5th year	Total cash flow	Average cash flow
300	400	400	600	2000	400
−400	0	400	1000	$ARR = \dfrac{400}{1000}$ $= 40\%$	
248	300	273	372 *		
−479	−179	94	466 ↑ NPV		
192	205	165	198 *		
−568	−363	−198	0 ↑ NPV	* Discounted cash flows can be obtained from specially prepared tables.	

Financial modelling

In the calculations (*left*), many of the figures are estimated and subject to significant variation.

Computer models can be constructed which allow extensive sensitivity analysis, enabling the variables to be changed and a number of different scenarios to be selected.

Such models, often equipped with DCF calculations as a standard feature, project future profitability patterns. You can then ask: 'What will be the outcome if any of the assumptions were changed?'

Remember that the figures are only predictions and are sensitive to many fluctuating forces. If the accountants turn down your project on the grounds of their calculations, try your own sensitivity analysis. Examine the numbers again and again.

And what about non-financial factors: can your company afford not to invest in a new product, especially when competitors' actions make it imperative? Supposing your plant is becoming obsolete? Do not hesitate to question the accountants' calculations when your business sense disagrees with them.

is paid back after three years. And the quicker the payback, the less the risk to the project. However, this method does not take into account the cash flows after the payback date.

● The Average rate of return (ARR) method averages out the cash flow over the life of the project, five years in our example, giving a percentage figure for the average return on the initial investment. Here it is 40%. And the higher the figure, the better the profitability.

● The Discounted cash flow (DCF) method accounts for more variables and so is more complex but more accurate. Unlike the payback and ARR methods, DCF measures the time-value of money by translating future cash flows into their net present-day value (NPV).

The discount rate selected represents the company's desired rate of return. It will normally equate either to the projected cost of borrowing money or to the return earned on present projects. Often this figure will be increased to allow for risk.

At 10% the project shows positive discounted cash flows and at 25% it breaks even. The decision to go ahead or not would use these estimates and all the other business related factors known to one's company.

A 10% rate, probably an underestimation, gives a net discounted profitability of £466,000 after 5 years; a 25% rate, probably an overestimation, means the company would break even over the life of the project. The discount rate at the break-even point is known as the internal rate of return.

Are things going wrong?

Major financial problems rarely occur overnight and do not always mean that a company will fail. They do, however, indicate that top management has problems, and the company will fail if management is not able to deal with them. Some indications that management is not up to the challenge are lack of management action, failure to manage the accounting function and poor budgetary control.

Company failures are management failures. Lack of success is reflected in the accounting information, but it is a symptom of ineffective management not a cause.

Top management needs to deal with present problems and future plans. Financial directors are essential participants. They must ensure that the

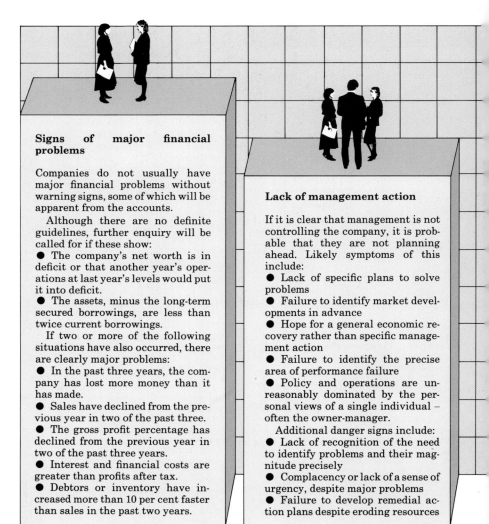

Signs of major financial problems

Companies do not usually have major financial problems without warning signs, some of which will be apparent from the accounts.

Although there are no definite guidelines, further enquiry will be called for if these show:
● The company's net worth is in deficit or that another year's operations at last year's levels would put it into deficit.
● The assets, minus the long-term secured borrowings, are less than twice current borrowings.

If two or more of the following situations have also occurred, there are clearly major problems:
● In the past three years, the company has lost more money than it has made.
● Sales have declined from the previous year in two of the past three.
● The gross profit percentage has declined from the previous year in two of the past three years.
● Interest and financial costs are greater than profits after tax.
● Debtors or inventory have increased more than 10 per cent faster than sales in the past two years.

Lack of management action

If it is clear that management is not controlling the company, it is probable that they are not planning ahead. Likely symptoms of this include:
● Lack of specific plans to solve problems
● Failure to identify market developments in advance
● Hope for a general economic recovery rather than specific management action
● Failure to identify the precise area of performance failure
● Policy and operations are unreasonably dominated by the personal views of a single individual – often the owner-manager.

Additional danger signs include:
● Lack of recognition of the need to identify problems and their magnitude precisely
● Complacency or lack of a sense of urgency, despite major problems
● Failure to develop remedial action plans despite eroding resources

information that management needs is provided. They should explain the financial consequences of company policy and emphasize the effects of indecision and delay on any proposed changes.

Without effective management, companies cannot react to problems or rectify mistakes. The most common mistakes are:

● Overtrading, ie trading beyond the financial capacity of the business
● High gearing, or leverage, ie too high a proportion of the cash used to run the business is borrowed
● A 'mammoth project' accepted without considering whether the company has the financial and management resources to see it through to a successful conclusion.

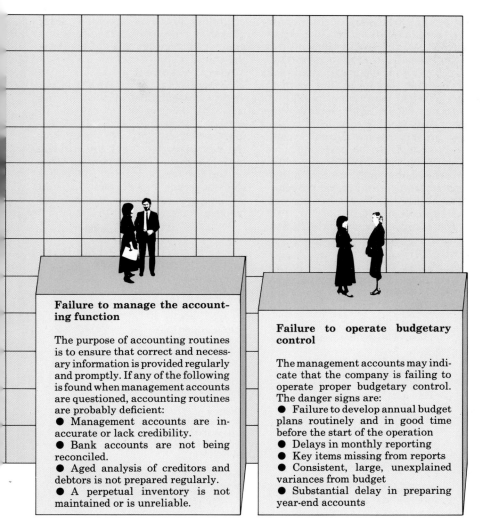

Failure to manage the accounting function

The purpose of accounting routines is to ensure that correct and necessary information is provided regularly and promptly. If any of the following is found when management accounts are questioned, accounting routines are probably deficient:
● Management accounts are inaccurate or lack credibility.
● Bank accounts are not being reconciled.
● Aged analysis of creditors and debtors is not prepared regularly.
● A perpetual inventory is not maintained or is unreliable.

Failure to operate budgetary control

The management accounts may indicate that the company is failing to operate proper budgetary control. The danger signs are:
● Failure to develop annual budget plans routinely and in good time before the start of the operation
● Delays in monthly reporting
● Key items missing from reports
● Consistent, large, unexplained variances from budget
● Substantial delay in preparing year-end accounts

Investing in people

Personnel concerns, first and foremost, the human aspects of any organization. It aims to get the most out of manpower resources.

As a manager, you are responsible for good relations with your staff. It is important that you recognize Personnel as an integral part of the management process and understand how the function can contribute to your effectiveness.

The development of Personnel

Since the early years of this century the personnel function has passed through various stages, elements from which remain in most personnel departments and help to explain its role.

Personnel began as a concern for the physical and social welfare of working people. The next development of Personnel responsibility was recruitment against a tight specification of tasks to be performed; provision of on-the-job training in routine tasks; and the application of output-related financial incentive schemes – all within the framework of company systems and procedures.

Increasing levels of regulations, procedures and controls, and the use of coercion and money as the primary tools of motivation, led to widespread workforce militancy. In the negotiation on wage rates, bonus rates and the application of working agreements, Personnel operated as intermediaries and conciliators.

Since the 1950s behavioural science has been included in the personnel function.

In the 1970s employment legislation brought a new role for the personnel function: specialist legal adviser and protector of the company against the consequences of breaking the rules.

Modern Personnel

Personnel plays an interpretive, advisory and administrative role, and it is also being asked to respond to external pressures such as demographic trends that force changes in the labour market. They are still the 'people experts'. The purpose, so often prescribed for Personnel, of getting the best return for an organization on its investment in people, is crucial to modern industries.

Recruitment

Personnel's role includes manpower planning and should cover:
- Liaison with the appropriate manager to agree job description and specification of the type of employee required
- Preparation of advertisements
- Screening of replies
- Assistance with the interviewing of candidates
- Associated administration including checks on references

As a manager, use Personnel to help you find the best recruits.

Clearly define your needs so that Personnel can draw up a job specification. Leave Personnel to sift applicants and draw up a short-list. Take advantage of their interviewing expertise to help you with final interviews.

You and Personnel

The primary responsibility for good staff relations rests firmly with you, the manager. However effective the personnel department, it cannot do as much good as you can.
● Ensure that you are closely involved in issues affecting your staff.
● Demonstrate your commitment and loyalty by solving your group's personnel problems or by making sure they are dealt with correctly.
● Seek advice from Personnel on how to apply the organization's formal procedures to everyone's benefit.
● Don't hide behind procedures laid down by the personnel department. If you have to resolve questions that don't fit the guidelines, work out your own solution.
● Avoid searching for a rule that determines what you might do before thinking out for yourself what is best.
● Don't think, 'I cannot do this because Personnel won't allow it.' Rethink your particular problem.
● If Personnel's answer is right for your staff, consider the decision as yours.

Induction

Personnel's objective in the last stage of the recruitment process is to help managers familiarize new employees with the company and its environment quickly. They should provide information on:
● Physical layout and facilities of the workplace
● Key company rules, procedures and philosophies
● Products and services
● Key personnel

Functions of Personnel

The functions and duties are to:
● Supply expert and up-to-date advice, interpretation and support on managing people.
● Run a comprehensive administration section which provides usable information for management.
● Provide expert recruitment support for user departments.
● Provide advice and support on the induction of recruits.
● Help identify training and development needs and set up the required programmes.
● Understand and apply the principles of job evaluation.
● Provide a framework for assessing staff performance which allows the company to identify training needs and promotable people, and enables individuals to identify their career prospects.
● Ensure that all departures, whether by resignation, retirement or dismissal, are managed in accordance with statutory provisions.
● Have a detailed understanding of employment legislation and its implications for the organization.
● Give authoritative information on personnel-related company procedures and agreements.
● Ensure the consistent implementation of remuneration and benefits policies and develop them in line with company needs.
● Handle company welfare provisions, including the counselling of staff on personal problems.
● Have a general knowledge of government social services, how they apply to employees and how benefits are claimed.
● Understand the ways in which common, civil and criminal law affect the employment contract.

Supporting and advising

Almost any set of published accounts will include somewhere in the chairman's statement a variation on the theme of 'Our most important asset is our people'.

It is doubtful, however, if Personnel has ever fulfilled its promise to make a positive contribution at strategy level to the success of the organization. Clearly there are exceptions, generally where the executive responsible for personnel has qualities of excellence, personal credibility, conviction and breadth of vision.

It is argued that only infrequently does Personnel attract the calibre of executive with the flair and power to capitalize on a challenging, complex role. Technical excellence is not therefore matched by managerial excellence. However, there is an increase in graduates entering the profession, and in professional qualifications.

Links with the organization

The potential strength of the personnel department comes from its support and advisory roles. These bring it into contact with all line and functional heads. Credible individuals can therefore wield considerable influence.

Typically, a well-developed personnel department will report through its senior executive to the head of the organization without necessarily being represented on the board of directors. If it reports to a manager at any lower level, it will probably have insufficient credibility and weight to achieve anything worthwhile.

To perform its support functions, the primary administrative responsibility of the department is to maintain accurate records of individual employees. These should contain both personnel and detailed operational information.

Training of some sort will be required for every employee, however informal, at some stage in his/her career with a company.

As a manager, you should seek support from the personnel department for training your staff in basic or specialist skills, and for supervisory and management training.

To appraise the job performance of your subordinates, you need sound understanding of what each job is about in terms of purpose, goals and targets. You should find out how well people are doing their jobs and if action is needed to improve performance.

To appraise job potential, consider whether subordinates are challenged, whether they accept responsibility and can view their jobs in relation to others.

Support function

To get the best return for an organization on its investment in people, Personnel must recruit better people and ensure that they are better trained and developed.

From the employee's point of view, Personnel can provide advice and assistance with personal problems, for example domestic, financial and legal difficulties, acting as a sort of in-house citizen's advice bureau.

More money is wasted on training and development than on any other aspect of the personnel department's work. There are only two reasons for training anyone: to make them capable of performing their job to a satisfactory standard, and to equip them to handle changed responsibilities either as a result of promotion or of redeployment.

Getting the right people trained in the right things is a difficult (and expensive) process. It requires the company to define its manpower needs now and in the future. It also requires individuals to know their strengths, to indicate their interests and ambitions and to analyse their shortcomings with complete honesty.

The department is frequently the designer of, and usually the coordinator or the adviser on, the appraisal system. Performance reviews should allow the organization to identify the good, the bad and the average and thus to plan the future use of resources at its disposal.

In the process, individuals should be helped to agree on tasks and objectives and advised on how they are themselves perceived by the organization and what their future holds. It is important that employees know both their duties and their prospects.

Training and development

A straightforward procedure should be applied before committing any funds to training:
- For all employees involved, identify what it is that they cannot do that they need to be able to do.
- For each need identified, specify on-the-job or off-the-job training and design or locate an appropriate programme.
- Agree criteria in advance for assessing the results of the training. This can be very difficult for management development courses, many of which rely on the gesture of faith that 'some good will come of it'.
- Ensure that senior management will support rather than thwart employees who return from training courses charged with new ideas.

Performance and promotion

A constructive appraisal scheme helps managers to improve their performance and that of their staff by:
- Demonstrating the value of all work done.
- Ensuring that managers and employees appreciate each other's position.
- Showing staff how to build on personal strengths.
- Identifying training needs.
- Drawing attention to employees with potential.
- Identifying any staff disharmony and rectifying it.
- Providing information on which to base future manpower plans.

Operating successfully

Companies have widely varying ideas on what their personnel policies should be and how they should be applied. The case studies (*opposite*) are not intended as ideal approaches to resolving these issues. Rather they are indicative of what can be done, given commitment and vision by managements and workforces.

The procedures, rules and contractual arrangements surrounding the employment of staff inevitably deal with sensitive legal issues and have a potential for disaster if they are misunderstood or misapplied. Personnel has a clear function to interpret the written word and to know the precedents for its application.

State legislation has increasingly affected the formulation of personnel policies and procedures and has introduced financial and other penalties for companies that fail to comply with its requirements. This has become important for personnel specialists who now need to understand the underlying statutes and their interpretation in the courts to be able to steer the company away from trouble.

Of particular relevance are the rules relating to redundancy and other dismissals and the anti-discrimination laws relating to sex and race.

Industrial relations

The most obvious involvement of the department is in the negotiating process. This is conducted either by direct involvement with the delegated authority of the chief executive or Personnel acts as adviser to other managers who are seeking to resolve disputes or reach agreement on issues. Because interests are normally highly polarized, the process itself has become highly formal and proceduralized.

Other activities under this heading include joint consultation, employee participation programmes, handling of grievances and disciplinary matters.

Departures

Whether due to dismissal, redundancy, retirement etc, departures involve Personnel in an advisory and administrative role to ensure:
● All benefits and entitlements are explained and paid.
● All internal procedures have been followed.
● The file on the individual is updated and retained for future reference.
● Statutory requirements have been met.

Most managers are happy to allow the personnel department to handle staff departures. Make sure that Personnel has all the relevant facts.

To minimize disruption to your department, arrange short-term cover for the vacancy or reorganize so that the vacancy disappears.

If a replacement is needed, start the recruitment process as quickly as possible.

TOSHIBA

Creating staff commitment

At Toshiba, positive staff relations are based on a recognition that, in employing somebody, a relationship has been entered into. Management expects commitment to the company in return for treating every employee as a valued member.

Staff are selected for their enthusiasm, idealism, attention to detail and expertise, as well as for their commitment. All are given the title 'production employee', which allows for flexibility.

There is no job grading and evaluation scheme. Every employee is expected to wear a company-issue blue jacket at work and to eat in the same restaurant.

Each working day begins with a five-minute meeting to discuss problems, ideas and solutions. There are also monthly meetings of the whole manufacturing department, addressed by the Production Director, and six-monthly meetings of the whole company, addressed by the Managing Director.

Employees are trained to be quality conscious and self-checking. Production figures and quality level performance are freely displayed.

The result is low staff turnover, low absenteeism, minimal lateness, a cheerful workforce and production on target.

The belief that each person should feel important has brought Toshiba enviable production results. Their corporate philosophy and attitude to personnel work as well, if not as naturally, in Plymouth as in Tokyo.

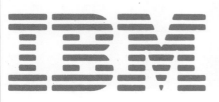

Supporting the manager

At IBM, the personnel function has little real power. Its role is to provide line management with a framework of personnel policies and practices. Ultimate responsibility for the management of IBM's people lies with the line managers.

Trust and confidence have been built up at all levels of line management. Managers are committed to IBM's personnel policies.

Full employment is offered to everyone. Employees whose jobs and skills are eliminated by economic or technical change are offered alternative jobs. In return, employees have to be prepared to move or retrain.

All IBM employees have the same conditions of service and benefits; every employee's performance is assessed against objectives; everyone is paid according to merit.

A central communications department ensures that information reaches all line managers, who are encouraged to hold departmental meetings. Opinion surveys are conducted on a regular basis.

Only if the system fails is the personnel function called on to adjudicate or make recommendations.

IBM recognizes that the company's aspirations will be realized only with the help of a workforce whose own aspirations are recognized by the company.

A personal strategy

The 1980s was a decade of unrelenting change in new technology. Few organizations can claim that technology did not have an impact, no matter how minor, on the way they manage and conduct their businesses.

This continual flow of developments in new technology tests the organization's ability to absorb new changes. Some developments may require a radical rethinking of how the business is run and organized. Cash dispensing machines in high street banks are an example of how technology has brought fundamental changes in business practice.

Technology cannot be viewed in isolation from the business. It should support strategic and operational needs. In some industries it has been used to strengthen links between distributors and retailers. In retailing it has become a critical day-to-day tool for merchandising decisions.

Technology stretches the manager, too. Keeping on top of new technology in a period of unrelenting change requires time, energy and constant commitment. Every new development brings opportunities to improve the way a business is conducted. However, these opportunities can also create a diversion for the inexperienced manager.

Managers who excel in this fast-moving age are those who are not frightened by new technology. They do not see it as a threat or ignore its impact, but embrace it and turn it to their advantage. New developments stretch a manager's ability as strategist and decision maker. Some tasks can be delegated to the experts but the manager needs to keep on top of new technology and ensure that it supports key needs of the business.

Key areas of focus for the manager

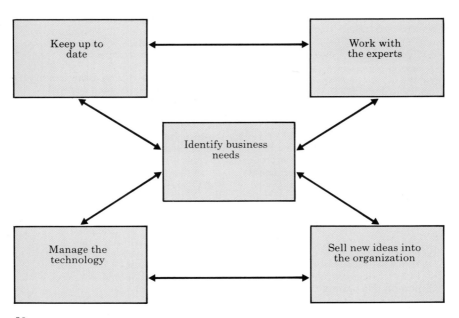

The diagram opposite highlights five key areas of focus for the manager. They are as follows:
● Identify business needs. Examine the way your business operates and continually challenge working practices and relationships with customers, suppliers and staff. Explore new ideas regularly. Explore the use of technology to achieve greater efficiency, effectiveness and quality.

Pick up ideas from staff meetings, from bottlenecks, from information that is difficult to get or contradictory, by reading about innovative uses of technology in the press, internal reports etc. You might ask the internal audit department or an external organization to look at the whole business to identify opportunities.
● Keep up to date, particularly with developments in your own industry. Your business cannot afford to fall behind with new technology – doing so may expose your organization to considerable risks. If changes are happening too quickly, make fewer changes in the short term.
● Work with the experts and try to develop a good relationship with them. They can help you achieve your goals with new technology. Be ruthless about what you need and make sure that you get the technical solution that you require.
● Sell new ideas into the organization. Don't underestimate the time and effort needed to put new technology in place. You will only get results if you and your team are committed. Prepare your team for the change and don't cut corners on skills training or support.
● Manage the technology to get the results that you want. Develop a mature attitude to new technology. It is there to support the business. Security is important. Don't encourage your staff to find ways round a system.

A personal computer can enhance personal productivity and flexibility.

Some words of caution

You may find that not all of the changes can be absorbed at the same time. The experience in the 1980s highlighted a number of reasons why organizations failed to realize the full benefits of new technology:
● Failure to understand the problem and to explore the underlying business processes and information requirements that were to be supported.
● Failure to define and agree on the business requirements in a way that was understood both by users of the technology and the technical experts.
● Failure to define the scope of the new systems and to manage user expectations.
● Failure to maintain the involvement of users throughout the process of developing new systems, from identifying priorities to planning and implementation.
● Failure to cope with and respond effectively to resistance from the top or from employees. Some organizations found the pace too fast.

Technology is an expensive resource in itself. Mistakes can have an even more costly impact on the success of subsequent projects. Start with a small idea where success is assured so that later ideas are received well.

Determine the priorities for your organization and select the ideas which will have the greatest impact on the business.

Business needs

To ensure that technology supports your business, you need to start with a solid understanding of the business process and of the value that technology can add. What are the critical success factors? What are the relative strengths and weaknesses?

The key to success is continually to reappraise the elements of the value added to your business in terms of cost savings and customer satisfaction.

Focus on the potential opportunities for your business. Only if technological change adds value should you consider adopting new technology.

● **Working practices** Challenge current practices. Can technology be used to increase productivity? Can repetitive and mundane tasks be automated? Would this achieve cost reductions and improve quality?

● **Relationships** Can technology be used to transform business relationships? Can you provide electronic ordering links to your customers? Can you use electronic banking to make your liquid funds work harder? Aim to achieve new ways of working with customers and suppliers.

● **Customer service levels** Can technology help your business to attain improvements?

● **Competing effectively** Are your competitors investing in technology? Have they managed to bring down running costs as a result?

New technology can push and pull in many directions, you will need to identify the priorities. Which is likely to give you the greatest benefit at the least cost?

Business needs

Always start from an understanding of what your business does and what it needs. What are the targets in terms of market share and profitability? This information will allow you to assess new developments.

Applications

What part can technology play in achieving goals? Look for areas where technology can help. Identify gaps in information and challenge existing working practices. Once you have identified the application then you can seek the technical solution in terms of software and hardware.

Software

Improvements in software occur constantly and offer new ways of supporting your particular application: beware of changing for the sake of changing. Consider enhancements in terms of the improvement in efficiency that they could bring about. Implementing even minor changes can take up considerable resources.

Hardware

Changes in hardware are generally related to machine performance. They will be stimulated by your need to process data faster, store more data or run enhanced software or applications.

Developing ideas

Turn your best ideas into a well-thought-out written proposal. This will help you to sell the idea upwards and to your information technology department. A proposal in writing will

---

Keeping up-to-date

● Be aware of technological developments in your industry.

● Develop a good relationship with suppliers and your information services department. Ask them to keep you aware of major developments that may affect your department.

● Don't delegate everything to the specialist in your group or department.

● Take time to create and innovate.

● Take part in meetings on developments in new technology.

● Attend exhibitions and briefings specific to your industry.

also help later when you want to specify your requirements in detail to a supplier.

Include the following in your proposal:
- A statement of what you want to do.
- How you intend to do it, how much it will cost and what benefits you expect to achieve.
- What technical help you will need.
- How you plan to implement the project in terms of timescales, dates and deadlines, and resources required.
- What equipment, staffing levels and technical support you will need.
- Specific information about the software and hardware required.
- How you will handle maintenance, system security and training.

Once your proposals have been formulated, you will need a sponsor who will be receptive to your ideas and who will help you obtain the necessary approvals.

Getting expert advice

When you need technical support, there are a number of sources of help available. People and organizations have generally developed expertise in technology at various levels of depth.

Departmental expert

Depending on the nature of the department, the expert varies from the most accomplished user to a member of the management team. This is generally the first port of call for most technology-related support. He or she will also probably purchase new equipment and provide training.

If the expert is part of the management team, he or she will set the IT strategy for the department and analyse and define solutions to management problems.

Internal IS/IT function

The structure of internal IT functions varies widely from one business to another. In most centralized organizations, there will be two or three distinct groups providing systems development and technical support.

- The help desk, whose function is to provide constant telephone and onsite support to any user in the organization. In most cases the help desk acts as a channel. Your call will be analysed and you will be put in touch with the appropriate specialist.
- Internal consultants are the technology experts who will provide information on key developments in their particular skills area. It is their job to keep abreast of new technical changes and develop new systems.
- Systems suppliers range from a high street dealer selling personal computers to a major systems house with a wide range of technical consultants. Many systems suppliers will provide pre-sale consultancy advice which you may find is reflected in the ultimate cost of the system.

High street dealers sell standard equipment and software packages. Some only sell to businesses and provide a range of software and maintenance support services.

Large systems houses provide technical consultancy and solutions to systems requirements. They generally have teams of programmers and analysts who develop applications for clients and sell hardware.

Most suppliers have incentives to sell particular brands of hardware and software, so the advice that you get may not be totally impartial.

Management consultancies

These organizations tend to offer advice on information systems issues in the context of business needs. Some provide support for overall IS development with an understanding of the business information requirements of each key function. The best of them can help exploit IT systems for competitive advantage in a wide range of industries. Most of these consultancies operate as part of large firms of accountants, although some management consultancies operate alone.

Working with the experts

At some stage, you will need the advice of the technical experts. Before you decide on a technical solution you must determine exactly which approach is going to give you the results that you need and then ensure it is within your budget and timescale for implementation.

It may be preferable to buy a ready-made system which you can tailor to specific needs. If managed well, this is a cheaper option than developing a system from scratch, but it may not give you exactly what you need.

Working with experts will help you decide the best course of action, but you should be aware that not all experts are independent of the solutions they offer. If this is a worry, you should look for an organization that can provide an independent appraisal.

In essence, your technical solution will be based on one of three options.

● **In-house development of major systems** When developing or enhancing systems, it is standard practice to follow one of the specific methodologies created for this purpose, since they provide a disciplined approach. For a system to be successful, the users must play a major part, together with in-house IT staff, contract staff and external consultants.

● **In-house development of small systems** As personal computer technology has become more powerful, there is an increasing trend to develop small-scale systems that satisfy departmental needs. These systems can be designed by in-house IT staff or by experienced users.

● **External purchase** For a majority of common applications, a number of software packages now exist which can be run on the latest hardware technology. This is often a preferable route where the requirements are fairly standard, such as simple accounting systems. Many of these

---

CASE technology

The 1980s have brought CASE tools to maturity. CASE – Computer Aided Software (or sometimes Systems) Engineering – exploits the power of the computer to automate techniques of systems development, to maintain multi-dimensional models of systems requirements and to generate systems from the detailed definitions. Good CASE tools enable the user and the developer to collaborate over interactive diagrams which specify requirements. CASE tools are also being used in the area of redevelopment engineering.

Information systems life cycle
Business-focused systems development must come from the top of the organization down. Truly effective developments of information systems start with an overall view of what the business's priorities are for exploiting information. Development projects vary and cannot follow a rigid step-by-step approach. It is therefore essential that the framework for the systems development you adopt is flexible enough to recognize this.

The full life cycle encompasses a number of phases.

1 Planning
● Understand business strategy.
● Identify the needs for information.
● Gain consensus on priorities.
● Develop a strategy plan for information systems to support information needs.
● Evaluate the contribution made by existing systems.
● Construct an architecture for future systems.
● Formulate a plan of action (a strategic information systems plan).
● Gain commitment to start on the first steps.

2 Analysis
● Confirm the scope of the project.

systems have been designed so that they can be modified. Effective use of a package solution often entails adapting your business processes to the package.

A standard tendering and procurement process is generally followed when acquiring major systems. The stages involve developing a statement of requirements in terms of the business application, inviting tenders from a shortlist of suitable suppliers, evaluating the proposed solutions, and agreeing a purchase contract.

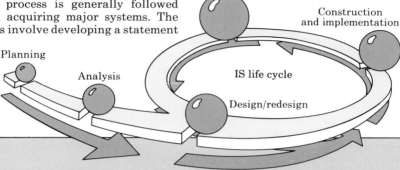

Planning

Analysis

Evolution

Construction
and implementation

IS life cycle

Design/redesign

● Analyse requirements jointly with users and IS analysts.
● Document the results in an unambiguous form. Using modelling techniques and CASE tools is the best approach.
● The analysis must be sufficiently detailed to cross-check data and process definitions.
● Decide on the scope of computer support in the business area being analysed.
● Plan the design of the system and ensure commitment of the sponsor.

3 Design
● Design the 'externals' of the system – how will it appear to users as a business system. Use prototyping techniques if appropriate.
● Design the 'internals', the technical design.
● Plan for detailed testing.
● Design the environment (IS and clerical) in which the system is to run.
● Plan the transition from old systems.

4 Construction and implementation
● Construct the system using a combination of techniques, ideally using an automatic application generator. Alternatively, write program code in a source language such as COBOL, or use a fourth generation language, or convert existing code to a new language.
● Test each new system or enhancement comprehensively.
● Plan the implementation.
● Train the users.
● Plan the future evolution and maintenance of the system.

5 Evolution
Most of the life of any system consists of use rather than development. All systems evolve in use to meet business requirements, to provide enhanced facilities or to fix inadequacies. The choice of development method and tools contributes greatly to the ease or difficulty of supporting an evolving system.

6 Redevelopment
Modern technology, through an extension of CASE tools, has made it possible to extract the structure and logic from existing systems. These can then be used as the basis of new systems maintained in a manner that makes modernization and integration with other business systems much easier.

Managing the technology

Your people and the technology are a resource partnership that must be organized to meet the objectives of the department or organization. The link is critical and there is no simple formula for success. Do you create a group of specialists who look after the systems or do you equip everyone with the skills? What are the key roles?

The leader is critical in introducing any change. The leader is not necessarily the most senior person but the most respected practitioner, in many cases the head of department. Visible endorsement from this person will influence less committed users to overcome fear and initial resistance.

The champion will drive new technology through to implementation. He or she needs an understanding of the business processes and how technology can help and strong interpersonal skills to smooth initial difficulties and win over reluctant users. Success or failure will rest mainly in this person's hands.

The systems administrator Once a system is up and running, there will be an on-going need for updates and reviews of system performance. These tasks fall on the systems administrator or manager. They demand a combination of technical and administrative skills and so may be split between a number of individuals.

The data administrator Sometimes it is necessary to appoint a data administrator. This person is vital in organizations that hold large volumes of data over various systems, to integrate the systems and ensure consistency across the organization. This role should also ensure that the data produced supports the business and provides the information required.

The security manager should be an independent person who can ensure that the data is safe and that the loss of a key user will not affect your investment.

The roles that you need will depend on the skills and experience of your team. Do not accept an organizational structure until it has been explained to your satisfaction.

Finally, don't set up committees unless you have to. Use task-oriented groups to implement solutions to fix problems.

Championing change

If as a manager you are asked to champion new technological change, what would you do? Where would you focus your efforts?

● **Sponsorship** An opinion former is critical and your most powerful ally. You may need more than one. Obtaining and maintaining ongoing commitment may be difficult, but it is worth the effort. Keep the sponsor informed of progress at all stages of the project. Provide briefs for regular meetings.

● **Marketing** Determine your internal marketing strategy early in the project. What are the likely benefits to the users? How will they react? Ask them for their views. Involve them in key decisions so that they feel part of the system. Be responsive to any questions or concerns they may have. Be open about shortcomings in the system.

● **Education** At some stage you will need to set up the training plan for the system. Some of this will be based on the features of the system. Incorporate all of the manual procedures around the system. Think about the different types of users – do they have the same needs?

Cater for changes in responsibilities and build in adequate time for getting to know the system. Provide concrete real-life examples of work and listen to concerns. Think about who is going to do the training and whether *they* need training.

● **Support** In the early stages of implementation, support is critical. Set up a formal support structure if necessary. Allocate some time in your schedule for this function. Encourage users to learn from each other. Set up expert users for parts of the system.

Most important, respond quickly.

The strategic role

Truly effective systems must support the priority areas in the business and must integrate with each other. With a view from the strategic level of the whole business, you will ensure that that there are no gaps between systems. Systems built in isolation generally do not integrate well.

The most advanced companies develop and maintain a strategic view of business information needs. The process of matching IT possibilities against this plan generates ideas for the imaginative use of new technology for competitive advantage.

Business process redesign

As new technology is applied in your organization, it will challenge the way people work. New ways of doing the same tasks will emerge and you as a manager will need to encourage such innovation. The redesign of business processes is cyclical: as the momentum for change increases, so will the speed of this cycle. Challenging working practices in response to competition will become increasingly vital in the 1990s.

Reviewing a system

There may be a time when you will need to conduct a comprehensive systems review, perhaps because you are taking over a new system or because the present system has become too costly or cumbersome or slow.

Cost benefit analysis Identify relative costs and benefits of the system.

User satisfaction Determine the system's level of user satisfaction by finding out how much the system costs to run, if it produces the planned benefits, how frequently it has been changed and how much changes to the system cost. Determine also what relationship users have with the computer function.

When you have done that you should then review the methods by which computer charges are calculated and passed onto the users.

Find out what support, such as training and advice, has been set up and make sure that it is followed. Ensure that you are kept completely informed of all plans and progress variances, as well as problems and the reasons for them. Monitor all the various costs and benefits, and establish quality control procedures. Make sure that your objectives are met.

Checking performance Examine reports of the system's performance level. If they do not exist, initiate them on a regular basis. Then make sure that they are, as far as possible, produced on time. Ensure that users who need to share data are able to do so, that terminals are available as planned and response times are adequate. Find out what the technical experts think of the system. Is there a history of maintenance problems?

Security

Examine the physical and data security procedures for the system:
- Identify threats to hardware, software, data, networks and people.
- Ensure adequate documentation is available.
- Take protective measures, eg make sure you are insured.
- Check back-up and physical security procedures.
- Draw up a disaster recovery plan which includes:
- Working out the critical business functions serviced by the computer and the plan to be without them.
- Plan and try out recovery procedures.
- Set up a system of regular monitoring to ensure that you are not caught out by unexpected changes.

Customer relations

Marketing is surrounded by mystique. Definitions vary from 'corporate planning' to 'the preparation of a media schedule for advertising'. In the game of business one-upmanship, you will score heavily by getting the definition right.

The simplest answer to 'What is marketing?' is that it is the 'process by which a company satisfies the needs of its customers at a profit which satisfies its needs'. The word 'marketing' is associated with the street market, where vendors compete vigorously with other stall holders. They use the simplest of strategies to sell their goods.

In 1887, when Michael Marks opened his penny bazaar, he displayed all the necessary constituent parts of a successful marketing strategy. He was able to sell:

● The right products
● In the right place
● At the right price
● Promoted in the right way
● To the right people.

A century later, marketing is still a management discipline that lies at the heart of Marks & Spencer's existence as a business.

Yet in many companies marketing is the part of the organization that is developed last or cut first during cost-pruning exercises.

Companies frequently mount expensive advertising and sales promotional campaigns without reference to an agreed marketing strategy. These campaigns fail because the company has not asked itself what business it is in; which markets it should seek to enter; and how it should go about entering them.

In preparing a marketing strategy for products and services, you will succeed if you concentrate on one thing – the customer. It may seem obvious to say that without customers all other aspects of a business are superfluous; but ask any group of

---

The end product of marketing

To achieve the right mix of products and markets for the company and its customers, you need to:
● Analyse opportunities by asking: Who needs our products? What are our strengths? What are our customer needs?
● Set realistic targets by using a consistent basis for decision-making and planning. Then define roles and provide a sense of purpose.
● Develop a strategy by recognizing internal strengths and weaknesses and external opportunities and threats. Devise tactics to beat the opposition.
● Formulate your game plan according to resources.
● Implement and control: make it happen.
● Implement and control: make it happen.

---

executives what is the most important success point on which a business should focus its attention and they will answer: profit, efficiency, productivity, management information, sales turnover or technical innovation. Customers, it seems, are regularly forgotten.

Any business which does not satisfy its customer needs now and in the future, will cut itself off from its customers and its essential life-support system. It should ask its customers (directly or indirectly): what they think of existing products; what improvements/additions they would like to see; what unfulfilled needs they have; and what about value for money.

Marketing nurtures the essential relationship between the company and its customers, and the marketing function defines the methods by which a company selects the appropriate mix of products and markets with which to achieve its objectives.

Good customer relations are essential for the success of a business. They are achieved by:
- Asking the customer what his needs are before and after sales
- Good customer service
- Product margins which meet the company's objectives and give the customer value for money
- Relevant product development and innovation to meet customers' future needs and potential new markets
- Regular sales calls and entertainment proportional to sales potential

Too good customer relations can mean:
- Service costs too high
- Margins too low
- High development costs of products with limited market
- Late payments
- Too many sales calls
- High entertainment costs

Bad customer relations can be due to:
- Poor service
- Products seen as poor value for money
- No interest in customers' future needs
- Insensitive credit control procedures
- Infrequent sales calls
- Low entertainment costs

If the balance swings too heavily in either direction, the result is *loss of profit.*

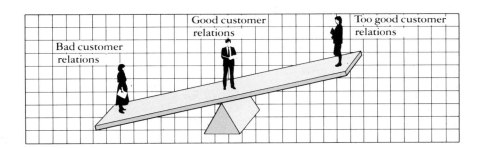

Market research equals knowledge of customer needs

Businesses change mostly as a result of movements in their customer base. A company's marketing activity should aim to understand and quantify those movements and achieve a continuous net growth in its customer base.

Past customers are often one of the easiest prospects for improving business. Study the sales history:
- Non-buyers may show a change in their regular pattern of buying.
- Slow buyers may show change in quantity or regularity of purchase.
- Lost customers can point to potential product or service problems.

Existing customers' buying habits give companies opportunities for selling-on or cross-selling. Ask:

- Are most of our customers in a single market segment/sector? Who else can we sell to?
- Are there opportunities to sell other products to existing customers? How can our products be improved or expanded?
- Can customers buy larger quantities more frequently? What else do they need?
- Are we dealing with the right person at the right level?
- Who are our competitors?
- How is our customer performing?

Future customers should be identified. Methods of targeting them include
- Market research in other sectors
- Prospect analysis for new types of customers
- Competitor research on products and services

Developing a strategy

The key elements of a marketing strategy are market segmentation, market entry and timing.

Market segmentation

This means breaking up the market into areas where the company can identify, promote or project its products and services.

No two buyers are likely to be satisfied by the same features. Because of the differences, each market segment will need different features to be promoted – even for the same product. Each – will provide different opportunities for the company to exploit.

Some well-used forms of segmentation are: customer, location and demand.

The purpose of segmenting the market is to identify areas which:
● Are suitable in size to justify committing resources
● Have potential for future growth and increased value
● Are not dominated by competitors
● Need the company's products.

Market entry

There are a number of ways of getting into a market; for example, the acquisition of a company which is already in the market; joint ventures and collaboration agreements; and sales and marketing techniques.

Timing

Timing can be the most critical element in marketing strategy. A company may have a good opportunity, an excellent product and may have the correct entry method and strategy, but unless the time is right, identified resources will be wasted and opportunities lost.

The important aspects of timing market entry are: demand patterns – cycles, seasons; education of end user; development of new products; and competitor activity.

The important aspects of timing a product launch are: lead time; setting up distribution; training staff; and production and stocks.

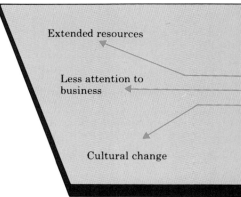

Extended resources

Less attention to business

Cultural change

The arena in which a company operates

Companies grow by:
● Developing and improving existing products and services
● Inventing new products and services
● Penetrating extended markets
● Developing new markets
● Diversifying where possible

Changing strategy

The following examples of marketing strategy illustrate the thinking which emerges from a well-formed strategic management review.

The Swiss watch industry was decimated by the digital revolution in watch making. Rather than competing in the descending price spiral in the mass market, 'Swatches' moved toward the 'design and fashion' end of the market, producing a product at low cost with the benefit of a strong tradition in the business.

Imperial Chemical Industries (ICI) suffered from the sharp decline in world markets in the 1970s. They were a traditional UK-based industry, dependent on the UK economy. Strategic management change indicated their wish to become a 'mid-Atlantic' company. They duly recognized both the importance of the US market and their need to strengthen links with the USA.

Marketing strategy

Once a company has products to sell, customers to buy them and a market in which to operate, its objectives should include:
● A review of internal strengths and weaknesses and external opportunities and threats
● Detailed research into the external environment and the potential market for the company's products and services.

The strategy should be formed from:
● Market segmentation alternatives: who/why?
● Market entry methods: how?
● Timing: when?
● Marketing mix: what?

Such a strategy is a plan which makes most use of the company's products, skills and services, and matches them against the needs of the customers who have a willingness to buy.

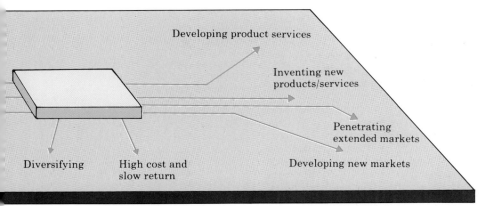

Developing product services

Inventing new products/services

Penetrating extended markets

Developing new markets

Diversifying

High cost and slow return

Many companies rush headlong into diversification in new markets, without fully exploiting the market for their existing products and services. Though potentially attractive, there are many pitfalls.

These include:
● Extended resources
● Less attention to existing business
● Cultural change necessary
● High cost and slow return

Success is achieved by consistently promoting and developing existing and improved products in present and extended markets.

Beware of the perils of diversification or change – stick to the existing strengths and promote them. Diversification should be carefully planned and controlled.

Preparing a plan

Once strategic market analysis is over and the products and markets chosen, you need to produce a marketing plan to make it happen.

Preparation

Successful marketing plans are developed by taking a disciplined approach to their preparation. Make sure that all key elements are considered.

A good marketing plan is a blend of the various aspects of marketing and selling activity, together with a commitment to meet the objectives of the strategy.

Like preparing to play a soccer match, you have to make certain that you have:
● The correct number of players in the appropriate positions
● The correct blend of attacking and defensive players
● Midfield creators and star strikers
● A suitable training and coaching scheme
● The right tactics to beat the opposition
● The 'sweeper' in the event of mistakes, and enough alternatives or substitutes on the bench.

Implementation

Marketing plans often fail because companies rely too heavily on advertising and promotional campaigns without enough consideration about the back-up services that are needed to respond to them.

A medium-sized car-hire company (£8M turnover) spent £0.75M on theme advertising which created a measured awareness of 95 per cent of those sampled. The company failed to capitalize on this awareness with structured campaigns and well-directed selling.

Growth was not sustained, and over a period of two years the company's gross contribution halved as other competitors attacked the market with heavily promoted schemes, well backed by service. The marketing plan was out of balance.

The eight-part marketing plan

Construct your marketing plan to ensure a balance.

Some sections of the eight-part marketing plan are more relevant in certain industry sectors than others. However, by going through a marketing plan in this structured way, you are forced to think of tactics and techniques which might otherwise be ignored.

1 Targets and objectives
Financial: turnover
Real term: units of sale (number); market share (%)

2 Product plan
Products: existing; improvement; development
Markets: existing; extended; new

3 Pricing plan
Prices: ours v competitors; trends
Margins
Discounts/rebates

4 Market information plan
Market research
Customer research
Competitor review

5 Sales plan
Direct: territories; distribution; prospects.
Indirect: distribution; networks
Controls: budgets/targets; reports

6 Promotional plan
Above-the-line: advertising through the media
Below-the line: printing; point of sale material; exhibitions
Public relations: free use of media; sponsorships
Direct marketing: direct mail; sales activities

7 Structure/staffing
Human resources
Training
Performance criteria
Incentives
Organization

8 Budget
To measure the performance of each of the above, linked to achievement of targets

Promoting excellence

BMW is an example of a company with a well-formed strategy and a sound, balanced marketing plan.

BMW cars compete in the upper end of the executive car market and, in all aspects of their marketing approach, BMW promote the technical excellence, quality engineering and reliability of their product.

Their dealer network is well supported by advertising and promotional aids. They promote an exclusive club for executives who are BMW owners. Fashion garments and regular magazines are available to owners.

By pitching their marketing effort directly at a particular market sector which aspires to ownership of BMWs, price is insignificant in relation to the product and its promotion. The average lead time in 1984 for delivery of their 3-Series cars was about four to five months, yet orders kept rolling in.

The promoted features of the BMW product far outweighed any marginal price benefit so heavily featured in promotional campaigns by the other mainstream motor car manufacturers.

Keeping the fizz

Perrier established itself in the luxury designer water market as a quality product. Originality and exclusivity are a clear advantage. A strong brand image separates it from other mineral waters. With a positive media campaign, Perrier could expand their market share almost at will – a marketing manager's dream.

But even dream companies are not immune to uncontrollable forces. In 1990 Perrier was forced by contamination to remove stocks from shop shelves. They reacted quickly and returned to the marketplace with new packaging that was clearly distinguished from the old. A firm market position and a strong marketing plan allowed them to recover from this serious setback. The vulnerability of any product can be minimized by a sound understanding of the market, and a marketing plan that reflects it.

Creating a structure

An organization must be structured to ensure that it satisfies the needs of its customers at a profit which satisfies its own needs.

The sales and marketing function in any company should be as structured as the other functions, but should not stop the development of 'product champions' and 'super sales people'.

In creating the organization structure for a company, the sales and marketing function is often covered simply by labelling executives 'sales managers' or 'marketing managers', with little thought as to the scope of their responsibilities.

The sales function

The direct sales effort should ensure that staff cover the territory where the customers are located. The size of a sales team depends on the number of calls needed to service the existing customers, regain lost customers and sell to potential customers.

Management has a responsibility to promote the use of sales techniques and to ensure a disciplined approach to produce value for the company.

The marketing function

The effort of marketing should aim for rigorous examination, analysis and promotion of the market for a company's goods/services. It should ensure that the company has sound, verifiable data on how its customers and the rest of the market are changing or behaving, and should be aware of competitors.

Marketing activities should support sales with research and promotion, and ensure that the sales resource spends more time with the customer. Market research must also contribute to product development.

Sales and marketing

The mix and relative weight of sales and marketing activities depend on the size and extent of the market. As in any structure or model, if one element is missing or incomplete, the rest will tend to be less effective.

Market research

Marketing plans and changes in direction should be based on verifiable data.

Analyse the last five years' performance and use forecasts and published indices to predict the behaviour of customers and markets in the future. Forecast at 'current prices'. Remember that every forecast you make will be revised. Sound research-based judgement will help you to be accurate in making key strategic decisions.

A review of performance can take one of the following forms.

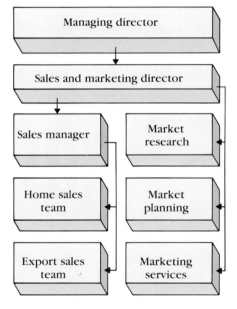

Small/medium companies often combine the sales and marketing functions under one director or senior manager, who has to ensure the correct balance of resources and skills is working for him/her and the company.

There will tend to be greater use of resources from outside. The most senior managers identify the need for these, and increase the overall skill of the function through their effective use.

1 External audit
The market: total market, size, growth and trends (value/volume).
Market character: developments and trends, products, distribution channels, customers/consumers, communication, industry practices.
Competition: size, share, standing and reputation; marketing methods, production capabilities, diversification, profitability, key strengths and weaknesses.

2 Internal audit
Sales: by location, type, customer, product.

Market shares: profit margins, cost rates.
Marketing mix variables: product management, price, distribution, promotion, operations and resources.

3 Customer research
Customer requirements and habits: some organizations use panels of sample consumers to gauge the acceptability of the product or change in product/price.

In industrial marketing, research is often ignored. Buyers are seldom asked about their current and future needs, or their views on the product.

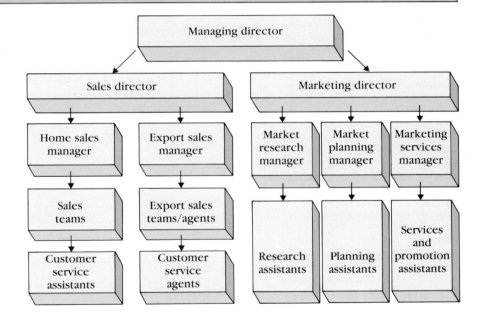

Large companies can afford the luxury of splitting up the sales and marketing activities and so manage them separately at a senior level.

In companies which have a high advertising budget, product managers take a dominant role relative to sales and sometimes work with media campaigns.

The sales function converts interest into real purchases and can include distribution. The marketing function supports this with promotion, research and product development input from the customer and the marketplace.

Because of the extent of their resources, large companies usually avoid having to depend exclusively on the help of external agencies and consultants.

Prospecting

Selling is the direct interaction between the company and its customer. Sales management training tends to concentrate on 'closing the sale', 'effective presentation skills', 'use of visual aids', and so on. The one aspect of selling which is often neglected is prospecting.

Before any direct selling activity or promotion takes place, it is important to allocate time and resources to prospecting for clients. Prospecting identifies buyers and makes the best use of time for other selling activities. It is the quality, not the quantity, of prospects that matters.

Market segmentation shows the area most likely to yield buyers, eg manufacturers with a turnover in excess of £5 million within 50 miles of your offices.

A prime prospect file is essential to any salesperson. Once achieved, canvassing is necessary only to 'top up' the prospect reservoir when the level drops; that is, once a prospect is converted into a customer, he or she ceases to be a prime prospect and is replaced by another.

The prospect file must be kept up to date and used systematically. A follow-up or bring-forward system will allow you to plan your time.

Selecting prospects can be done at the desk or by telephone. It involves a relatively low cost resource, compared with a field sales activity. Computers allow companies to build a database of prospects which can be used interactively for all sales objectives or changes in strategy. By using a computerized marketing database, you can analyse important factors such as source of prospect/lead, date last called, change in staff.

A sale in a new market sector can open the door to a number of new prospects in this sector. Remember that any customer might be interested in other products and services that the company can supply.

The prospecting process: Stage 1

Canvassing

The key elements in analysing potential customers are research and creativity. The research phase identifies the prospects, their size, location and type of business. Sources of prospects are various and often depend on product/service. Sources of data include:

- Electoral registers
- Trade directories
- Kompass directory
- Development agency directories
- End-user lists
- Other companies' sales ledgers
- Seminars/presentations on subjects of interest
- Chambers of Commerce
- Trade Associations
- Publications

The prospect file

To make informed judgements and successful sales visits, a prospect file, or marketing database, must include the following:

- Basic data: company name, address, telephone etc
- Holding company and structure
- Key personnel and decision makers
- Relationship with your company and previous contacts/jobs
- Financial data/performance
- Recent information/activities/appointments
- Actual sales/potential needs

Stage 2

Prime prospect selection

Time and effort can be saved by ruthless application of the following criteria:

● Need: no matter how convincing your sales talk, your time is wasted if you give it to a prospect who has no need for your product.

● Money: ability to pay for your product or service, ie being able to afford it and pay for it.

● Authority: you may successfully sell to a prospect, but make sure he has the authority to buy. Don't be misled by titles on business cards. Your time may also be profitably spent finding a star who may be a real buyer in the future.

If any of these three criteria is not met, the prospect must be discarded.

Stage 3

Hot prospects

These are prospects who have the need to buy – now.

They must be rigorously courted and sales effort must be concentrated on the period during which they are on heat.

This is the buying time, and the opportunity must not be missed.

Stage 4

Customer acquisition

The final stage of prospecting is when a prospect is converted to a customer and a sale is made. Remember selling-on and cross-selling.

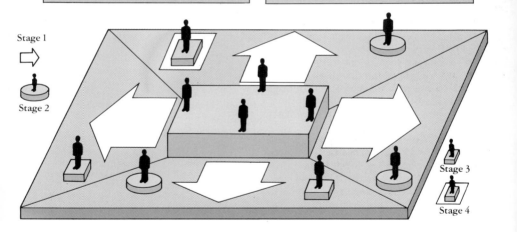

Stage 1
Stage 2
Stage 3
Stage 4

Prospecting has been described as a process to be handled mechanically, based on research. However, some elements require more creativity.

A novel approach to a prime prospect can often bring forward a need that has been lying dormant.

The successful salesperson keeps up a continuous flow through all four stages of the process and particularly concentrates on Stage 3, ie within hot prospects.

The effective salesperson also plans his or her time, or uses research in such a way as to encourage prospects from Stage 2 to Stage 3 at the same time, while topping up Stage 2 from Stage 1.

Increased use of the telephone to establish prospects in Stage 1 and Stage 2 has led to the more effective use of the salesperson's time in planning calls and other sales activities. Keep topping up and keep it moving.

Promoting the business

Even the best advertising campaigns will fail unless correct promotion has ensured a fully informed, enthusiastic and motivated public. Far from being an exact science, promotion means delivering the 'selling' message to the right public with appropriate emphasis and force.

The ingredients of promotion are: public relations, sponsorship, sales promotion and advertising. A well-chosen balance of these, related to stimulating the buying urge, is the aim of a good marketing strategy.

Promotion of a product, company or business is carried out by advertising or PR agencies, in-house PR or sales promotion staff. Their accuracy and sensitivity to the target market makes for good promotion.

Apart from the major manufacturers of consumer goods, business in general has lost, or never developed, the art of testing. However, test marketing, or testing a promotional technique, remains a most effective way of establishing whether:
● Research results are valid
● An idea is worth developing
● Customers' reactions to change are real
● Product development expenditure is justified.

Testing can ensure that expenditure on sales and market promotion gives the maximum value for money.

The form of promotion depends on the 'public' to be reached. The most important of these are customers and clients – established and prospective – on whose patronage the companies' financial success depends.

Increasingly, the financial community – banks, stockbrokers and shareholders – are gaining significance as a 'public'. And a vital and often overlooked group is company employees and their families; while for companies with ever-increasing environmental concerns, politicians are important.

Promotional activity

For any form of promotion, first set a sales goal and decide what emphasis to put on advertising, sales promotion, PR and sponsorship.

Promotional activity is used to:
● Create greater awareness in prospective customers' minds of the company and its products.
● Make buying easier by communicating product features/benefits.
● Sell products, services, ideas, businesses etc.
● Change opinions, attitudes and hence market shares.
● Inform in order to persuade.
● Retain current customers and attract new ones.
● Build company reputations.
● Increase number of sales calls.
● Upgrade priority and value of products and services.
● Reduce the cost of selling yet increase its value.

Effective public relations involve such things as announcements of expansion plans and new appointments, community and charity donations, and expert comment in the media on news items. However, while good public relations need good press relations, remember high media profile means that bad news as well as good news will be reported.

Sponsorship involves a company buying exclusivity for an event or sports competition, or lending its name to a product, to promote itself. Or it may sponsor an individual competitor or a team, as Mobil sponsor Benetton Ford cars in Formula 1 motor racing.

While sponsored events rarely succeed on their own, they usually present extremely good value. WD & HO Wills' sponsorship of the Embassy world

snooker championship gave them 75
hours of television coverage for only
£75,000, where equivalent advertising
would have cost £2,500 for 30 seconds.

Sales promotion offers the short sharp
incentive designed to change the habits
of customers and increase sales. They
include: 'road shows', featuring product
competitions direct to the public in key
salesrooms; financial inducements to 'buy
and try'; cash prizes and games of chance,
such as those employed by newspaper
groups and oil companies.

Advertising campaigns should be
regular and effective – they rely on the
correct message, choosing the best
medium and good timing. The message
must relate to what the customer wants
or needs to buy and what the company is

able to provide or supply.

The American Express 'That'll do
nicely' campaign was so successful, the
slogan entered everyday language.

The Perrier ads are so designed, they
only have to say 'O' and we all know
to what they are referring.

The Canon range of photographic and
business machine products, and Goodyear
tyres, are promoted at sports events all
through the year, and all over
the globe.

The medium must relate to the 'public'
in question – a costly national campaign
to woo customers in particular localities
may be far less effective than direct mail
or local advertising.

Finally, research and analysis of
previous sales peaks can assist in choice
of timing a campaign.

Selling

Good management is fundamentally about direction and control. Selling is no different.

Most salespeople, particularly in large companies, have a basic problem: they enjoy spending their time doing what they know best, with the products that are easiest to sell, and selling to those customers who are easiest to sell to. Direction, management and control are needed to ensure that selling time and cost are spent where they are most effective – on prime and hot prospects.

Successful sales managers and directors keep the pressure on their sales force by meeting regularly with them to review:

- Performance versus budget
- Key performance ratios
- Follow-up procedures
- Opportunities
- Competitor activity.

Incentives do not feature high on this list. Many sales managers spend too much time inventing elaborate sales incentive schemes, which the salesforce can manipulate to their personal benefit. Incentives must be geared toward the overall objectives of the marketing plan in terms of turnover and cost. When used, they should be short, sharp and regular, enhancing the overall sales effort, *not* detracting from it.

Sales incentive schemes are often an excuse for poor management of the sales resource. There are many lasting benefits in creating an effective team relationship within a sales force: shared experience is a benefit that does not arise from a totally competitive environment.

The other forgotten standard of performance is control of debt. A sale is not a sale until the debt has been paid. The sales force should chase up money owed to the company. It was responsible for the sale and should be responsible for assuring its payment – before team members are paid a bonus.

How well are we doing?

The key performance indicators of selling activity are:

Ratios
- Percentage sales:budget
- Enquiries:quotations:orders
- Percentage margins:sales

Sales activities
- Number of calls:length of calls
- Number of new prospects called/found
- Results on enquiries/quotations:conversions
- Credit control (age debt of sales)
- Frequency of calls per day/week/month etc
- Percentage discounts:sales overall utilization
- Number of customers and their value, actual and potential
- Administration of sales reports/prospects
- Submission of itineraries
- Deposits taken

Overall
- Cost of sales force/sales
- Sales value/order
- Orders to calls ratio
- Percentage discounts:sales
- Key account development
- Quality service assessment

Know your customer base. It may be most appropriate to spend 80 per cent of your selling/promotional activity with 20 per cent of your clients who account for 80 per cent of your turnover.

Beating the competition

Always overestimate your competitors – they are not sitting back letting you make the sale at list price and in a well-ordered process. In any competitive sale, get to know the clients better than your competitors do, and establish what influences their attitudes. Sales are not made to companies – they are made to individual people, whose attentions are being sought. The sales call report should be used as a source of information on competitors.

The sales call report

The cornerstone of most sales control systems is the prospect client call report. The example can be modified to meet the needs of most companies and covers the essential ingredients.

When it is distributed to the relevant people, it can help the communication process, and in particular:
- Establish customers' needs.
- Act as a bring-forward reminder.
- Ensure necessary action is taken by salespeople and support staff.
- Assist managers to control sales staff.

1 Who are you calling on?
This section is the basic reference which establishes if the call is being made on the decision-maker, or if it is exploratory. Salespeople are often diverted to an assistant who cannot authorize a purchase.

2 Why are you calling?
This section records the objective of the call and establishes the criteria against which results can be measured. By completing this section, the salesperson confirms that the call will represent effective use of time.

3 Result of the call
This section outlines the caller's proposal or presentation. The customer's response should be qualified, and any information, such as competitor activity or change in customer need, detailed.

4 Client/customer requirements
This section summarizes the prospect's interest and justifies the action to be taken.

5 Action required
All sales calls require follow-up action, including those which could result in a lost order. The salesperson will normally follow up the call. He/she will need to call on support services to prepare detailed quotations or despatch products and sales literature. The main purpose is to communicate the status of a particular customer.

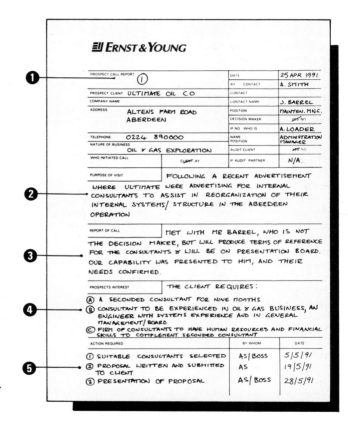

ERNST & YOUNG

PROSPECT CALL REPORT ①		DATE	25 APR 1991
	AY CONTACT		A. SMITH
PROSPECT CLIENT ULTIMATE OIL CO		CONTACT	
COMPANY NAME		CONTACT NAME	J. BARREL
ADDRESS ALTENS FARM ROAD ABERDEEN		POSITION	MAINTEN. MNG.
		DECISION MAKER	YES NO
		IF NO WHO IS	A. LOADER
TELEPHONE 0224 890000		NAME POSITION	ADMINISTRATION MANAGER
NATURE OF BUSINESS OIL & GAS EXPLORATION		AUDIT CLIENT	YES NO
WHO INITIATED CALL	CLIENT AY	IF AUDIT PARTNER	N/A

PURPOSE OF VISIT FOLLOWING A RECENT ADVERTISEMENT WHERE ULTIMATE WERE ADVERTISING FOR INTERNAL CONSULTANTS TO ASSIST IN REORGANIZATION OF THEIR INTERNAL SYSTEMS/ STRUCTURE IN THE ABERDEEN OPERATION

REPORT OF CALL MET WITH MR BARREL, WHO IS NOT THE DECISION MAKER, BUT WILL PRODUCE TERMS OF REFERENCE FOR THE CONSULTANTS & WILL BE ON PRESENTATION BOARD. OUR CAPABILITY WAS PRESENTED TO HIM, AND THEIR NEEDS CONFIRMED.

PROSPECTS INTEREST THE CLIENT REQUIRES:
- Ⓐ A SECONDED CONSULTANT FOR NINE MONTHS
- Ⓑ CONSULTANT TO BE EXPERIENCED IN OIL & GAS BUSINESS, AN ENGINEER WITH SYSTEMS EXPERIENCE AND IN GENERAL MANAGEMENT/BOARD
- Ⓒ FIRM OF CONSULTANTS TO HAVE HUMAN RESOURCES AND FINANCIAL SKILLS TO COMPLEMENT SECONDED CONSULTANT

ACTION REQUIRED	BY WHOM	DATE
① SUITABLE CONSULTANTS SELECTED	AS/BOSS	5/5/91
② PROPOSAL WRITTEN AND SUBMITTED TO CLIENT	AS	19/5/91
③ PRESENTATION OF PROPOSAL	AS/BOSS	28/5/91

Distribution

Good marketing means getting the right product to the right place at the right time. All the marketing effort put into achieving sales can fail at the last post – when you have to deliver the goods.

Marketing people have to balance the promotional mix to achieve the best value. These trade-offs are mirrored in delivery. With advertising, the objectives are market supply and customer service. Advertising moves people to products, and selling moves products to people. Physical distribution links these two.

Effective distribution techniques reduce inventory levels, free working capital and reduce borrowings. They should also reduce the time needed for delivery and the cost of transport as an element of the overall product price.

Businesses need to use their resources to the maximum. This causes a continual interaction and conflict between *time* and *capacity*. For example, it may be necessary, at times of product launch, to employ selective express carriers, but to change to distributors when a cycle of demand has been established.

There are four main channels of distribution.

Direct

Effective distribution relies totally on the ability to move the product in sufficient bulk at a frequency which satisfies the customer and results in the lowest possible unit cost.

The main issues that arise are method of transport: packaging of units; handling facilities at each end, and use of own transport/subcontractor.

The quality and reliability of the product is in the hands of the supplier throughout.

Owned warehouse

Strategically placed warehousing allows the suppliers to move large quantities of finished product at one time. The distribution warehouse may either be owned by the company or it may be a break-bulk distribution warehouse, where loads of the product are broken down into a number of smaller deliveries that are shared by a number of companies.

The supplier pays for stockholding, but gains the benefit of being able to supply in smaller quantities at more frequent intervals.

Wholesaler

As a distribution channel, the wholesaler is an intermediary who is paid a fee to act as a carrier or stockholder. Suppliers of consumer goods, from fast-moving consumer goods (FMCG), such as food, to white goods (refrigerators, washing machines, cookers) make frequent use of wholesalers as intermediaries.

Goods are *sold* to wholesalers at a discount on list price, enabling them to stock and distribute to their customers. They are assisted by the suppliers, who promote the product to their customers.

Suppliers may suffer due to the pressure of competition on wholesalers. However, the converse is equally true.

By promoting wholesalers and distributors, suppliers can gain access to large numbers of clients. Wholesalers who are particularly effective promote both their own business and that of the supplier.

Franchising

The ultimate channel of distribution is one in which the rights to sell, or indeed the rights to manufacture, are transferred to a company or an individual within a given marketplace. This simple, low-cost form of distribution, involves a great deal of high-cost support.

Successful franchising depends on the maintenance of quality standards, a clear pricing structure and the ability to negotiate franchises without a commitment to a costly support structure.

Exporting

For most developed industrial countries, the major growth markets will be abroad in developing countries. Successful exporting depends on:

- A firm understanding of the demand for products and services from the export market
- Selecting the market which fits the product and the resources you are prepared to commit to it.
- Sound marketing management

You should explore the market in terms of:

- The country's political stability
- Recent history and forecasts of currency movements
- Ease of communication.

Seek advice from those with experience. Most governments will help you with:

- Export-related market research
- Export paperwork
- Finding an agent with a successful track record
- Creating a joint venture
- Introductions to agents and manufacturers under licence.

Many established export consultancies offer to 'hold hands'. This service is particularly useful where language difficulties exist.

Finding the right agent for your product can be difficult. Good agents pick and choose their principals. You will have to sell yourself to them, but beware those who seek an exclusivity agreement.

Manufacture under licence agreements is often a low-risk way of penetrating a market, particularly one controlled by the importing government. But you need to ensure that you are not transferring technology and so are likely to lose all benefit after one or two years.

The right product in the right place at the right time

Selecting the product the customer ordered requires:
1 Correct inventory levels
2 The appropriate processing system
3 The right picking and packing system. Delivering the product to the customer requires 1, 2 and 3 plus:
4 The appropriate consignment note and labelling system
5 A reliable carrier, which can provide the required timed delivery service at the right cost.

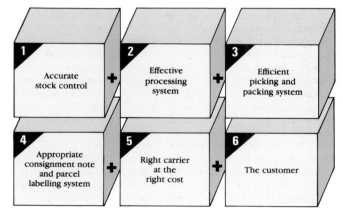

In the retail sector, linking the distribution chain has become a way of keeping close to the market and ensuring that the product is in the right place at the right time.

The Italian clothing manufacturer Benetton has replaced storage space with information. Most of its competitors have large in-store storage areas, but Benetton manages with very little. Its up-to-date electronic information systems allow changes in buying patterns to be reflected in new styles and colours within days instead of months.

Getting the right balance

The materials manager ensures that there is always enough raw material and stock available to support the forward production programme and its potential variances – but only just enough, since materials usually account for 50 per cent of a factory's throughput.

Too little stock can be obvious and embarrassingly public: customer orders fall overdue and can only then be recovered by working overtime. Most traditional materials managers err on the side of carrying too much stock to avoid being blamed for running out and delaying production.

The problems of having too much stock are less apparent. Stock has to be paid for, usually with borrowed money, which can mean high interest charges. It has to be stored, which uses up storage space and in turn costs money for lighting, heating and storekeepers.

Depending on the industry and type of material, stock either deteriorates with age or becomes obsolete because of design changes.

Materials management should not be overlooked in areas where services or skills account for the major portion of costs. It can be just as costly for a computer department not to have, say, adequate paper for printing as it is to have a machine operator run short of material.

Getting the right amount of stock

First, it is essential for materials managers to forecast what is going to be needed. This is best based on a forecast of sales of the finished product, which is then broken down to individual component levels via a bill of materials, although it can also be based on an average of how much has been used in the past.

Next, it is important to know what, and how much, is currently in stock. Obviously this changes from day to day as stock gets used and new deliver-

---

Effective materials management

To achieve this you need:
- An accurate sales forecast
- Up-to-date bill of materials
- Material requirements planning
- Efficient stock recording systems
- Routines for calculating buffer stock
- Constant measurement of performance against budget
- Regular comparison with industry standards

---

ies are received. So it is essential that materials management has an accurate and responsive stock recording system. In theory a comparison of how much stock is available against what is required will quickly identify how much more stock needs to be bought.

Stock bought into the company falls into two basic categories. Planned stock is made up of two basic elements: working stock needed in the raw materials, work-in-progress and finished goods stores to service the smooth running of the operation, and buffer stock, usually finished goods to accommodate variable customer demand.

Unplanned stock is in the system because things have gone wrong – a rejected batch, a cancelled order or incorrect forecasting. It is the job of the materials manager to minimize this stock.

Total stock – planned and unplanned – can be measured in two ways: it can be compared to previously set budget levels; or measured in terms of inventory turns – the number of times stock is used in a year, which is probably the best yardstick.

Some firms achieve as few as two or three turns a year, but the most efficient can get 20 or more. The difference enables working capital to be better utilized and the business to be more profitable.

How the warehouse at NWS BANK got the right balance

NWS BANK, a subsidiary of the Bank of Scotland, has a department which controls stationery and printed materials for its UK branches. In 1989 it had a stock level of £376,000, representing a stock turn of 2.2 times per year. As part of a cost-saving initiative, a different approach to materials management was implemented.

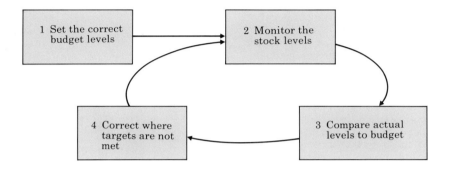

1 Setting the correct budget
Traditionally companies base their inventory targets on previous year's performance. NWS BANK, however, wanted to improve and therefore set targets not at 2.2 turns per year, but at 8 turns per year. This meant that they had to alter their inventory policy significantly – re-order levels, lead times and batch sizes.

2/3 Monitoring and comparing
Companies normally monitor global stock levels once a month, but to gain close control, NWS BANK monitored stock turns of each item each week. Problems could then be recognized early and corrective action taken.

4 Correcting
If a problem is encountered, the tendency within industry is to react by increasing inventory. If a supplier delivers late, buffer stocks are installed to insulate the company from the effects. In time, inventory levels build up to cover problems and inefficiencies.

Inventory
NWS BANK recognized that as they lowered inventory they would have to resolve the underlying problems. There is no single method of achieving this, but some common problems include long machine setting times leading to large batches, long supply lead times leading to supply uncertainty, poor quality supply, and unpredictable usage requiring buffer stocks.

However, by assigning inventory responsibilities to people who could actually make it happen, and with coaching and commitment, each of these problems was resolved.

The result
At the time of writing, NWS BANK were 6 months – half way – to achieving their target. Stock turns had increased from 2.2 to 5 and service levels increased from 80 per cent to 97 per cent. Warehouse space was reduced from 13,000 square feet to 8,000. This is a significant achievement, and is possible in most industries.

Almost paradoxically, a higher service level was achieved, with lower inventory. The reason is logical. Problems have to be eliminated to decrease inventory. Fewer problems mean higher efficiencies, which lead to higher service levels. Low stocks and good service can be achieved.

Purchasing

Purchasing is an important strategic function in most organizations. In manufacturing, the cost of purchased goods and services can amount to 30–80 per cent of total turnover. In the financial services it usually amounts to 50 per cent of management expenses. Therefore a professional approach to purchasing is essential to ensure you maximize the potential of your spending power.

The primary aim of purchasing should be to select and manage suppliers that will give you 100 per cent quality assurance, 100 per cent on-time delivery and a whole range of other value added services. Price is important, but not in the sense of what you pay. What is important is the value you get for the money you spend.

There are four key aspects to the management of suppliers:
- The size of the supplier base
- Selecting the right supplier
- Monitoring their performance
- Developing suppliers.

Too many suppliers are costly and cumbersome to manage and water down your purchasing power. Too few suppliers means overdependence and lack of flexibility.

To select the right suppliers, you must work with your technical and finance people. This ensures suppliers have technical approvals and financial strength, and are people that you can work with. Try to select suppliers that are nearby – this helps communication and problem solving and reduces transport costs.

Once you have selected a supplier, make sure that it performs to the required standard in terms of delivery, quality and price. Set standards, compare performance and let the supplier know how it is doing. In return, make sure your own house is in order – give suppliers accurate and timely information and pay them on time. Remember that cash flow is their life-blood as well as yours.

What is a buyer?

Good professional buyers are likely to have many of the following characteristics:
- Experience in the trade or industry, often with a degree or an appropriate technical qualification
- Sound interpersonal and communication skills and numeracy
- Professional training and experience in the techniques of buying and membership of the national purchasing institute
- Skill as well as credibility in negotiation
- Entrepreneurial spirit
- A sound understanding of your own and your suppliers' production processes
- Close links to sales and marketing, with a keen eye for changing customer needs
- Willingness to become involved in and manage lengthy and demanding relationships with suppliers.

What do buyers do?

Buyers must be sure to select the right supplier at the right price. This means identifying potential suppliers from:
● Personal experience and contacts
● Trade directories and journals
● Technical publications and trade fairs
● Overseas trade visits and embassies
● Word of mouth within the trade.

To pick the final supplier, buyers must weigh up the following factors to strike the best balance:

Reliability
● Recent track record with own and other companies
● Honesty, commitment and trustworthiness
● Financial stability gauged from the balance sheet
● Ability to meet imposed quality standards

Delivery
● Reputation in the industry for holding dates
● Type of packing and freight used
● Relative size of own company's order in supplier's eyes

Price
● Comparison with various other quotations/internal estimates
● Discounts, freight costs, duty
● Settlement terms

Responsiveness
● Ability to accept change
● Speed of reaction to changing demand patterns
● Supplier's after-sales service and ability to respond to problems

Effective purchasing

These are some rules which will help to ensure that buying is carried out effectively:
● On the basis of the 80/20 rule, spend most of your time working with the suppliers and on the goods and services which account for 80 per cent of your expenditure.
● Never focus simply on price. Look carefully at total cost, which includes transportation, storage, administration, exchange risk, value in use and return on investment.
● Remember, a price that is significantly lower than the average for the rest of the competition can often be an indicator not to select that supplier.
● Keep a track of material price increases and compare them regularly with indices published by government or trade bodies.
● Obtain the financial results of key suppliers to ensure that they maintain financial stability and continue to support your operation.
● Keep regular statistics on rejected goods, late deliveries and other supply performance and communicate performance to suppliers before things get out of hand.
● Always look for ways of reducing supply lead times. This means you can hold less stock and make your production process more responsive to customer needs.
● Build up your own supplier relationships and ensure that trusted members of supply companies make and keep personal commitments.
● Be aware of the levels and types of entertainment received by the buying staff and ensure that they are within sensible norms.

Receiving, storing and controlling stock

As a manager, you need to be aware of the importance of receiving and storing goods and controlling stock effectively.

Receiving goods

The layout and facilities of the goods receiving area play a significant part. Easy access to major road networks is essential and internal traffic should be smooth so that delivery vehicles can be turned around quickly. Drivers of supply vehicles may turn away if they cannot unload promptly.

The layout of the receiving area should ensure that off-loading can be carried out swiftly. Self-levelling docks may help the movement of forklift trucks; cranes or hoists may also be needed. The type of material and packaging, and the quantity and frequency of planned deliveries, are the important factors.

Good operating procedures are equally important. Plan a delivery schedule so that receipts are evenly phased. Suppliers who consistently leave deliveries to the last day of the month and cause bottle-necks should be re-educated – or dropped.

Make the first physical inspection checks in the receiving area to ensure that the right goods have been sent, undamaged, in the right quantity. A full quality-control inspection may also be needed.

In all instances, deliveries must be checked and damage or discrepancy notified immediately to the supplier and delivery agent. It is better to reject damaged goods there and then to avoid future haggling over responsibility for damage. Otherwise, the onus may be on your company to prove that the loss or damage did not take place in your charge or on your premises. When all checks are complete, the goods must be moved promptly to their final location. An organized receiving area is essential. Access should be restricted and issues made only from stores.

Finally, receipt of goods must be entered promptly into the company's stock recording systems. Most companies use VDUs or preprinted cards or forms for this.

Storing materials

Materials can be stored in a variety of ways, from cupboards to computer-controlled, robotically-operated ware-housing systems. Successful storage depends on several fundamental principles.

First is the amount of space needed. Having too much capacity can be as big a problem as too little: if space is available, it will be filled, and the company may carry excessive stock. If stock-holding levels peak and trough dramatically, as in the wholesale spirits trade before Christmas, consider renting temporary space to cover the peaks. However, hiring space can be costly and hard to control and should not be used to overcome long-term or permanent shortage of space.

Obtaining stock when it is needed is equally important in the space/volume equation. A full warehouse where stock cannot be drawn easily is not cost effective. Narrow aisles can make stock movement slow and expensive if movements are hampered. Store goods in the least space that allows good access. It is also crucial to know where everything is.

Not being able to find stock is as bad as having none. There should be defined areas for all stock, and each item should be stored where designated in a 'stock locator system'. Less obvious, there should be a secure area to hold reject material and goods requiring inspection. This ensures a company's quality standards are maintained.

Controlling stock

The process of taking material into a store, holding it and issuing it later should be simple, but several pitfalls can cause problems. These arise from allowing unauthorized personnel to have access to the stores. Materials collected in a 'panic' or for a special order can result in stock being moved, misplaced or damaged. Casual callers rarely update stock records, which then become unreliable and can lead to the use of 'private' records.

Stores areas should be enclosed and secure, and access should be restricted to authorized personnel. Accurate and up-to-date records are essential. Every movement should be accompanied by authorizing documentation, and recording systems, including stock location, updated immediately. A common danger is for stock to be moved hurriedly when the need is urgent, with every intention of catching up paperwork later.

All stock should be clearly labelled. Parts which look similar or have inadequate or missing identification can lead to mistakes. Poor labelling leads to inaccurate records and can seriously affect production efficiency and quality. If unlabelled material comes in, it should be 'quarantined' for identification by the inspection department.

Stock rotation is essential. Stores personnel should operate the FIFO principle: First In, First Out. If bins are refilled at the top and stock is issued from the top, materials at the bottom will not get used and will either deteriorate or become obsolete. If it is impossible to date-stamp each item, the physical layout of the warehouse should ensure that the oldest material is used first.

All movements must be supported with adequate paperwork and stock records must be updated. The same principles apply to both damaged and rejected material.

Recording stock

A vast number of systems can be used to record stock. They can usually be classified in three ways: bin cards, Kardex and computer systems. All depend on prompt and accurate recording of every physical stock movement. This often requires good staff training, particularly for computer systems, to ensure that no parallel 'private' systems operate.

Bin cards record quantities per bin or rack and are held in the stores area. They consist of a series of line entries for each receipt or issue, and a running balance of remaining stock. Updated promptly and accurately, bin cards give an effective picture of stock quantities. However, their major drawback is that details are not readily available to other departments.

Kardex systems are usually held centrally. They are similar to bin cards, but include more detail such as supplier and customer information. Their main disadvantage is the lack of ready visual checks. If a storesperson sees an empty bin with a bin card showing that there should be stock, immediate action can be taken. If the only record is the Kardex, the first sign of error is often when stock shortage occurs.

Computer systems are the most effective method of recording stock. Information is available on printouts or VDU screens, and on-line systems provide instant updating. The most important control is to ensure that, while any number of people may scrutinize records, only trained personnel should amend them.

Computerized systems are quick and easy to update, but transcription errors may occur. Check the audit trail of transactions and hold regular physical stock checks. Always keep back-up copies of data files so that restoration is possible if a breakdown occurs.

Production planning

The purpose of a production plan is to balance your requirements (orders in hand/sales forecasts) against resources (people, materials, machines) so that the company operates at maximum efficiency and profitability.

All managers should be aware of the need to plan the actual manufacture of the company's products.

Order sequencing

The first action required to formulate a production plan is to sort the orders or forecasts received into a sequence, according to the dates by which they are required.

Next, the orders have to be broken down to establish what components need to be bought or made to complete the order. From this the production control department can determine what material, machines and labour hours will be needed and the earliest possible date for final production.

This is a crucial process, since although there may be standard lead times, circumstances may alter from day to day, even hour to hour, and being short of just one component can delay the whole order, leaving the factory with excessive levels of unfinished work in progress.

In drawing up an order plan, it is essential to consider total factory loading, especially if the company makes a wide range of product lines. Unless each line is loaded evenly, one part of the factory may be working flat out, paying premium rates for overtime, while in other areas people and machines will be standing idle.

In most manufacturing processes there is a period of non-productive time when orders are changed over. Requirements for the same or similar parts should be batched together to minimize downtime and to achieve greater output.

The final results of this balancing process should be an order schedule which can produce goods at a profit and satisfy the customer by the

---

Key elements of an order plan

● Putting the orders into a sequence according to dates desired by customers
● Breaking down orders into constituent details
● Balancing mix between product lines
● Batching orders together to achieve economies of scale
● Keeping a balance between high and low margin orders
● Keeping the customer informed of delays

---

efficient use of available resources. Inevitably, there will be times when orders either cannot be produced on time, or only at an unacceptable cost. In such cases the customers must be informed.

It is better to lose a single order but keep a good customer than to gain a reputation for unreliable delivery promises and so lose customers in the long term.

Obtaining the best balance of resources at the same time as satisfying customer demands is a highly complex operation.

Production scheduling

In any production process, it is usually impossible to state precisely what can be produced with given equipment, materials and manpower.

Only the industrial giants can afford computer power to formulate the best production plan, according to the wide range of possible resource allocation against a sequenced order plan. Most companies have to rely on more simple systems, coupled with the flair and experience of their individual managers.

However, as computerization becomes cheaper and more powerful, companies should regularly consider whether they can benefit from the mini- and micro-based systems appearing on the market.

Production scheduling is simpler if machinery is highly specialized rather than multi-purpose. Within the priorities of the order plan, production planners should ensure that all machines are loaded to the maximum possible and that downtime (because of, say, order changeover or gaps in the production sequence) is kept to the minimum.

When planning material availability, production planners should ask:
● What material is required and when?
● Is the material available in stock now?
● Can the material be made available in time for planned start of production at an acceptable cost?

Using available labour to the maximum is a complex factor for the production planner. Particular equipment may require specialist skills which are limited to a few operatives. It may be a holiday period or a time of year when absence through sickness is traditionally high.

The workforce may also resist changes in shift patterns or levels of overtime working. In most cases, the flexibility of labour is dependent on the prevailing state of industrial relations.

When all else fails, despite the risk of encouraging potential competitors, subcontract work out. Other companies operating in the same activities may have spare machines and manpower capacity, or may have the right materials available. Reversing the process (ie by taking subcontracted work in) can also be a useful way of levelling out workload troughs.

The final result of balancing all the variations in resources against demand should be a clear plan for production of what work is required to be done and when, and a clear statement to the sales function of when individual orders will be completed.

Key elements of production scheduling

● Component requirements according to the priority of the order
● Minimization of machine downtime
● Material requirements planning based on accurate stock recording systems
● Maximum use of available labour hours
● Use of subcontracting to smooth workload peaks and troughs

Balancing resources and customer needs in a production plan

To get the right balance between customer needs and resources, you need to consider the following, broken down under four headings:

Orders
● From customers
● From sales forecasts
● For stock or sub-assembly
● Broken down into details

Priority
● Sequenced into order of date required
● Special requirements identified
● Customer satisfaction maintained
● Batched into similar groups
● Evenly balanced load

Availability
● What machinery is required?
● Is material available, or can it be procured in time?
● Is there sufficient labour with the right skills?
● Can work be subcontracted if necessary?

Cost
● Balance of high/low margin orders
● Effect of premium payments on profitability
● Downtime costs from excessive changeovers
● Cost of subcontracting

Production control

A production plan is rarely, if ever, carried out in all its details. Machines break down; suppliers' promises are broken; and people fall sick, take holidays, leave the company or go on strike.

The function of production control is first to ensure that production is maintained in line with the production plan wherever possible; and second, to respond to the things which do go wrong and rework the plan in order to get back on schedule.

The production controller monitors the supply and production process to ensure that there is always accurate up-to-date information on what per-formance has been achieved and what actions are required to maintain performance. Where deviations from the plan are spotted, corrective action can be taken at an early stage to overcome the shortfalls.

Regular checks must be made on material availability and not just on the day it is due. A supplier's promise given several weeks before may not be kept, so there should be a programme of routine follow-up to keep a check on this. This should be backed up with an equally regular programme of stock checks.

The production controller needs to be constantly aware of what labour

Things that can go wrong in production . . .	. . . and how to correct them
1 Machine breakdowns	1 Service contracts; planned preventative maintenance; machine hire.
2 Poor production quality	2 Repair and rectify; concessions from design engineering.
3 Low productivity	3 Productivity bonus schemes; incentive schemes.
4 Unforeseen shortages	4 Use other materials; fresh deliveries; modify or rework other parts.
5 Reject material receipts	5 Modify or rework; concessions from design engineering; replacement deliveries.
6 Supplier strikes	6 Use alternative suppliers; security stocks.
7 Transport breakdowns	7 Use alternative freight methods (eg air freight for sea freight).
8 Absenteeism	8 Improved labour relations; overtime; additional shifts.
9 Overtime bans	9 Use temporary labour; recruitment; improved labour relations.

'This machine's broken down. It'll take weeks to repair.'

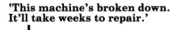

'I've run out of brackets. The buyer says they were due in yesterday.'

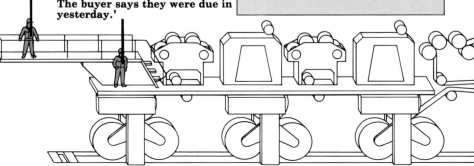

hours are available, how the operation is performing in terms of quality and productivity, and even what social events are taking place. Planned overtime may be suddenly cancelled when a big sporting event is unexpectedly rescheduled.

If machines break down, outside contractors can be brought in to repair them quickly. If not, machines can be hired or the job may be subcontracted for completion. Materials can often be bought from other sources or other materials can be substituted.

Defects can sometimes be rectified, and design engineering may agree to the use of off-standard components if they do not materially alter the finished product. Extra overtime, additional shifts or even temporary labour may overcome a potential shortfall in available hours.

Customers can often accept a later delivery date, or accept part shipment of an order, if treated correctly. In all cases, they must be made aware of the status of their orders.

The process of checking, reworking and rescheduling must be continuous to be effective.

The original plan must remain the key objective. Changes should be made only if they are totally unavoidable.

Maintaining production at JCB

JCB, the UK earth moving equipment manufacturers, were faced with a total shut-down of their highest volume production line as a result of a protracted strike at the premises of their sole engine supplier.

By using up the buffer stock they had held in case of such an occurrence, they were able to put in a crash engineering development plan to redesign the unit to use an engine from an alternative manufacturer.

The speedy redesign combined with an extensive material procurement exercise meant that JCB were able to fit the new engine and so maintain the production of their vehicles.

Threatened stoppage at Ford

Ford Motor Company, in Dagenham, England, were threatened with a complete stoppage to their assembly line, at the time producing 1,000 vehicles a day. A shortage of steering wheels prevented vehicles being driven off the line.

A squad of mechanics was used to drive cars into the park and remove the steering wheels, which were then used as 'slaves' to drive off more cars. Although they had fields full of cars, production was not stopped, and fitting new steering wheels when they became available was relatively simple.

'I'm not working late tonight. It's the beginning of my holidays and I promised to be home on time.'

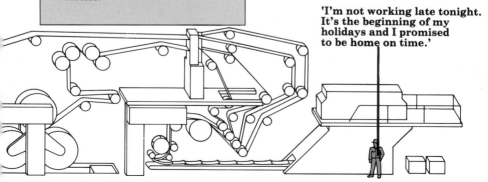

Manufacturing management

The volume, variety and complexity of day-to-day production problems, most of which require on the spot decisions, make manufacturing management one of the most difficult tasks a manager will face.

In most large operations, the manufacturing manager, in addition to the materials management functions described in pages 110–121, is likely to be responsible for:

● Production management
● Works engineering
● Quality performance
● Labour relations.

Production Management

The production manager must ensure that maximum output is produced for minimum cost by keeping the work force and the machines as fully occupied as possible. Since production costs often form the largest part of a manufacturing company's total costs, this is a key task.

Once production control has loaded each machine or process to its fullest extent, the production manager, through superintendents and foremen, must ensure that the operating performance is maintained using numerically quantifiable factors.

For machinery this is relatively easy since actual speeds and output can be readily compared against original design standards. Measuring output performance from the workforce is not so easy, and usually requires a set of standards, established by the work study department, to be used as a yardstick.

There will always be problems to be dealt with, from machine breakdowns to material and manpower shortages. It is the production manager's skill at getting around these problems, by rearranging the details of the production plan, which determines his success or failure.

Works engineering

Failure to produce to standard usually means that a machine needs repair or adjustment. The works engineering department therefore should organize a programme of regular maintenance repairs and refurbishments to ensure that machine performance is consistently kept up to standard and that predictable problems are avoided.

There are, of course, always unpredictable breakdowns. In very large operations such as automated assembly lines or process systems these can be extremely expensive if not corrected immediately. To minimize such downtime it is often advisable to have a back-up squad of maintenance engineers permanently on standby to deal with any emergencies immediately.

The works engineering department is also responsible for ensuring that the layout and flow of the factory processes are planned to give maximum efficiency, and for utilizing new technological advances to improve the manufacturing process.

Quality performance

Although it is inadvisable for the manufacturing manager to be given overall responsibility for quality control he/she will, nevertheless, be responsible for quality performance. There is a significant difference between these two concepts which everyone in manufacturing needs to appreciate.

Quality control is the planning and checking process by which a company aims to produce good quality products, whereas quality performance is making sure that this happens in practice. It should, for instance, be obvious that quality control inspectors can only check to determine what does or does not come up to standard, but it is the production workforce who make good or bad quality products.

The manufacturing manager is responsible for ensuring that good quality is produced regularly and that the workforce have enough pride to want to produce good quality.

Labour relations

The manufacturing manager must often be part psychologist and sociologist, as well as a trained engineer, to get the best out of his workforce. Establishing and maintaining good labour relations brings higher morale and greater productivity.

Perhaps the most important factor in this process is to establish a firm and consistent style and framework within which to operate. It is generally accepted that being too harsh in your relationships with workforce and unions leads to poor cooperation and morale.

However, being too easy-going can have a similar effect since it leads to a loss of respect for management's right to manage. Worst of all, though, is the manager who is tough one day and soft the next, because nobody knows what is expected of them. The workforce can become confused and resentful.

It is essential, therefore, that manufacturing managers develop their own operating style, make sure it works and stick to it. This will improve their ability to handle those occasions when hard decisions have to be made (such as dismissal) in a rational efficient way understood by everyone.

One of the major stumbling blocks in all labour relationships is remuneration. Some key rules which may be a guide as to how to handle this thorny problem are:

● Pay levels that are too low by comparison with local industry may encourage the most able workers to leave.

● Levels of pay that are too high will make products either over priced or unprofitable, in both cases leading to a loss of orders.

● Bonus or incentive payments should be achievable, but not automatic.

● Bonus and overtime pay should not be so large a percentage of total pay that the loss of it, at times when orders are slack, causes discontent.

Establishing effective relations with your workforce means adopting a consistent approach to:

Style – firm, without being too harsh or too easy-going

Remuneration – not so low that it bars recruitment, nor too high that it reduces profitability

Incentives – a spur to higher productivity, not a reward for basic productivity

Manufacturing strategy

The good manufacturing manager, having dealt with the immediate daily problems and crises, must ensure that sufficient time remains to spend on planning medium and long-term strategy.

Most efficient companies have a long-range corporate plan. Within this plan all their subsidiary activities are carried out and collectively directed toward the achievement of the company's prime objectives.

These overall objectives are most likely to be broad-based, such as increased market share, improved profit margins, introduction of new products and so on. It is the manufacturing manager's primary responsibility to develop a detailed strategic plan for the manufacturing department to support these objectives.

The manufacturing manager must constantly take numerous factors into account, but there are some important, specific areas which should normally be reviewed.

Automation

Buying new machines or introducing robotic techniques into the department may well improve product capacity and efficiency but both need to be coordinated within the context of the company's overall capabilities.

For instance, there may be insufficient funding to finance the capital investment and pay for depreciation and maintenance charges. Or automation might have an unwelcome adverse effect on staffing and labour relations.

As in other aspects of management, it is important to maintain a close liaison with all other departments to ensure that strategic actions are mutually compatible.

Sourcing

Significant cost savings may be made by subcontracting work to outside companies with specialist equipment and expertise, instead of replacing old plant with new capital equipment or hiring more skilled labour. Even so, this may have an adverse effect if it leads to underutilization of current plant and labour and so increases unit costs. Subcontracting may lead to labour relations problems and additional 'one-off' costs if redundancies are required.

Consolidation of facilities

If there are several different manufacturing sites all operating under capacity, or several underutilized machines producing similar products, it may be sensible to consolidate the work at fewer sites on machines which can then operate more productively.

Again, subsidiary factors must be considered, such as availability of specialist skills and equipment, disruptions to labour relations, closure costs and so on. The most profitable course of action may even be to reduce margins and prices in order to sell more and so produce more efficiently in greater volume.

Systems

New computerized systems may lead to improved efficiency and control but will themselves cost money and require time to be spent on training and implementation.

Horror stories abound of firms who have abandoned sound manual systems in favour of sophisticated computer systems only to find that they do not work as intended. It is crucial that any new systems implementation be specified and planned in minute detail, and that there are always back up plans in the event of any failures.

Purchasing

New and cheaper sources of supply should be a key objective of the purchasing department. However, before sanctioning any major resourcing action the manufacturing manager should weigh up the total costs of purchase, freight charges, quality standards, inventory carrying costs and so on, to ensure that the sourcing decision is commercially sound.

It is also essential that, when developing their own strategies, the other departments in the company are fully aware of manufacturing's plans and limitations. For example:
● Sales targets should take into account capacity constraints to ensure that they are realistic and achievable.

Imagine, for instance, that part of the sales strategy is to increase the sales of Product X by 20%. But Product X is produced on a specialist machine already working to full capacity. Something will go dramatically wrong unless investment in new equipment is included in plans, or the target increases are reduced in sales plans.

● Design engineering will continually try to improve the design of the products made. And so it should not introduce new materials, tolerances or techniques without confirming them as practical possibilities.

● The finance department should be fully aware of the details of labour relations and incentive schemes before embarking on new payroll systems.

Despite the pressures of immediate daily problems, the manufacturing manager must set aside enough time in the working day to address these long-term requirements. This often involves regular planning meetings and keeping in daily contact with other heads of departments.

Similarly, he/she must ensure that subordinate managers prepare lower level plans so that internal departmental meetings can agree the overall manufacturing strategy.

Regular consultative meetings with your own fully briefed staff are essential to formulate a strategy for the long-term development of the manufacturing function. This strategy must dovetail with the company's corporate plan, and be the centre for all the manufacturing department's future detailed actions.

Obstacles to successful strategies

Any good strategic plan must recognize that forecasts and theories do not always turn out as predicted, and therefore should be regularly reviewed and amended in the light of changing circumstances. For the manufacturing manager some of the key areas in which problems may arise are as follows:

● New equipment or machinery may not arrive on time or may not initially perform up to specification. Putting additional contingency allowances into the overall plan can often ensure that such delays do not disrupt the plan.

● New computer systems often contain unforeseen bugs and operating problems which need to be ironed out before they can work effectively. Any plan to introduce new systems should therefore include the maintenance and parallel running of the old systems until the new ones have a clean bill of health.

● Even the best of suppliers can suffer from breakdowns, strikes or closure. The trauma that this can cause can be alleviated by ensuring that security stocks of key items are held. When possible, the supply of critical components should be split between two sources.

● Internal labour relations problems can disrupt the best laid plans. The only way to prevent this happening is to work consistently, and on a daily basis, at maintaining sound labour relations.

Nationally organized disruptive action, however, may have nothing to do with a local plant but, because it affects the labour force, can seriously jeopardize its performance.

● Plant and machines may still break down, despite the regular maintenance efforts to prevent this from happening.

Innovation, research and development

All companies must look constantly to the future. They cannot afford to rely on the thinking that what works today will continue to do so tomorrow. In the business chain, changes occur all the time – from products, equipment and plant to the workforce, suppliers and customers. New opportunities ignored by your company will certainly be exploited by its competitors.

Every organization needs innovation. This is its life blood. While access to new technology can always be gained by negotiating licensing agreements with other companies, your organization will always need to work on stimulating innovation and creativity.

The vast majority of organizations, however, cannot afford to formalize their perspective on the future by establishing a permanent research and development (R&D) department. And many large companies with such R&D departments have shown how hard it is to innovate.

Size, complexity and bureaucracy can all stifle initiative and creativity, making the passage of new ideas through the organization too cumbersome.

If an R&D department is set up, its research may be pure and/or applied. Pure research has no specific end in sight except to discover more detail about a certain field, eg finding out the electroconductive properties of silicon compounds.

Applied research attempts to solve specific problems or needs that have been identified beforehand; if controlled properly, it provides positive and beneficial results. Exploring the practical uses of the electroconductive properties of silicon would be applied research.

The research will usually be carried out within predetermined budget costs. Where costs overrun budgets you will find you have to be ruthless in cutting off research projects – don't be tempted to spend just that little bit more.

Where does innovation come from? The simple and best answer is from the culture and attitudes of the people in the organization. Accepted methods and practices must be constantly analysed and challenged; the freedom to look for and exploit new opportunities must be encouraged.

Few ideas come from blinding flashes of realization; innovation and creativity are not simply erratic and spontaneous. The Polaroid camera, for example, was not the result of an isolated brainwave. It was the logical development of existing procedures and products, the result of hard team work in an encouraging environment.

The stereotyped picture of R&D activity is one of people in white coats beavering away for years in laboratories on complex problems and emerging with an end-product amid cries of 'Eureka!' This is not true. Remember:

● Keep R&D simple and fruitful by regularly testing new ideas in actual working practice.

● Problems such as customer complaints, incomplete production processes and the encroachment of competitors all provide opportunities for innovation.

● Don't neglect your strengths – they must be developed in tandem with problem solving. IBM, for example, woke up in time to use their strengths to dominate the personal computer market.

● Keep close to your core activities. Don't stray too far from what your business is about, but at the same time don't be so inward-looking that you constrain your ideas.

Sources of inspiration and innovation

Consistently examine and systematically harness any ideas emerging from the core of your business. Discover what you can about your company's customers, employees and environment by asking:

Customers:
● What are they buying and why?
● What do we do well that they like?
● What improvements or variations would they like to see?
● What complementary products or services would interest them?
● How are their needs evolving?

Employees:
● Are working methods keeping pace with new technology and materials?
● What skills are needed?
● What skills are available but are at present underused?
● What feedback are production and sales getting on problems and quality?
● Which processes cause problems? Should they be abandoned or improved?

Environment:
● What social or demographic changes are occurring?
● What spending patterns are emerging?
● How is the public's spending power developing?
● What is happening to attitudes, perception, needs and lifestyles?
● How are our competitors developing?
● What niches in the market are our competitors exploiting?

Social and demographic changes

By finding out what the social trends are and by examining the statistics concerning people's lives in their communities, new niches can be revealed.

McCarthy and Stone saw that after retirement elderly people wanted to live independently in their own homes. They also needed to live in a sharing and caring community. Thus McCarthy and Stone evolved the idea of sheltered accommodation.

In satisfying the needs of an increasing number of elderly people, McCarthy and Stone became the leading UK supplier of sheltered accommodation in the private sector. A constant eye on economic and social trends allied with strong commercial management have secured this. Notwithstanding the worst housing crisis for 40 years, they are still leading the market because their original assessment was correct – 10,000 people still retire every week.

Achieving the right balance

Discovering who you are, what organization will suit you and how businesses function, are the essential prerequisites to your career in management. But real management begins only when you take over your specific responsibilities and the team that will help you handle them. It is then that you start to tackle problems on a day-to-day basis.

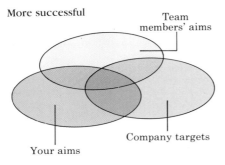

More successful

Team members' aims

Company targets

Your aims

Your ultimate responsibility as a good manager is to help the organization achieve its goals, whilst ensuring that your own targets, and those of the individual members of your team, are also attained. This is a tall order.

Business objectives can often be achieved only at the expense of personal aims. The result may be a high turnover of personnel.

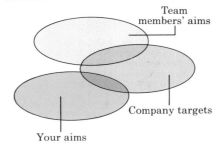

Less successful

Team members' aims

Company targets

Your aims

Your people can be happy and fulfilled but results do not necessarily follow. Achieving the correct balance

will take continual effort. Answers may be found, but they will need constant reassessment. No solution will work in every situation.

Your work will be challenging, complex and unscientific; it will demand general knowledge and specific skills. And the relentless pace of work means you will be in constant danger of being superficial, spending time on brief, varied and piecemeal activities. This is normal. Don't expect it to be any other way.

Your job has many aspects. Some of them will be compatible while others will appear conflicting. You may find yourself pulled by apparently opposing forces.

● Managing vs administering
In the ebb and flow of the organization's work, you must actively shape events, determine a direction and ensure that it is followed. You need to motivate your team to follow your lead and stimulate them to find their own direction. In short, you must take responsibility.

On the other hand, you need to be able to respond to events and interpret the actions of others. You need to be able to absorb them and ensure your team's activities stay on course. Logic, order and method mean smooth administration but you must ensure that your efforts do not stop there.

● Effectiveness vs efficiency
These aspects of your work may appear similar but they are not. The effective manager tries to advance team efforts toward corporate goals, regularly asking: 'What have I added to the business today?' Progress and results are the ultimate measure.

Being efficient and busy may actually disguise a lack of real progress. Responding to daily demands and having your desk clear at the end of each day do not always mean anything worthwhile has been achieved.

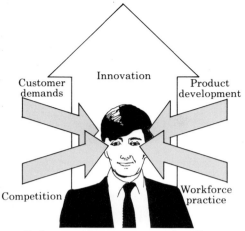

product development and workforce practices to customer demands and competitors' progress.

● Overseeing vs doing

You will often be tempted into getting involved in the tasks your team has to perform – either because the tasks are exciting or familiar. However, you must manage the people, not the task. In other words, manage the action but don't do it yourself.

The transition, from doing something you have always done well to organizing others to do it, will be your toughest challenge.

A portrait of the skills of a successful manager would include a whole spectrum of qualities. The following sections give you some useful ideas on how to cope better with your challenges, from leadership and communication to motivation, delegation and decision-making.

● Innovating vs preserving the status quo

You may be good at the supervision of activities, systems and processes, but managing includes creating time to think, experiment, research and generate tomorrow's ideas.

Genuine innovation relies on your ability to read all the signs in your business environment, from trends in

You will have your own personal aims and needs as a manager. But remember that those who work with you have also entered into a contract with the organization. They will give a lot if handled correctly. They will want something in return and not just a decent salary. They, too, seek meaning in what they do and have enduring values. These must be nurtured *by* the organization *through* you.

129

Leading your team

The ability to lead is vital to managerial success. Yet leadership is hard to define. Military leaders are often compared with business managers and other commercial leaders. Indeed, both types have clear objectives, roles and responsibilities and may share similar qualities, such as vision and the ability to handle a crisis. But there are important differences.

War is an extraordinary situation, requiring authoritarian leaders to command subordinates to take required action and achieve objectives.

Modern business managers, on the other hand, need to be democratic, creating consensus in their teams on objectives and required action. Like their military counterparts, managers motivate their team members by encouraging ambition, the desire to achieve and a wish to contribute to the collective good of the business.

Leaders of people

Some managers may seem born leaders. Most have the potential to develop the skills of organizing, planning, scheduling, setting goals, making decisions, solving problems, communicating, negotiating and supervising.

However, there is no known way to train people to become leaders, although it is evident leaders need such qualities as integrity, honesty, enthusiasm and the ability to express themselves clearly – all of which must be demonstrated consistently so that subordinates may see and subsequently respect them.

Leadership in management necessitates pointing the way ahead; leading from the front is far better than pushing from behind. While many leaders are often solitary, go-it-alone, visionaries who impose their world-view on others, managers must take their people with them. They must work with their team, both reflecting and using the team's collective strength as well as employing the strength of their own personal vision.

Effective leadership

The list of qualities a leader will need is long. While many appear daunting, most are achievable.

To lead your team you need to:
● Look for tomorrow's problems and issues today to detect signs of changes and pitfalls.
● Learn to adapt to change, to embrace it and turn it to your advantage.
● Set high standards as well as clear objectives.
● Think clearly but allow intuition to influence rationality.
● Create a sense of value and purpose in work, so individuals believe in what they do and do it successfully.
● Provide a positive sense of direction in order to give meaning to the lives of team members.
● Act decisively but ensure your decisions are soundly based and not just impulsive.
● Set the right tone by your actions and beliefs, thus creating a clear, consistent and honest model to be followed.
● Keep your composure and learn to wait for the right time to make decisions and take actions.
● Provide an atmosphere of enthusiasm in which individuals are stimulated to perform well, find fulfilment, gain self-respect and play an integral role in meeting the organization's overall goals.
● Be sensitive to the needs and expectations of team members. Pay regular attention to communication and on-going training.
● Define clear responsibilities and structures, so collective effort is enhanced not hindered.
● Recognize what best motivates each team member and work with these motivations to achieve standards and objectives.
● Do not constrain the team but determine the boundaries within which they can freely work.

Leadership as empowerment

Successful managers tend to alter their leadership styles to be appropriate to themselves, their teams, the nature of the problem and the situation itself.

Managers' choices relate to the amount of authority exercised and the degree of freedom given to the team. Most managers would probably use one of these options:

1 Make a decision the team accepts.
2 'Sell' a decision before trying to have it accepted.
3 Present decisions but respond to team's questions.
4 Present a tentative decision, subject to change after team input.
5 Present problem, get team's input, then decide.

6 Define limits within which team makes decision.
7 Manager and team decide jointly. One question managers ask themselves is 'How can I get things done properly while exercising my authority less directly?' John Kotter of Harvard Business School lists five basic kinds of power: to reward, to punish, power from authority, power from expertise, and referent power, the influence attached to a manager because he is admired and liked.

As organizations change, the manager's leadership styles must also change. Managers need freedom to think strategically by delegating operating authority. The successful learn to empower their team without abdicating responsibility.

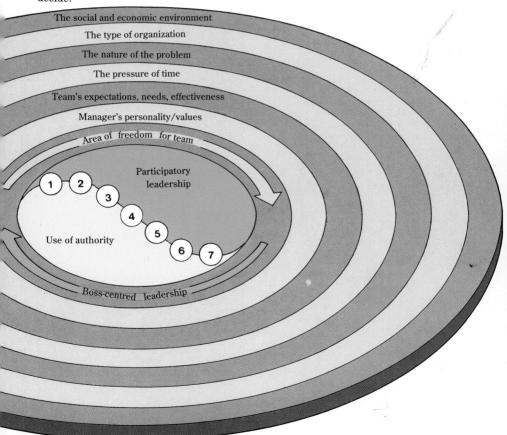

The social and economic environment
The type of organization
The nature of the problem
The pressure of time
Team's expectations, needs, effectiveness
Manager's personality/values
Area of freedom for team

Participatory leadership

Use of authority

Boss-centred leadership

tting it across

manager, you exist through your ...unication with colleagues and their subsequent observations about you to others inside and outside the organization. Communication has two important aspects: first, the maintenance of personal relationships, and second, the efficient transmission of messages.

You may, of course, choose not to communicate. If, for example, your opinion is sought at a particular meeting, your absence may imply lack of support. If attendance is obligatory, silence may have the same effect.

You can communicate in different ways and so it is necessary to be clear about the aim of your message before choosing a medium for it. Ask yourself: 'Who needs to receive the message? What is their working environment? What do I want to happen, and how soon?'

Be clear and brief

Get into the habit of being clear and coming to the point – explanation, if it is necessary, can be provided later. Avoid verbosity, obscure language and irrelevant details in any form of communication. The same applies to jargon, statistics, or references (unless they have been specifically requested).

Written or 'presentational' communications will often be received by more people than the person for whom they were intended. So write in a language that the least expert of your audience will understand.

'Get it on one piece of paper' is sensible advice. Write messages as briefly and clearly as possible. This will save your own time and the reader's, and give the message a better chance of being understood.

Don't write a memo if a telephone call will suffice. Making daily lists under headings, 'see', 'telephone', 'write', 'fax', etc, and allocating time to each, is good training for effective communication.

Think before you communicate

Before communicating ask:
- What action do I want?
- What is the main aim/purpose?
- Who will receive it?
- What is the recipient's likely attitude to the subject?
- How much do they need to know?
- Is my timing right?
- What is the main subject?
- Are the major points clear?
- Is the tone/language appropriate to the subject?
- Is there enough/too much detail?
- Is the action required clear?
- Does the recipient know what to expect?
- Is there any ambiguity?
- Have the facts been checked?
- Will I need to follow it up?
- What is the best medium for my message – memo, telephone, meeting in person?

Crossed lines

Ambiguous communication can cost the business money and waste time; it can also lead to faulty decisions as the following apocryphal story illustrates:

A young man was put in charge of the FBI's stores and stationery. Keen to make an impact, he decided to save on costs by reducing the size of memo paper.

These new sheets were in operation and one of them landed on the desk of J. Edgar Hoover himself. He disliked it on sight – the margins on both sides were too narrow for him. Across the top he wrote, in some irritation, 'Watch the borders'.

His purpose was misinterpreted. For the next six weeks, it became incredibly difficult to enter the USA by road from either Canada or Mexico!

Irrelevant messages are counterproductive, as are irrelevancies and information which does not lead to progress or action. Repetition of main aims and objectives can be helpful. A questioning approach – 'Do you have the latest sales figures?' – establishes the receiver's state of knowledge, and gets to the point quickly.

Unnecessary detail should be avoided. Decision-makers want to know *what* will happen, and not always why. Ask yourself if the detail adds to the meaning of your message – if not, it is noise.

Unplanned interruptions disturb concentration and confuse communication. But if the message imparts urgent news, such as 'our competitors have just launched a new product', then interrupt.

Uncommitted chatter indicates boredom and if meetings generate a lot of it, lack of purpose is often the cause. Is the presentation meeting necessary? Is the right communication medium being used? One-to-one contact or a memo might be more effective.

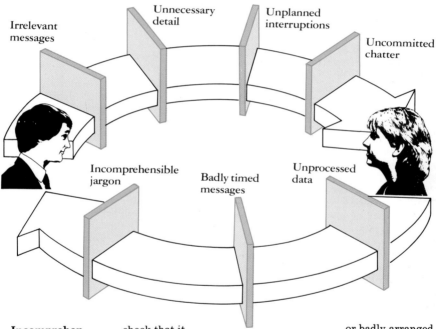

Irrelevant messages

Unnecessary detail

Unplanned interruptions

Uncommitted chatter

Incomprehensible jargon

Badly timed messages

Unprocessed data

Incomprehensible jargon is one of the more damaging forms of 'noise' and can lead to faulty decisions. Avoid using jargon yourself and, if others use it, ask them to repeat it in plain English. But some jargon may well be essential. If you must use it, check that it means the same to all with whom you communicate.

Badly timed messages will prove to be unproductive. Always find out the recipient's state of readiness (eg by asking secretaries or others) before giving information. Don't ask for detailed or expert advice when someone is in a hurry to leave. Always give bad news at a time when a considered response can be given.

Unprocessed data or uncoordinated or badly arranged information is annoying to the hard-pressed manager. Technology frequently worsens the situation by providing delivery systems for messages which speed the transmission of data and increase its volume.

One-to-one

A high proportion of an effective manager's time is always taken up with one-to-one communication with staff, peers and superiors. It is wrong to evade this responsibility through the use of written communication.

The advantage of meeting person-to-person is that you can get instant feedback about your plans and ideas. Also, you are better able to generate enthusiasm or commitment if you deal with someone face-to-face.

Show that you value others by paying attention to what they say.

Listening may seem easy but in fact it involves attention, hearing, comprehension and memory. You can check its effectiveness by asking for a summary of the conversation.

If a conversation has been wide-ranging and discursive, it is a good idea to clear up any ambiguity by summarizing it.

Remember, you have to be especially alert when someone is communicating with you in person, in order to ensure that you give the right response. You may be asked, on the spot, to change your views to support or endorse another's proposal; to share responsibility or blame; or to make a snap decision.

In a one-to-one conversation you can get colleagues to promote change; to help with problems; to relinquish power or authority; or to praise or reprimand. Modern communication systems allow easy one-to-one access to people many miles away.

Timing is important: make sure there is enough time available and that other commitments will not drag you away. Spend the first part of the conversation checking your respondent's current state of mind. You will be in a better position to win valuable support.

If your timing is wrong, then the best thing to do is to abort the discussion and try again at a more auspicious time.

Instant feedback

The advantage of one-to-one communication is that it enables you to gauge reactions instantly. Check understanding and ensure agreement and commitment by asking:

● Do you agree with my proposal?
● Can you meet the deadlines?
● Do you have enough relevant information?
● Have we the resources?
● Are there other aspects to the problem?
● What are implications for budgets/costs etc?
● Do you have an alternative proposal?
● Do you want to discuss the matter further?

By including such questions and dealing with the answers there and then, you will resolve important issues in the most effective way.

Communicating without words

Body language is not simply a set of standard, non-verbal signals which correspond to certain emotional states, such as fear or anger. Everyone makes individual gestures which indicate the current state of, or a change in, their emotions or attitudes.

Smart managers consciously study those they deal with to become familiar with their postures and gestures and work out what they indicate.

Body language will not give a precise insight into people's thoughts and emotions, but it may give important clues.

A salesperson who consistently fails to recognize that a customer scratches his forehead, say, when he is unhappy, loses a negotiating advantage.

Communicating with Jung's four types

Carl Jung observed four types of people: 'thinkers', who traffic in facts and figures; 'intuitors', who are creative and deal in ideas; 'sensors', who are action-centred people; and 'feelers', who are governed by feelings and emotions.

Obviously, the personal psychology of people should influence the way you communicate with them. Try to assess your respondent's personality and prepare your message accordingly. If you are a facts-and-figures person, you may need help in preparing a proposition for the approval of, say, an emotional, 'feeling' type.

Pumping ideas across to a facts-and-figures person may not achieve the desired action or agreement. But by converting the verbal idea into a well-constructed memo you may confer the status of fact upon it and win support.

The responsibility is with you, the communicator, to choose the right 'idiom' or language if you wish to gain others' support. Teams will have within them very different psychological types, and you should spend time understanding these types, to produce an effective group commitment. Good communicators spend a lot of time 'lobbying'.

Thinker Intuitor Sensor

Feeler

'Feelers' tend to be concerned with the 'health' of the organization, and to gravitate toward Personnel and PR. Issues of image, reputation, environment and ethics have more appeal to them than turnover and profit. They often bring interesting alternative values and judgements to balance a purely commercial proposition.

Speak to them in terms of the 'values' and 'significance' of issues.

'Thinkers' are dispersed widely in organizations and specialize in analytical thought. They like order, and are suspicious of disorganized thinking and information. Often regarded as 'custodians' or 'regulators', their support gives respectability and adds security to a concept. They are careful, logical and rational and are attracted by arguments supported by data and measurable values.

'Intuitors' can be instinctive and intolerant of 'reams of data'. They enjoy being told about problems and being left to work them out. They seldom take suggestions beyond concept stage, and need back-up from those good at action. Innovation is their forte but they may be bad at getting down to details.

Timing is vital when you want to communicate with intuitors: make sure they are 'switched-on'.

'Sensors' are resourceful and work-orientated. They are useful members of any team, although sometimes inclined to get plans into action before they are properly completed. They tend to be more interested in the 'how', rather than the 'why', but are often highly motivated.

You can usually get to the point fairly quickly with sensors, since they are almost always in the mood to 'do something'.

135

Effective writing

The advantage of written communication is that it enables the recipient to retain and study information for as long as is necessary.

It also allows many people in different places to read the same message simultaneously. But it does lack immediacy and gives no chance for instant feedback.

Don't think you are being diligent just because you write a lot of letters and memos. Before you write something, ask yourself what it is you want to achieve. Consider whether personal contact might be more effective. Only use the written word:

● If you wish to remove the need for personal contact
● To supply information that would otherwise take too long to reach all who need it
● If material needs to be kept for future reference (as in a contractual letter or a report)
● If you need proof that you have taken action
● To register or emphasize your views.

Use a structure

Organize your facts and arguments before thinking about how to express them. Then draft your material. Reduce information to manageable chunks; present your ideas in an ordered sequence. If the ideas are complex, try to clarify them with examples or analogies.

Check that the treatment and length are appropriate to the subject matter as well as to the recipient. You may be able to cut out verbiage by using headings or summarizing points in note form.

You should be able to justify every word, sentence and paragraph. Finally, read through the finished draft, putting yourself in the place of the receiver.

For a report, the different structural elements might include: summary, findings, conclusions and your

Winston Churchill on brevity

Churchill issued the following memo to his government departments in August 1940:
'i The aim should be reports which set out the main points in a series of short, crisp paragraphs.
ii Often the occasion is best met by submitting not a fulldress report, but an *aide-mémoire* consisting of headings only, which can be expanded orally if needed.
iii Let us have an end of such phrases as these: "It is also of importance to bear in mind the following consideration ..." or "Consideration should be given to the possibility of carrying into effect ..." Most of these woolly phrases are mere padding, which can be left out altogether, or replaced by a single word. Let us not shrink from using the short expressive phrase, even if it is conversational.'

recommendations. But these are interchangeable and dispensable, depending on the subject.

Make it readable

George Orwell wrote 'Never use a long word where a short one will do ... if it is possible to cut a word out, always cut it out ... Never use a foreign phrase, a scientific word or a jargon word if you can think of an everyday English equivalent.' He also had the common sense to add: 'Break any of these rules sooner than say anything outright barbarous.'

Remember that your written output will usually have to compete to be read, so be brief whenever you can: short memos get read; short sentences are understood. Combine the two and you are winning.

Brevity is particularly appreciated by senior management, who often have to do their reading in cars, trains and planes and do not want to be burdened with mounds of paper.

The effective memorandum or report is a well set out, structured document that puts its message across succinctly.

Copy lists should be restricted to those who need to know. Otherwise, you may seem aggressive or appear to be showing off. If you want people not directly connected with the subject to know, send them a copy with a covering note.

Headings/titles enable the recipient to read quickly and efficiently. Titles can obviate the need for an introduction. The memo or report can get straight to the point.

Origination details can be important, especially if the memo/report is one of a sequence. Don't make the reader wait to the end to discover who wrote it.

Don't classify written communication if your message is confidential. If you want something to be widely read, mark it 'Confidential'! Restriction is best achieved by a selective circulation list, and sealed envelopes marked 'Addressee to open'.

Categorize the memo/report to alert readers to its purpose and help them organize their time: 'File report', 'Discussion paper', 'Action sheet', 'Meeting minutes', 'Report and recommendations'.

Summarize each major section of a long document. Provide a summary of conclusions at the beginning or indicate in the contents where it is to be found. A busy manager will read the conclusion first.

Numbering of pages, paragraphs and notes should be consistent and simple: 'page 3, para 12' is better than, say, 'Findings, section 4 II (b)'.

≣ ERNST & YOUNG   ■ Internal Correspondence   ■ Rolls House London Office

		August 6, 1991
To	Divisional Sales Managers Head of Purchasing Financial Controller	
From	J Smith, Marketing Department	

USING OUR PURCHASING POWER TO IMPROVE SALES

Contents	Page
	1
Background and Objectives	
Main findings of Survey	2/3
Summary and Recommendations	4/5
Detailed report	Appendix

Background

The Marketing Department has conducted a survey amongst the sources of supply of raw materials and components for our products. It has revealed that, although many of our suppliers purchase some of our products, few make use of the whole range and some deal exclusively with competitors. The purpose of this report is to recommend a plan for improving the incidence of reciprocal trading with our suppliers.

Objectives

I believe we should aim to:

a) Identify suppliers as a distinct market segment in order to direct a sales and marketing campaign at an area where we should already enjoy some goodwill. (We have over 150 regular suppliers with an estimated sales value to us of £1.5m per annum).

Subject headings direct readers to what concerns them most, makes reference easier in meetings and provide visual relief on the page.

A contents list alerts readers to what follows. Leo B. Mayer, the movie mogul, said, 'Tell 'em what you're gonna tell 'em, tell 'em it, and tell 'em you've told 'em.'

Wide margins on both sides of the page, generous space at the bottom and also between paragraphs allow readers to make their own notes.

Effective reading

Day by day, as a busy schedule consumes more and more of your time, a pile of reading material steadily mounts up. This growing pile may contain, for example: internal and external reports about the business and its competitors; newspaper and magazine articles; technical update material; memos, publicity and circulars; letters to be answered, and promotional material.

You may feel increasingly guilty because these remain unread, and that you may not be keeping up to date or doing your job properly. Yet even if you could find time to cope, you know that you could not absorb it all.

Reading effectively is a skill all managers need in their repertoire. Even though it may be true that three-quarters of our knowledge is gained through our eyes, this skill is not simply a question of reading faster. There is more to it than rapidly consuming all the reading matter arriving on your desk. It is important to understand what you decide to read.

Effective reading means assimilating written information quickly yet comprehending the essence of the printed word and absorbing and interpreting it according to your needs. It takes a lot of practice to develop but it reaps its own rewards.

The wise manager never allows reading material to accumulate but deals with each piece as it arrives. Focus on what you or the business needs to know and then ask: Is it important or urgent, or can it be dealt with later? Important material demands that you find the time to give it proper attention. Urgent but unimportant material may be delegated.

Whatever the material, you must develop a technique of reading effectively: selecting what is essential and skimming what is not; knowing what to look for; concentrating in bursts and saving most of your energy for more important material.

Improving your reading

Adopt a positive attitude: motivate yourself to improve the effectiveness of your reading – you must want to get better at it and feel you can. Don't seek overnight improvement, but practise regularly without becoming obsessed by the problem.

Above all, accept that you cannot read everything. Constantly remind yourself to be ruthlessly selective. This may mean not being technically up to date in all areas of your business life. Ask yourself regularly where it is essential to stay up to date.

Once you have decided:
● Read the headings or index and get an idea of the essence.
● Skim the whole before reading any particular piece first.
● Review the conclusions or summary before starting on the detail.
● Read the introduction carefully: it may indicate which parts of the detail to avoid.
● Annotate as you go through. Do not wait for a second detailed reading; you may well forget what your first thoughts were.

Avoid the following bad habits:
● Reading word for word – don't fix your eyes on one word at a time; let your sight move along the words at a constant rate and take in several words at a glance.
● Reading aloud to yourself – don't subvocalize the words; let the words talk to you.
● Lack of anticipation – don't rely on every word to give you the sense of what is being said; anticipate as much as possible – effective readers require few clues to recognize what comes next in a sentence.
● Reading the same sentence or paragraph over and over – you may legitimately discard any piece that holds no interest for you. But if there is something in the words you want to understand or absorb, by all means dwell on it.

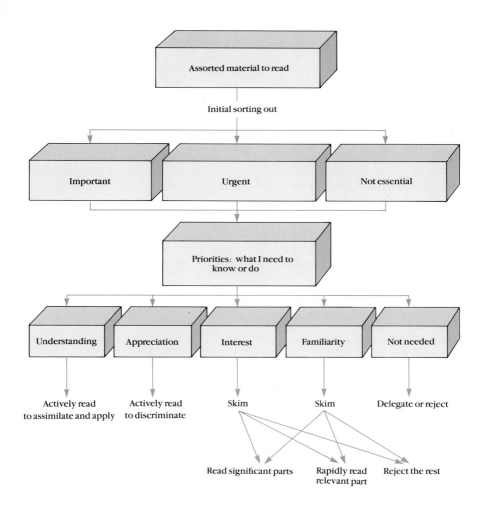

Categorizing reading matter

Try to sort your daily reading as it arrives: decide what your priorities are and then read; take notes if necessary and digest the information and ideas. Don't give up – the longer you persevere, the more you benefit.

Ask questions as you read and answer them yourself – for example:
● What is my purpose in reading this? What am I looking for?
● What is it about? What is the detail saying? What are the main ideas?
● How significant is it to me? How can I use what I am absorbing to be a better manager?

At first, it will be difficult to read and question at the same time but, with practice, the dual activity will become a habit. Keep a positive attitude and have a flexible approach – information and ideas are not readily communicated to the negative or fixed mind.

Presentations

The public presentation of new concepts, ideas or information with visual aids involves all the communication skills: writing, speaking, body language and imaginative illustration.

An understanding of *why* the talk or presentation is being made will lead to how best to prepare for it. If the presenter knows the subject and can explain it simply, even a complex technical or financial problem can be understood by an intelligent audience, using simple visual aids such as blackboards, flip charts and overhead projectors.

But if, for example, the sales force is to be briefed on a new product and motivated to achieve ambitious selling targets, then all the dramatic effects of a topline presentation are called for. In all cases, visual aids must be informative in themselves or give support to the spoken word.

Presenters have to cope with the indifference and inattentiveness latent in all audiences. To help overcome these barriers, take particular care with scripting and delivery.

Scripting

Prepare and write your presentation in full. Always bear in mind the type of audience you aim to convince. Organize your facts in a logical sequence, choose clear language, and balance the length of your sentences. Consider where and when you want to make key points and emphasize them.

For heavily illustrated shows, detailed scripting is essential to co-ordinate voice and visual aids. For less complicated presentations, reduce the script to notes or to headings written on cards. Use the method with which you feel most at ease.

The script allows you to time the length of your presentation. Keep it short. The worst speakers are those who claim never to need scripting and then ramble on interminably.

Make sure your script matches the occasion and the audience.

Delivery

Your personality is the key to the success of any talk, speech or presentation. Vitality and enthusiasm count most.

A good speaking style helps. Practise, using a tape recorder to give yourself feedback and to help improve clarity and correct speech mannerisms. Face the audience and talk *to* them not *at* them; sound natural and spontaneous. Project your voice so that those at the back can hear every word. Vary the pitch and change tempo to keep the audience alert.

Signpost important points by pausing before or after them. Add emphasis by raising your voice slightly or by using a gesture.

Visual aids

General

DO:
- Ensure that visuals contribute to your presentation. They should add impact and aid comprehension.
- Ensure any written words are clearly legible.
- Allow time to set up and check equipment.
- Use visual humour with care.

DON'T:
- Use coloured pens or chalk which are hard to see; avoid red.
- Use visual aids as notes.
- Let the visuals upstage the speaker.
- Spend large sums of money on professional visuals until you know what you really need.

35 mm slides

DO:
- Use them for emphasis and explanation.
- Get them professionally produced if possible.
- Use a pointer for big screens.

DON'T:
- Darken the room so much that you lose touch with the audience.
- Let the slides compete with your script.

Room layout

Cabaret For audiences up to 30. Encourages participation, good for workshops and discussion in smaller groups. Ensure that everyone can see the visuals and the speaker.

Boardroom Similar to U-shape, but for smaller numbers.

Cinema For large audiences, and where you do not want to encourage audience participation. May be necessary when complicated or sophisticated visuals are used. Audience has nowhere to put papers.

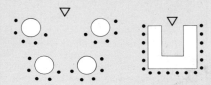

U-shape For audiences up to 30. Encourages participation from the whole group. Not effective for workshops.

Other Any room layout can be used as long as it is suitable for the speaker's material. For example, a senior shop steward or army commander may find that his talk is best received by people gathered round and standing up.

Flipcharts

DO:
- Write in large capitals.
- Be concise.
- Display pages so that you can refer to earlier points.
- Use them for 'brainstorming' sessions.
- Prepare them beforehand if your spelling is bad, or if your writing can be difficult to read.

DON'T:
- Write your own word if the audience has given you one.
- Leave flipcharts up when you move on to the next topic.
- Clutter the flipchart.

Overhead projector

DO:
- Use bullet points rather than paragraphs.
- Keep points concise.
- Have your slides produced professionally rather than writing them by hand.
- Use a large type size.

DON'T:
- Leave them up too long.
- Skip points.
- Crowd them with information.

Video

DO:
- Get professionally produced material.
- Make sure you introduce the video and debrief it afterwards.

DON'T:
- Treat it as light relief.
- Use it at a time when the audience may switch off, eg after lunch.

Blackboard

DO:
- Write clearly.
- Add and rub out as you talk.
- Use yellow chalk to increase visibility.

DON'T:
- Use one if you need to preserve the visual information generated.

Working/architect's models

DO:
- Use them in the right context, eg showing a factory plan or office reorganization.

DON'T:
- Allow your audience to become too participatory, unless you want your scheme redesigned.

The grapevine

As a manager you will never have control of more than a part of the communication process. Paradoxically, the part to which you have direct access diminishes as you rise in the organization.

Your subordinates will begin to tell you only what they think you wish to hear; your policies will probably be amended somewhere within the subculture, and eventually you will lose access to the 'grapevine'.

However, if you are clever, the labyrinthine nature of communication can be exploited to earn more consent for your policies and effect faster distribution of your message.

In reality, official memos, reports, statements and policy documents constitute only the tip of a company's communications iceberg – they reflect intent, rather than practice.

Unofficial networks

Organizations create formal structures for communicating vertically: a superior will pass decisions down. To cooperate efficiently, peers usually develop their own structure for lateral communication: a highly efficient, semi-official bargaining network which ensures the instructions and policies of senior management are adapted to suit middle management.

The aptly named 'grapevine' gradually entwines itself around the entire hierarchy of an organization, and is often international.

To most organization's employees, a management statement is seldom taken seriously until it is confirmed by the grapevine – or, more often, the statement confirms an already widespread rumour. Effective managers are aware that their policies often have greater 'street credibility' when channelled through the grapevine, and they act accordingly.

To communicate effectively, you should have reliable two-way access to the grapevine, via intermediaries. Through 'moles' and 'mouths' you can

---

Why use unofficial channels?

● To soften the blow of unpleasant news ('Profits are down; the incentive scheme may not pay out').
● To check reactions to a proposed project.
● To alter or adapt someone else's unwelcome plans, without officially opposing them.
● To add credibility to, or gain acceptance for, official policy.
● To improve your image ('She's actually extremely competent').
● To win advance support for a negotiating position.
● To weaken someone else's bargaining position by stimulating opposition in advance.
● To lift the morale of, say, a team or a department ('We're doing better than expected').
● To lower expectations ('Apparently, we're doing worse than expected').
● To communicate disapproval to subordinates or peers, thus protecting them from the stigma of a more public warning.

---

test reaction to ideas, receive information on others and control rumours helpful to your objectives.

You should create or join a number of networks at your own level so that policies and orders can be subtly modified to suit working objectives.

Because the main value of the grapevine is to help you gain positive reactions to policies which may otherwise generate hostility, the point of access is critical. It is no good having your 'mouth' leak information to someone who is negative about management. To circulate information quickly, you may want to inject information at several levels.

Remember that unofficial networks are often used by outsiders. Many a company's share price, for example, has responded quite unexpectedly to rumours from within.

Using the grapevine

Don't believe that communication will work because it is orderly. Stratified layers of command can make orders unrecognizable.

Chief executive decides and orders a course of action without adequate consultation with other senior management or middle managers.

The middle management network meets: Manager 1: 'This may destroy my relations with the union.' Manager 3: 'If we adapt the instruction slightly ...' Manager 2: 'I'll support that and look after the communications.'

Manager 2 issues instructions to the workforce, and briefs his 'mole', a union official, 'A', who has access to the grapevine, to give support to '2's' instructions to 'B', 'C' and 'D'.

Later, at an official consultation, 'A' feeds back how successful the chief executive's initiative has been. This supports '2's' official report. The chief is happy and possible difficulties have been avoided.

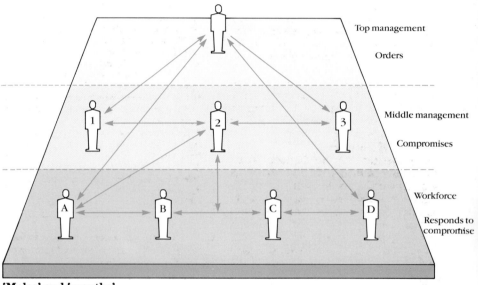

Top management

Orders

Middle management

Compromises

Workforce

Responds to compromise

'Moles' and 'mouths'

All managers trying to gain access to the grapevine need intermediaries.

Moles are, essentially, listeners; they feed back reliable grapevine information to managers. They give access to grapevine data from which your status would debar you. They also reflect opinions about you and your policies.

Moles are only effective if no one knows precisely whose mole they are. Since they are almost certainly being used by the grapevine to feed information back to management, they are likely to be working at an executive level, with easy day-to-day contact with the workforce.

Secretaries, personal assistants, trainees, or promotion-seeking junior managers all make excellent moles. But recognize that they may modify the information which they give you.

Mouths are people in whom the possession of a secret creates an irresistible urge to communicate. They are useful when your views will be found more credible if received indirectly.

Mouths are opinion leaders at all levels. They receive and project messages, and the grapevine is *their* network. They can contribute to the value of the grapevine by preparing people for change before it happens. Chauffeurs, liftmen, filing clerks, long-serving employees, even supervisory or junior management people can be mouths; but they should not be regarded simply as tools of management.

Do not always rely on the same moles and mouths. Protect the identity and reputation of people who assist you in this way.

143

Preparing and chairing

Well-conducted, productive meetings which deal with relevant subject matter efficiently are a sign of good teamwork, a high level of morale and commitment, and typify a healthy organization.

To the individual in such an environment, the meeting is both a challenge and an opportunity. Good performance at meetings can lead to increased responsibility and advancement. Also, the meeting provides a chance to bring group experience to bear on a particularly difficult subject.

'What do we need to know?'
Gathering or disseminating information is a crucial starting point when managing any new project. The purpose of the meeting is to share knowledge between all team members, establish lines of authority and responsibility and reinforce objectives. Often referred to as 'briefing', this meeting is also useful in defining problems. A strongly chaired 'formal' style is preferable.

'How are we getting on?'
Progress reviews are essential to good project management or customer/supplier relationships. Meetings are held at regular intervals as demanded by the project. Individuals work on an agreed agenda; cross-questioning and open discussion are vital ingredients, so skilled chairing is needed. Most of the participants will know each other, so a 'planned informal' style is the most appropriate.

'What's wrong? What shall we do?'
Sometimes it is necessary to break down discussion of problems into two separate meetings if time permits: one to define, and one to solve, with an interval in between to examine alternatives. An informal style is best because the issue is often too urgent to allow elaborate preparation. Informality also helps to avoid the allocation of blame, and the time-wasting justification this often causes.

For the meeting room you may need: name cards for participants; a soundproof, air-conditioned room; telephone messages taken externally; pads and pencils; a flipchart; copying facilities; electrical sockets/extension leads; a large table, extra chairs.

If chairing the meeting:
● Be more concerned with the process than the content. Keep the meeting moving to its conclusion and stay out of the discussion. If you have a strong interest, delegate the chair during that issue.
● Protect the weak, control the strong.
● Don't watch the speaker, watch the audience for reactions.
● Ensure a result – identify the issues, and agree on the means of their solution.

Don't be in a hurry to speak. Let others make their case, then construct yours by logically summarizing their views, concluding in favour of your own.

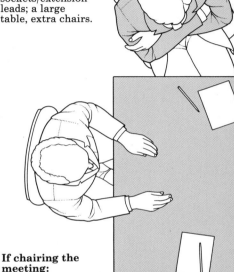

● Agree deadlines for progress reviews; set date, time and place for next meeting.
● Send good action-needed notes promptly to each participant.

Develop your skills of improvization, be aware of what is going on and, if necessary, use your contingency plans. The unexpected may lead to a better result.

If you know that someone else shares your view, let them speak first and then follow on, supporting their strong points, and adding any points they may have missed.

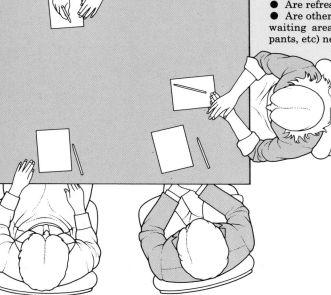

Meeting preparation

● What is the meeting's objective?
● Who needs to attend?
● When and where is convenient?
● What style should it be?
● Should information and agenda be precirculated?
● Are any special facilities (audio/visual aids) needed?
● Do topics need ranking/timing?
● Is there any conflict of interest?
● Is prediscussion with individuals required?
● What kind of record/minutes/action-needed notes are most suitable? Can a participant handle recording, or is secretarial help needed?
● Are any new members joining the group; do they need briefing?
● Are refreshments needed?
● Are other facilities (car-parking, waiting area for part-time participants, etc) needed?

The people who achieve most at meetings are often those who say least. But behind the economy of words lies detailed preparation and careful monitoring. Before the meeting it is essential to:
● Read pre-circulated literature carefully and question any contribution you do not understand.
● Be clear about your objective, and find out who supports and who opposes your view; lobby your supporters.
● Plan your contribution but prepare to be flexible. All plans need contingencies.

Always appear reasonable; keep a sense of humour (not flippancy); an intense approach exhausts and alienates others. Loss of cool usually means loss of argument.

Listen to all contributions; opponents may present you with openings; there may be aspects of the issue which were not covered by advance literature.

If you do not know the answer to a question, do not attempt to bluff. Promise an early reply or, if possible, ask permission to get the information at once.

Achieving results

True 'brainstorming' meetings are rare because people have difficulty lifting their sights from current problems and real innovators may fear scorn from their peers.

Meetings called to generate ideas require sensitive steering but, when successful, can be of immense value; ideas are the food of business growth. Informality is invariably the right atmosphere for such meetings (lunch can provide the setting). Remember, *encourage* the ideas to emerge.

Arbitration – one of the rarest and most valuable skills – puts great responsibility on the chair. Meetings to resolve difficulties or conflict require forethought (often careful lobbying of participants to find out attitudes and positions).

Meeting style should be a tactical decision of the chair, or of the person who calls the meeting, in order to achieve the desired result. Remember, consensus may not be the object if all it does is submerge conflict.

Earl Mountbatten of Burma was highly skilled at meeting technique. Alan Campbell-Johnson, his press attaché in India, recalls that he used a meeting to reach agreement on an issue, the contentious features of which had already been ironed out in personal discussion. If, during a meeting, there was unforeseen dissent, he took the matter off the agenda for personal treatment afterwards.

In this context, staff meetings, both when he was Supreme Allied Commander and Viceroy, were held on an almost daily basis, part of a continuous process of diplomacy.

How to perform well at meetings

● Listen actively: practise this skill. It leads to good questions, improves group understanding, keeps meetings good humoured.

● Give direct replies: keep the meeting to the point to avoid wasting time.

● Clarify issues: 'Are you saying that you can provide this material by the end of the month ...?'

● Summarize progress: 'It's now 3.30 pm, where are we ...?'

● Restate important points: 'So let's confirm ...'

● Be prepared to change your strategy if necessary.

● Be supportive: 'That sounds like a good idea ...'

● Confront issues: 'Are we really prepared to ...?'

● Question critically: 'What exactly do you mean ...?'

● Bring with you accurate supporting data.

● Make sure the meeting is not interrupted by telephone calls, except in emergencies.

● Avoid interrupting.

● Don't be afraid to make your feelings known.

● Refrain from distracting behaviour such as pencil tapping.

● Don't talk to your neighbour during a presentation.

● Never lose your temper, except deliberately.

Formal meetings

Committees, boards of directors, large briefing groups and some project progress meetings follow this style. Often it is the only way to control large groups covering varied topics. Rigid, structured agendas, time allocated to subjects by agreement with participants, and firm control of time and relevance by the chair are essential.

Informal meetings

These can be *ad hoc* — 'It's time we talked' – or a sub-group of a formal meeting. Typically, they are convened to deal with specific issues, rather than a whole subject. Little notice is needed; the outcome should be a plan, a solution, or a request to hold a larger, formal meeting (talks about talks). Can be as small as two people, or as large as six.

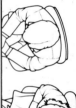

Planned informal meetings

For the planner, these are the most useful meetings. You decide the objective, select the participants, prepare your case and deal with people singly or in groups. To avoid random results, misunderstandings and wasting time, all your business contacts should be thought of as planned informal meetings.

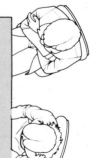

Using internal resources

Consultation is a way of testing what impact an action might have on others before you commit yourself to it. Consultation is used to assess risk, create consent or conduct arbitration.

Consultation is essentially a process in which one party seeks the views, knowledge or advice of another. As a manager you may want to use consultation to overcome potential resistance to a decision you have made, or to use the knowledge of your staff to help implement your initiatives in more effective ways.

If, as a manager, you have set the right climate for your team and your colleagues, people will feel able to consult with their bosses, peers or subordinates on a regular basis. An open style of management will promote consultation as a normal facet of business behaviour and not as a sign of ignorance or weakness.

Indeed, the consultation process can have positive benefits for you and your team. People should be encouraged to seek and accept consultation, especially on issues which may have far-reaching consequences.

Benefits of consulting

Handled properly, consultation can have positive results. It helps you to:
● Test reactions to risky or threatening ideas.
● Check feasibility: if you are too close to an idea you may not be able to recognize that it just would not work in practice.
● Look for compatibility with other people's plans and projects. It is surprising how often the same idea occurs to people working in the same organization at the same time.
● Seek advice: there may well be people who are experienced or expert in something you are coming to for the first time.
● Get agreement: an idea or suggestion which meets with favourable early reaction is well on the way to agreement.
● Sharpen up your own thought processes by highlighting parts of your initial unsound thinking.
● Reveal extra pieces of the jigsaw you failed to recognize which either complement your original thoughts or reveal ideas counter to your original direction.

Direct and indirect consultation

Consultation is multi-directional: you can consult directly or indirectly with your boss, peers and subordinates. But you must be clear about what you want to achieve and whether it is feasible.

Consulting upward: if you consult your boss directly about an idea, it may give the impression that what you are really seeking is approval, not consultation. Instead, you could float the idea informally over lunch. Your boss is bound to give you an indication whether the idea is, in fact, worth pursuing or not. If the idea originated from a peer or subordinate, give him/her credit: it will encourage people to come to you with ideas and improve your reputation as the person who gets the ideas moving.

Consulting sideways: when you consult peer colleagues directly, you risk their stealing your proposal/idea; or if they oppose it, you give them time to think of ways of blocking you. Instead, you could take your idea to a superior to whom you have access. Get it approved and then take it to your colleagues, making sure that they know it has the superior's backing. This will give it authority and stop anyone stealing it.

Consulting downward: subordinates unused to consultative management may experience confusion or suspicion if suddenly consulted directly by a superior – 'Why should the boss want to consult a junior person like me?' Also, they may tell you what they think you want to hear, not what you need to hear. Even worse, they might see it as a sign of weakness on your part – 'Surely you can make your own decisions without having to consult a subordinate?' Instead you could get your secretary or personal assistant to float your proposal for you: your subordinate is more likely to react honestly and you can act on the feedback.

Pitfalls of consulting

The risks of consultation are:
● You waste time. If an idea has been in your mind for some time, it is often impossible for someone else to understand it quickly.
● Those whom you consult may not have anything positive to contribute. The ideas you glean when you consult are often ones you have already rejected.
● You may end up antagonizing those you are consulting because they suggest ideas that you have already rejected; or because you do not follow their advice.
● Your idea may get stolen by someone else. Innovation and creativity are often in short supply and people may take your idea and call it their own.
● Consulting with your boss may leave him/her with the impression that you are not fully in control of your situation.
● Consulting with your subordinates may similarly be seen as a sign of weakness. They may feel that you ought to know, which could diminish your standing as leader.

Consulting successfully

Develop your skill at consultation, to enhance your own solutions as a result of others' contributions.
Remember to:
● Give your good ideas time to mature in your own mind. Don't rush off to consult others every time you have a brainwave, but...
● Get used to floating your ideas at an early stage in their development.
● Don't get into consultation if you have no real options. If you are committed to an idea and are expected to implement it, don't consult on its feasibility, make it work.
● Find one or two colleagues whom you can use as regular sounding boards. In time they will come to know you better (and vice versa) and the consultation process will be speeded up.
● Be genuinely prepared to change up to the point that you commit yourself. Once committed, try not to entertain doubts.
In the last analysis, consultation does not change the basic responsibilities – the decision is always yours.

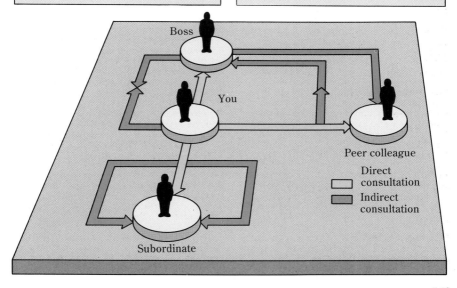

Boss

You

Peer colleague

Direct consultation

Indirect consultation

Subordinate

Seeking outside help

An organization will often bring in management consultants to deal with problems it has either not encountered before or whose solution demands resources it does not possess. Consultants are commonly thought of as having the missing piece of expertise that will complete the jigsaw or solve the problem.

But it is not simply a question of providing technical expertise. Consulting is more than that. It involves the difficult process of acclimatizing quickly to the organization and its problems; gathering information and checking its relevance; bringing together the interested parties and persuading them toward making a particular decision, then taking a course of action. Consultation is an art, not a technique.

There are three main reasons why companies bring in consultants.

The need for extra resources
There is only a finite amount of time in a working day or week and good managers need it all. This means that important projects requiring a period of concentrated effort may be delayed because of everyday demands. Bringing in consultants to deal with a specific task can be the answer.

The need for objectivity
Before making a decision on a problematic issue, you have to weigh up the pros and cons carefully. Managers may find that the issue in question has become such a bone of contention within the organization that reasonable and detached advice cannot be found internally. Equally, they may be too close to the issue to be able to stand back and contribute usefully.

The need for expertise
Problems may arise or decisions may have to be taken which need a depth of knowledge and experience that is lacking within the organization. Good consultants can provide the necessary expertise without lengthy familiarization programmes.

There are a number of less tangible benefits that consultants can help to provide.

The role of consultants

Good consultants are friends (not foes) to the client organization. They might have been brought in by head office, but they must work *with* the client to generate long-lasting, sometimes radical, solutions.

Jani Jack is a leading manufacturer of industrial and commercial cleaning systems, including equipment designed to meet the stringent hygiene requirements in hospitals and operating theatres. 70% of the turnover is exported to places such as Germany, France and Scandinavia. To ensure continued profitable growth, they asked Ernst & Young to review their manufacturing operations. The consultants brought external expertise resulting in proposals to radically change the manufacturing operating procedures. These were to result in:

● Halving of inventory
● Lead times cut from 8 weeks to 3 days
● Productivity increased by 6%
● Space reduced by 20%

Inventory reduction

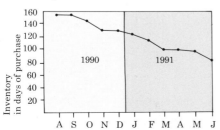

Productivity increase

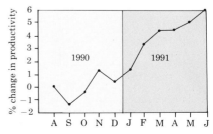

Reassurance

A company may want to invest a large sum of money in acquiring new machinery or other assets, and may seek a second opinion from consultants to confirm it is doing the right thing.

Insurance

Say that an organization wants to spend millions on a project. Its shareholders are anxious as to whether the board of directors is spending the money wisely. The latter can take out an insurance policy, as it were, by enlisting the advice of top consultants. This will ease the worries of the shareholders as well as spreading the responsibility if anything goes wrong.

Sounding-board

Senior executives who have to make crucial decisions often find it difficult to consult within the organization because it might call into question their ability or competence. Nevertheless, they still need a sounding-board to assess the quality of their decisions; this can be provided by consultants, contracted on a long-term basis.

Reservoirs of information

Companies and their executives are often so involved in the day-to-day running of their affairs that they cannot see themselves as part of the overall picture or compare themselves with other companies/executives. Consultants can provide a survey of industrial practice. They hold up a mirror in which the clients can see where they stand in relation to others.

Catalysts of change

The answers to clients' problems are often to be found underneath their noses and not in some magical expertise that consultants are supposed to have. In such an instance, it is the consultants' job to sift the relevant information, list the facts and get the clients to confront what they have previously been ignoring.

An internal report may give the same facts as the consultants' report. But if you are paying the consultants a lot of money for their time, you have a greater incentive to do something about the problem.

To achieve these benefits, the client and consultants agreed that large batches were not economic; machine set ups could be reduced, and methods of working integrated. It was a tribute to the open mind of the client company (at all levels) that such radical changes were readily accepted.

Having agreed the strategy, the next step was to plan for the future. A 'way forward' was devised, consisting of a series of workshops the purpose of which was to work *with* the client's organization to 'make it happen'.

Employee involvement was the key to the success of implementation – shop floor operators know and experience the daily problems on the shop floor. This also ensured commitment and gave 'ownership' of the new factory concepts to the workforce. The consultants were retained to provide facilitation expertise, ensure continuity, act as a catalyst and contribute to the steering committee.

Layout before

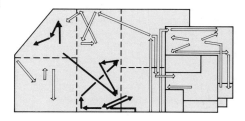

Layout after
20% space saving

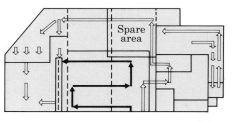

The formal approach

Negotiation is the process of arriving at mutual satisfaction through discussion and bargaining. Managers negotiate to settle differences, vary agreements or terms, or to value commodities or services. Although there is a large area of overlap with 'cooperation', as different interests emerge among 'cooperators', negotiation is required to resolve conflict.

For negotiation to succeed, each party must genuinely desire agreement, which can be expressed as a lasting contract. Agreement that cannot be applied is useless.

Solutions must be viable or the negotiators – who are only representatives of an interest – will lose their credibility and authority, and lack of lasting agreement will result.

Negotiators have to perform several skilled functions. They must be able to plan in the knowledge that they may not be allowed to proceed in the sequence they desire.

The case relating to each point of the negotiation must be prepared as if the other parties did not exist. Every argument should be complete. Negotiators must be flexible enough to argue cases in context and according to the priority given them by the other side.

Good negotiators understand how to resolve conflict. Denying the conflict antagonizes the opponent. Accommodation is dangerous – it is the slippery slope to appeasement and leads to submission. Domineering behaviour intensifies resistance.

There is no single comprehensive theory governing the complex practice of negotiation, although some of the world's foremost business education establishments – notably Harvard – devote much effort to developing strategies to help negotiators achieve positive results.

Three major theories of practice have emerged in the last two decades, namely 'positional', 'principled' and 'situational' negotiation.

How to negotiate

The art of negotiation is to avoid reaching a fixed position too quickly. Well before meeting, messages should be exchanged.

Negotiation should then follow a well-prepared, logical sequence:

1 Introduction
Be sociable with the other party and set a tension-free atmosphere.

2 General overview
Confirm both parties' broad objectives and feelings. Assess any differences between your positions.

3 Background
Review proceedings leading up to the present negotiation. If you have different interpretations of the 'facts', iron out the differences.

4 Definition of issues
Specify in detail what you want to resolve, if possible starting with an issue on which agreement is probable. Link issues if advantageous. Specify if one issue can be settled only if another is also resolved.

5 Negotiate the issue
Start by asking for what you want. Both parties want as much as they can get, but both must accept that goals may have to be modified. Conflict should not be avoided – it ventilates the issues and leads to settlements.

6 Compromising
Give, to get something in return, but make sure you give points at a consistent rate. If compromising becomes difficult, go 'situational', exchanging messages outside the meeting ground through others.

7 Settlement
'Agree on what you have agreed.' Unless agreement is fully understood by both parties the settlement will not last.

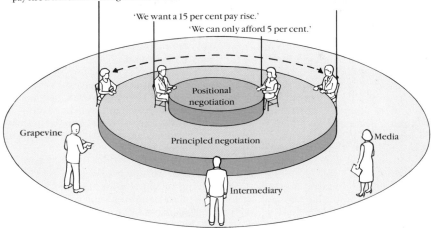

'We are prepared to accept a 10 per cent pay rise if it means avoiding redundancies.'

'We can afford to give a 7 per cent rise if productivity is improved.'

'We want a 15 per cent pay rise.'

'We can only afford 5 per cent.'

Positional negotiation

Grapevine

Principled negotiation

Media

Intermediary

Situational negotiation

Types of formal negotiation

In theory, there are three distinct types of negotiation. The distinctions are less clear in practice. For example, situational negotiation usually takes place before both positional and principled negotiation.

Positional negotiation is the traditional form of negotiation. Participants often work to a tight mandate. If their positions afford no compromise, the result will be deadlock. Success is usually achieved only after all aspects of opposing positions have been explored to try to find common ground.

Typical examples include, union/management bargaining, disputes between customers and suppliers and boundary or territorial difficulties.

Principled negotiation is the 'Harvard Model' whereby negotiators are encouraged to search for the underlying principles which support 'positions'.

This is a more relaxed and creative process for the negotiator, who is briefed to deliver objectives, not solutions. Principled negotiation depends on detailed identification of all the various options. The will to succeed is often greater than in positional negotiating, because both parties feel a sense of achievement rather than loss.

Principled negotiation degenerates into positional negotiation or deadlock if emotions are allowed to cloud the issues at stake.

Situational negotiation usually takes place before both positional and principled negotiation in the form of leaks to the press or via the grapevine. It is an indirect and pre-emptive form of negotiation. Sending messages via a third party before a meeting can prevent wasting time. Deadlock can be avoided and solutions quickly found.

Internal bargaining

Most managers dislike the process of negotiation, believing it to be a clash of wills from which only one conclusion is certain—both parties will lose something. But negotiating is a feature of almost every bargain struck in every workplace.

Managers regularly have to negotiate – with peers, the boss and subordinates – especially as giving and taking orders becomes a less acceptable aspect of business behaviour.

In theory, conflicts are resolved by reference to who is 'right'. Reality is much more complex, with its systems of favours done and owing.

Internal negotiations are much more difficult than external ones. Each agent has his/her own idea of what is best for the company. This, coupled with individual needs and relationships, heightens the potential for conflict. The loser in the negotiation may work in the same building, doing a similar job. The loser may be the winner in the next negotiation, may be a rival for promotion, a close friend or a bitter enemy.

Therefore, if you don't have to negotiate, don't. If cooperation can be achieved without bargaining or compromise, accept it. Don't believe that you have to negotiate every point, complicating the manager/subordinate relationship by encouraging negotiation of the most trivial matters. It is your duty as a manager to foster a climate of cooperation.

All parties to a negotiation must perceive that they have needs which can be satisfied. When one side does not acknowledge having needs, the other side must demonstrate that such needs exist. In other words, needs may have to be 'sold' to the other side.

Timing is an obvious and frequently overlooked point with two main aspects:
● Is it the right time for the organization to accept the idea that you are trying to implement? Premature forcing of an issue weakens your negotiating position.
● Is it the right time to tackle the individual(s) to whom you must speak? Is he/she under pressure, busy, depressed or bad-tempered? Being sensitive to the mood and receptiveness of others can prevent sound ideas being rejected for the wrong reasons.

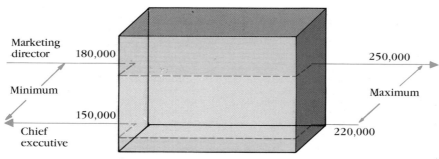

(Figures in pounds sterling)

Define your objectives—most negotiations centre around finding a mutually acceptable mid-point. In the annual budgeting round, for example, the marketing director's objective may be to obtain an advertising budget of £250,000, while the chief executive's objective is to keep it down to £150,000. Both parties must have a range in mind.

Settlement is likely to be reached somewhere in the blue shaded area between £180,000 and £220,000.

Achieving win/win

There is a greater need for both sides to win in internal negotiations. One danger is that argument often centres on who is doing the best job for the company.

Negotiators who adhere rigidly to a fixed position can succeed only by causing some form of damage to the other party and are, effectively, not negotiating. The damaged party will find all sorts of ways, either subtle or blatant, of getting revenge. This will be to the detriment of company efficiency and staff harmony.

To arrive at a win/win solution:
● Honesty is essential. Because both sides tend to know each other very well, ploys, privileged information, strengths/weaknesses, may be difficult to exploit.
● Don't embark on negotiation with all the emphasis on your own needs – 'This is what we want', 'When are you going to start supporting our efforts?' Try to analyse and understand the needs of the other party. Be prepared to accommodate these other needs, unless doing so weakens your own bargaining position or jeopardizes your negotiating strategy.
● Don't deal with internal issues by full frontal confrontation. Try to don the velvet glove rather than wield the iron fist of authority.
● If you choose to be cynical and sceptical, do so only to expose the weaknesses in a position. Don't act the part of devil's advocate to repay some previous hurt or to establish a reputation with a patron.
● Remember that egos surface more readily on internal matters and often lead to power struggles to justify worth or position in the hierarchy. Don't expend effort trying to prove yourself to others, perhaps to the detriment of the point at issue.
● See the other party's need for help to resolve their losing position if a win/win situation is not achieved.

Leverage factors

The party with the greater need is in the weaker negotiating position and must analyse factors which might provide additional leverage:
● How much you need the other party.
● How much the other party needs you.
● What you know that the other party does not.
● What the other party might know that you don't.
● What you both know that you don't want exposed elsewhere.
● The time pressures on both parties.
● The extent of peer group involvement and influence.
● Fear of failure, loss of prestige, or the heaping of disgrace on either side.
● The effect on future plans (win the battle, lose the war).
● The need to be right, to win praise or recognition.
● The ability to influence formally or informally both your peers and superiors.
● The ability to make the other party feel guilty.
● Deprivation of freedom of action.
● Threat of boycott.

Having assessed as far as possible the strengths and weaknesses of both parties, ask yourself:
● What strengths does the other party have that could be a source of worry to me?
● What strengths do I have that will worry the other party?

The above may seem to be tinged with cynicism and aggression. It is. Negotiating is not a parlour game.

If this all seems too uncivilized, an alternative way of redressing an imbalance of needs is for the weaker party to create needs for the other party. Bear in mind motivational needs and that needs occur over time. A previously solved problem may resurface, or a possible future problem may be identified.

Staff selection and interviewing

Recruitment is an important managerial task because you will usually have to live with the results for a considerable time.

Good managers rarely delegate the process entirely and usually stay close to all its stages since the candidate's personal commitment to them (as opposed to a department of personnel) can be achieved only through close involvement in the appointment.

If a member of staff leaves or is promoted, don't automatically recruit a replacement. Make sure that the work cannot be absorbed internally without affecting quality, morale or productivity.

If you have to recruit, first define the job, taking into account its function, the duties and responsibilities involved, and the skill, knowledge and experience needed. Check whether past job-holders had specific difficulties, the pay and conditions package, and the way the job interacts with other members of the department.

Once you have defined the job, ask:
- Is this a long-term role?
- Can it be filled internally?
- Does it demand any specialized knowledge?
- Is it likely to attract high-calibre applicants?
- Can it be merged with other responsibilities to make it more attractive?

Decide where to pitch the job, and draw up a job specification, listing job objectives, status and reporting relationships, main tasks/responsibilities, available resources and support and any problems associated with the job.

Then work out a 'person specification', listing essential and desirable skills, qualities, background experience and qualifications. This information can be used to issue an internal 'job vacancy' memo and to produce a recruitment advertisement.

Interviewing is expensive, so make sure the job information is accurate and evocative of its 'feel'. For example, don't ask for 'aggressive achievers' if the organizational culture is a conservative bureaucracy.

To decide whom to interview, compare CVs against the person specification. Remember, not all criteria can be assessed from a CV, particularly personal qualities. These should be explored in depth at an interview.

The interview

Read the applicant's CV carefully before the interview, and plan the areas you wish to explore.

Interviews are difficult and demanding because no two people are alike. Some express themselves better in writing than in conversation. So if the job does not demand great speaking skills, don't be overimpressed by eloquence. Stick to relevant qualities.

You will need skill, tact and understanding to make an interviewee relaxed enough to proffer information from which you can assess potential. Get interviewees to talk about real situations they have been in, rather than asking how they would react in hypothetical ones.

Sympathetic listening and well-timed, but open, questions encourage honest responses; trick questions, a rigid interview structure, an impatient or bored attitude, do not. Interviews are a two-way process. You are selling the organization as well as finding out about the interviewee.

Follow up the interview by preparing a short list. Write promptly to candidates who are not on it. You will need to take up references, but check with the candidate when this will be appropriate. As one of the referees is likely to be their current employer, it would be awkward to request a reference before they know the person is moving.

If you think a candidate who narrowly missed your job would do well elsewhere in your organization, pass the particulars to a colleague.

Interviewer tactics

● Plan the interview but be prepared to be directed by the candidate's answers.
● Take brief notes; expand later.
● Get the interviewee to enlarge on the facts given on his/her CV.
● Be alert to the interviewee embellishing the facts.
● Don't ask questions which produce only yes-or-no answers.
● Listen and be seen to listen.
● Ask for career aims and compare them with past experience.
● Be sure applicants have had a chance to reveal all relevant information.
● Allow candidates to question you.

Interviewee tactics

● Dress smartly and look the part.
● Support answers with examples.
● Act as if you *want* the job.
● Say *how* you have gone about work.
● Be sure you can answer questions on career and personal objectives.
● Show, with examples, how you have previously handled challenging situations.
● Give concrete examples of your work performance.
● Be honest: you can be checked, and it may not be worth getting a job on the basis of untruths.
● Be ready to ask the interviewer questions.

Assessing candidates

After the interview, you will have a mass of data to evaluate. You need to compare the candidates both impartially and consistently. Look back to the job criteria you have drawn up. How well did each candidate meet the criteria? If more than one interviewee meets the criteria, it may be worth considering any other skills or qualities they demonstrated at the interview which may be a bonus in this job. This may be useful in deciding between strong candidates.

Planning succession

Organizations are dynamic. Continual movement is dictated by the ever-changing demands of the marketplace, and by people's desire to improve their careers. As a manager, you have a duty to meet these changes by accepting and encouraging promotion and other opportunities.

But you should also ensure that as you or your staff move up (or out to other jobs), so the void is filled by a competent person, capable of working to the high standard you expect from your department.

What happens to you also has a bearing on your staff. If you don't plan to have your own job successfully filled as you move on in the organization, the inefficiencies that are likely to develop in your former department will call into question your ability as a leader.

Even if you have moved out of your company, your old employer's succession problems may affect your career: your new boss may be watching to make sure you don't create similar problems.

Planning subordinates' succession
The skilled and self-motivated people in your team will probably receive overtures from other companies as well as chances to move up their company's ladder.

You need to anticipate and cater for the gaps left when good staff are sucked into the promotion tube, rather than be pitched into crisis by sudden departure.

You will also have people who are not obvious candidates for promotion – staff who should not have been hired, are past their best or who are content with their level of skill/responsibility.

People may fail to live up to expectations; some will get stale and lose their motivation. You cannot afford to compromise quality and efficiency to accommodate their tarnished performance. Succession planning has a definite role to play here, too.

Anticipate and plan for staff changes

To plan succession effectively you need to look ahead at least three years. Planning on such a time scale will equip you to deal with departmental change and succession much better than if you tried to cope with the whole problem during a three-month notice period.
● Show you care about your people's careers.
● Encourage staff to be open with you about their ambitions.
● Be alert for signs that staff need or want to move.
● Be broadminded about departures: help staff to leave pleasantly.
● Help staff in their promotion search within the company.
● Talk frankly about the negative as well as the positive factors.
● Encourage people to seek new challenges if they have become stale/bored in your team.
● Be your own talent scout by keeping your eyes open for people who might slot into your team.

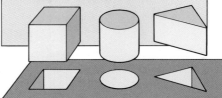

Recruiting from without

You may need to recruit from outside to fill an important slot in your team. A different approach or new ideas/skills can be positive for your team.
The personnel department
Personnel can be helpful, if they know the market for the type of expertise you require, and can support you in your search for a successor. But they may advise you to use external agencies (especially if you want to tempt someone from a competing company).

Planning succession

The development, by you, of a first-rate second-in-command is beneficial to the company because:
● Management does not waste time or money searching for and interviewing your successor.
● Departmental morale is raised by internal appointments.
● Continuity is maintained.
● If extra staff are needed, it is at a more junior level and so less costly.
● The 'culture' of the department is more likely to remain intact.

You should look for potential successors when your career is on the up and your prospects are bright. If you leave it until you are facing setbacks and difficulties it looks like a tactical retreat or resignation.

If you have to make an appointment from elsewhere in the company or externally, you may need the help of a consultant or an agency to find the right person.

Such an appointment is best made in advance of your move; indeed, if a role can be created prior to, rather than as a result of, your move, so much the better.

Lord Rayner and Richard Greenbury

On announcing his intention to retire, Lord Rayner, chairman of Marks and Spencer, named Richard Greenbury, a solid figure with a strong presence, as his successor. Greenbury is seen as the product of the M&S corporate culture – building upon Rayner's electronic ordering and invoicing systems (the most elaborate in British retailing) to keep Marks & Spencer up to date and in touch.

Greenbury left school to take a job as a management trainee at M&S and eventually became one of the youngest-ever managing directors at the age of 41. His experience was broadened by nine years as a non-executive director of British Gas.

Emerging in 1988 as chief executive officer – a subtle M&S upgrading from his previous title of chief operating officer – he took over as Chairman and Chief Executive on 1 April 1991.

Register companies

These companies keep lists of people in specialist occupations (retail, electronics, food etc) who want to change jobs.

Such companies save the cost of advertising and can be a good source for recruiting junior management.

Recruitment agencies

Agencies offer a mixture of 'register' and advertising. They screen candidates before producing a short-list. The client pays in advance and for the advertising. Agencies are widely used for recruiting middle management.

Recruitment consultancies

Consultants, retained to advise companies on how to develop their personnel, undertake the recruitment of middle and senior management.

Executive search ('headhunters')
'Headhunters' advise companies on key strategic posts. They are increasingly responsible for the most senior appointments in commerce, government, industry and the professions. They differ from other agencies in that they enter actively into the marketplace and use a network of contacts to build up a 'talent list'.

The need for training

In the early stages of your career up to manager level, training will be largely task-related: the acquisition of technical skills, professional knowledge or specific techniques.

As your career develops, and you become responsible for task-related training of others, it is crucial that you are on top of your basic job skills. At the same time you need to acquire those business-related skills that lead to a better understanding of the management process as a whole.

Broadening your knowledge

You should become familiar with the operational activities of related functions in the organization. If, for example, you are a manager in the production department, you need to appreciate the working of the finance, marketing and sales departments. As your responsibility for others increases, so should your knowledge of the organization as a whole.

Throughout the development of your career, you should keep up to date on technology and on legislation relating to the workplace.

The acquisition of business-related skills, such as effective decision-making and problem solving, increases with job experience so that by the time you have become established in the manager's role your ability in these areas should be well developed. People-related skills – the ability to motivate, influence and lead – are in highest demand in general corporate management.

Learning by doing

People learn to perform well from a close observation of 'role models' and from being in challenging situations which require initiative and positive leadership.

You should recognize that formal training courses are not the only source of learning. Ambitious managers actively seek learning experiences to acquire knowledge and a broader range of managerial skills.

Those around you in the workplace (and you yourself) are judged on performance and specific tasks. Qualifications and attendance at training courses do not guarantee a climb up the corporate ladder.

Because most of your time is spent on the job, the best way to train yourself is to seek challenging tasks and projects. Aim to get a variety of experience by transferring to well-led and pressured teams on other projects or in other departments. Don't stagnate, but don't over-specialize; build up a wide range of knowledge.

If you seek ever-greater responsibility, you will increase your management experience while improving your technical skills. A record of performance and achievement will be of greater influence in getting you promotion than any number of academic qualifications.

Formal training

Your ability to cope with specific technical skills can be helped greatly by undergoing formal training. But it is up to you to ensure that you maximize

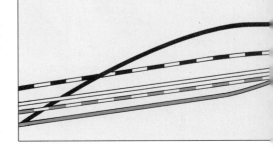

Acquiring skills and experience

In the early stages of your career, you need to concentrate on acquiring skills that enable you to carry out specific tasks and to be given feedback on how well you have performed them.

the usefulness of this training.

You should analyse your needs and career objectives first, and only then approach the training department. If their proposals match your objectives, needs and timescale, then accept them. Make sure training is geared to you as an individual.

Check the quality of the courses, and that they will meet your needs. Ask colleagues who have been on the courses before you about their content and practical relevance to the job.

If the training department cannot match your needs, then consider going to an outside training organization. Many training departments augment their own work in this way. But check out the quality of an outside course thoroughly before committing your time and the company's money to it.

You should augment formal training by reading around your subject and by discussing your work, at appropriate moments, with peers or senior colleagues. Watching how acknowledged 'experts' perform can also be helpful.

Questioning your development

To ascertain your training needs, ask yourself:
● What are my strengths and weaknesses?
● Which weaknesses can and should be improved? Which strengths could be enhanced further with skills/ knowledge?
● How did the organization's 'high fliers' get on? How did they acquire their skills/knowledge/attributes?
● Where did successful managers gain experience? (It is likely that little of it will have come through formal training.)
● Is the skill/technology used in my industry stable or changing? Am I keeping up to date? Is my company successfully meeting the challenge of change?
● What have I learned in the last two or three years? How much more am I likely to learn if I remain in my present job?
● Is what I am learning likely to enhance my present/future employer's opinion of me?

By the time you reach first managerial level, you need to concentrate on strengthening your skills in other disciplines related to the business and to your work. Keep up to date with basic skills so as to train others, but acquire a broad understanding of your business that will further your career.

People-related skills, leadership, motivation, team building, delegation

Business related skills, eg communication, desision-making, time management

Knowledge of other functions, eg finance, marketing, sales

Technical skills, basic knowledge

Once your have become established as a manager, your ability to motivate, influence and lead will be in ever-greater demand. Communication skills become increasingly important.

General knowledge, eg health and safety, industry/trade affairs

Finding effective training

The training function helps individuals, and therefore organizations, improve on quality, competitiveness and productivity.

In a recent survey, a German manager said: 'The same machines and equipment can be bought by anybody; success in the market can only be won by those who have a labour force capable of using them to their advantage, and being constantly trained to improve their performance.'

This strong belief in training is exemplified by such companies as Marks & Spencer, Mercedes, British Airways and Siemens, where members of the workforce are regularly engaged in self-development training programmes.

In the USA, top high-tech companies like IBM, Xerox, Boeing and McDonnell Douglas spend between 2.5 per cent and 3.5 per cent of sales revenue on training; and Britain's highly successful financial services industry invests a like amount.

Benefits of training

Training should produce profitable results both for the company and the individual. But how do you know when you are being given good training advice?

The training function should essentially provide a source of experienced advice to guide you in your personal and team decisions. You should feel you are dealing with people who are close to the business, who understand the direction of its corporate development and who have access to, and the support of, senior management.

Trainers should be active in the business, encouraging managers to be part of the training process, they should have recent experience themselves of running part of it. Indeed they may, in the long term, return to line management.

The training function should test ideas, encourage change and seek out tomorrow's issues. It should have the honesty to let you know when training is *not* the solution to your problem. Career development, organizational issues or recruitment may need attention.

There is a thriving training industry that provides specialized and general independent support for organizations who do not possess a training function or who wish to augment their existing one.

Internal or external training

There are no hard and fast rules determining whether you should go for outside training or not: you must choose according to needs.

Look at your own internal training function; try to evaluate its performance. If it scores highly with other colleagues on performance, initiative and relevance, then you would be well advised to work with them.

Internal training has its advantages; those involved will usually have accurate, up-to-date knowledge and understanding of the real problems of the business. This should mean that they are well placed to pass on realistic and relevant thoughts on how to solve the problems.

External training, on the other hand, is noted for objectivity and breadth of experience (from other working environments). It provides a fresh, outside view of problems and a proven training 'product' and approach. Participants gain credibility within their own companies based on experience, knowledge and research.

It can often deal with subjects in greater depth of specialization. Your own training department should be able to recommend good organizations whose services match your needs.

For any training programme to be effective, everyone in the department should be committed to it and supportive of its aims. Such commitment is essential if you are to avoid the problem of trainees arriving back from a training course, eager to apply its lessons, only to have their enthusiasm crushed by colleagues who have not undergone the same 'conversion'.

If you are seeking an external training programme, talk to a number of training organizations about your needs. Ask them how their product has been applied by other clients with similar needs. Talk to the other clients. Not until you are satisfied that your needs or those of your people can be met should you proceed.

A trial with a test candidate may give final reassurance that the course is relevant, applicable to your industry and speciality and, above all, transferable to your workplace.

Take care that the external trainers have knowledge and insights into your actual problems and issues, and avoid the academic approach which deals with how things *should be,* rather than how they *are.*

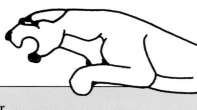

Jaguar

Jaguar, the luxury car manufacturer, achieved a remarkable turnaround in the first half of the 1980s under the leadership of Sir John Egan. The whole company had become dispirited by bad results, by the fact that its once high reputation for quality had fallen, and by its loss of identity when it was absorbed into the Leyland Group. Employees could no longer take pride in their uniqueness. There was doubt whether Jaguar would survive – the need for change and strong leadership was evident.

Egan decided to stick to basics. He made quality the number one concern, followed closely by productivity. Customers were surveyed regularly, new manufacturing technology and quality circles were introduced. These circles were significant. They involved everyone and helped to restore a sense of pride and belonging, and a flow of ideas for improvement emerged. Communications were improved in other ways as well, with Sir John himself taking a prominent role in inspiring the employees. The entire battery of internal public relations approaches, meetings, videos, newsletters, etc, were used. Training became widespread, and the company education centre produced learning materials which employees could use on their own. New reward and share ownership schemes were introduced.

The company reached high customer satisfaction index ratings in the US and a new high-performance model was successfully launched in 1986–7. There have been difficulties, largely currency problems, and these contributed to some industrial relations concerns. In 1990 Jaguar was acquired by the Ford Motor Company which has the ability to provide much greater technical resource. The company has now established a solid foundation for restoring the glory of Jaguar.

Selecting and shaping

Two types of team usually exist within an organization. The 'formal' team is the department or section created within a recognized structure to pursue specified goals.

'Informal' teams are created to deal with a particular situation; their members have fewer fixed organizational relationships, and they are disbanded after performing their function.

Both formal and informal teams need to be led by managers who give as much thought to team relationships as to the task the team has to perform.

Teams cannot be created simply by analysing the demands of work or the project and assembling a group of people who appear to have the relevant qualifications and experience. Teams have certain features that include:
● Shared or agreed aims
● A common working 'language'
● The ability to manage relationships as well as tasks.

Choosing the right team

Selecting and shaping teams to work on projects is one of the most important and interesting roles of management, and requires skill and sensitivity. Among your staff you will have people who are vague conceptual thinkers, 'workaholics', those who need the task spelt out, and others who can process work limitlessly.

Select or build a team of people with compensating strengths and weaknesses. Make careful decisions about project teams and pairings; don't allow combinations that have worked well in the past to continue simply from force of habit. Try to match each individual's talent to his/her task.

To arrive at a good team you will need people who, for example:
● Create useful ideas
● Analyse problems effectively
● Get things done
● Communicate well
● Have leadership qualities
● Can evaluate logically

● Have technical abilities
● Can control work
● Are good at writing/speaking.

Decide in what proportion these skills are needed for the task in hand, and select staff accordingly.

If you inherit a ready-made team, go through the same process to see if you need to reshuffle or reinforce it.

Developing your team

Building a group into a team requires skill. Maintaining the health of a team and developing it demands constant attention. Your group will never become a team unless you put considerable effort into ensuring that differing personalities are able to relate to, communicate with and value the contribution of their colleagues.

If you are in charge of a team, you have the responsibility to develop your people. Training is not simple. You will find disparity between the time it takes people to learn new, unfamiliar skills and the time needed to develop innate skills.

As team leader, you will have the strongest influence on your team. People will not do as you *say*, they will do as you *do*, so be sure to set examples that you want followed. If, for example, you want good cost control and keen, competitive buying in your department, don't indulge in long, expensive lunches with suppliers.

Remember, too, that real life at work includes time pressure, conflict, personality clash, change and stress.

Work types

Many have tried to categorize the types of people who work in organizations. The chart (*right*) is based on the work of Meredith Belbin at Henley Management College, UK.

When selecting a team you should be aware that these various 'work types' have differing behaviour characteristics that need to be taken into account.

Work type	Typical features	Positive qualities	Allowable weaknesses
Plant	Individualistic, serious-minded, unorthodox	Genius, imagination, intellect, knowledge	Up in the clouds, inclined to disregard practical details or protocol
Resource investigator	Extroverted, enthusiastic, curious, communicative	A capacity for contacting people and exploring anything new; an ability to respond to challenge	Liable to lose interest once the initial fascination has passed
Monitor-evaluator	Sober, unemotional, prudent	Judgement, discretion, hard-headedness	Lacks inspiration or the ability to motivate others
Implementer	Conservative, dutiful, predictable, competent, loyal	Organizing ability, practical common sense, hard-working, self-discipline	Lack of flexibility, unresponsiveness to unproven ideas
Completer-finisher	Painstaking, orderly, conscientious, anxious	A capacity for follow-through, perfectionism	A tendency to worry about small things. A reluctance to 'let go', not very keen on delegating
Team worker	Socially oriented, rather mild, sensitive, perceptive, diplomatic	An ability to respond to people and to situations and to promote team spirit	Indecisiveness at moments of crisis
Shaper	Highly strung, outgoing, dynamic	Drive and a readiness to challenge inertia, ineffectiveness, complacency or self-deception	Prone to provocation, irritation and impatience
Coordinator	Calm, self-confident, controlled	A capacity for treating and welcoming all potential contributors on their merits and without prejudice; a strong sense of objectives	No more than ordinary in terms of intellect or creative ability
Specialist	Studious, dedicated	Expert knowledge, services the team	Not interested in general management, does not think of him-(her)self as part of the team

Developing an approach

Changing circumstances, variable resources and constant compromise are the realities of the workplace. Systems and methods for managing teams or solving problems provide you with a starting point and a framework in which to operate.

But, as a manager, you must never forget that (most of the time) you have to get the job done with the people and resources at your disposal.

The key to any situation is the way you handle your staff. This is difficult because people's behaviour is affected by numerous factors, not only by individual characteristics, ranging from timid introversion to rugged individualism, but also by cultural attributes and social skills.

All these have an important bearing on the complex web of relationships within the team. As the manager of a team you should lead rather than drive and show rather than tell. Your task is to encourage your team to practise reasonable and supportive behaviour so that problems and risks are dealt with in an objective way, and

A systematic approach

To get work done, good managers develop a systematic approach like the following advocated by the Coverdale Organization. The process should be flexible so that the various stages can be interchanged.

1 The assignment
Define the task before briefing your team, creating objectives or assigning responsibilities. In practice, however, it is often difficult to arrive at a conclusive definition. Don't agonize: accept your best attempt but be prepared to modify it if it is necessary.

2 Aims
Clarify aims by asking your team:
● Why is this task necessary and important?
● What is our actual objective?
● What specific criteria should we meet?
● How will we judge that our objective is satisfactorily met?

In most instances, team commitment to the task will be higher if the members are involved in this initial process.

3 Information
When the manager and team are as clear as possible about what they need to achieve, they can then explore ways of achieving it. As this stage it is helpful to:
● Pool ideas
● Draw on previous experience
● Identify particular skills
● Note skills that are wanting
● Check available resources
● Plan to get information
● Explore risks/benefits of options.

This process will vary from a crisp analytical meeting to a messy but creative brainstorming session.

4 What has to be done
When it becomes clear what the preferred option is, the team should list what steps, stages or sub-tasks will be involved to complete the task. This is a useful prelude to detailed planning.

5 Planning
It is your job to ensure that everyone on the team knows exactly what to do. Specify in detail who is doing what, where and by when it will take place.

the team's personal skills are engaged to their full potential. The team will have to deal with:
● The egos and the weaknesses/ strengths of individuals
● The 'expert' syndrome: 'I know because this is my area of special knowledge'
● Relationships/circumstances constantly changing.

To manage teams successfully, you must pull back from the task in hand – however appealing you find it or well qualified you are to deal with it – and

examine the processes that create efficient teamwork.

Find out what it is that makes your team greater than the sum of its parts. You will help the process if you:
● Have a consistent approach to solving problems
● Take into account people's characters as well as their technical skills
● Encourage supportive behaviour in the team
● Create an open, healthy climate
● Make time for the team to appraise its progress.

This is a two-way process, however. Check that people understand their responsibilities as well as their tasks.

6 Action
The team carries out its tasks as separate individuals or as a group. You may feel a need to be involved with certain specific tasks, especially as you may have the best idea of how to perform them.

But you *must* maintain an overview. Monitor what is going on and check progress, spotting snags and adapting the plan to overcome them.

You cannot do this well if you are constantly involved in the action. Your team will need you to maintain a certain distance so that you can guide and direct.

7 Review
As the assignment progresses, allot time to check the quality of the work done.

When completed, carry out a detailed review on what happened, so that future assignments can benefit from past experience. Look at the difficulties and what went well and would be worth repeating in future projects.

Supportive team practices

Listening
● Pay attention; respond positively.
● Don't interrupt; look interested.
● Build on proposals; ask 'clarifying' questions.
● Summarize to check your comprehension.

Cooperating
● Avoid coercion and acrimony.
● Encourage others to give their views; compliment good ideas.
● Give careful consideration to proposals different from yours.
● Offer new ideas openly.

Challenging
● Continually refer back to the problem-solving process and aims.
● Question assumptions in a reasonable manner.
● Review progress of objective, team relationships and time.

Understanding motivation

An understanding of what motivates people is crucial to the creation of productivity and profit. But people's needs and wants are complex and difficult to define. Priorities differ from person to person; individual aims change over time.

Money and status are important motivators but they cannot be relied on exclusively. The theories put forward by behavioural scientists provide a useful way of thinking about people's needs and wants.

In the first quarter of this century, the American F. W. Taylor established his 'scientific management'. This involved breaking down jobs into simple but repetitive tasks, providing a thorough training, isolating individuals from distractions and each other, and paying good wages, with bonuses for productivity over predetermined levels.

In the short term, production gains were significant; in the long run, these gains fell away as people reacted against being treated as machines.

Though the 'scientific' approach has largely been discredited, some managers still give too much attention to basics, such as pay, and not enough to the personal needs of the workers.

In contrast to Taylor, A. H. Maslow concentrated on human needs, which he saw as five-fold:

1 Physiological – food and shelter
2 Safety – security of home and work
3 Social – the need for a supportive environment
4 Esteem – status and having the respect of others
5 Self-fulfilment – the need to realize one's potential.

As each goal is achieved, so the next is sought. Thus, at different stages of your career, you will have differing values, depending upon your progress along the 'hierarchy of needs'.

In a publication of 1959, Frederick Herzberg added to Taylor's and

---

The real motivators

Money obviously plays an important role in motivation. But there are many non-financial motivators that are equally or more important:

● Achievement: most people want the satisfaction of making a meaningful contribution. They are rarely content to plod along mechanically.

Managers who recognize this and provide opportunities for others to attain their individual levels of achievement will frequently be surprised at the results.

● Recognition: it is a natural inclination to want your effort recognized. Praise and feedback stir people to achieve even more.

● Advancement: early theories suggested that people are basically uninterested in work and need a combination of carrot and stick to react. Herzberg's researches showed that this is not generally true. Most people want to move on to more challenging situations and will continue to make increased efforts to cope with them.

● Interest: the chance to practise skill or use intelligence at work motivates most people.

● Responsibility: most intelligent, skilled employees are happy to accept responsibility and authority. They do not need to be forced.

Maslow's work by introducing the important idea of 'hygiene' factors. If these are absent, they can lead to dissatisfaction and so prevent effective motivation. The more obvious hygiene factors involve:
● Organizational policy and rules
● Management style and controls
● Retirement and sickness policies
● Pay and recognition of status.

Herzberg thought that, although 'hygiene' factors were important, they did not have lasting effects on motivation; other positive 'motivating' factors must be present.

The myth of 'Organization Man'

Despite the work of behavioural scientists and a number of studies conducted in the workplace, managers persist in the belief that they are differently motivated and more committed to the organization than their staff. This theory has been effectively debunked by recent findings.

The table (*below*) shows what management, subordinates and their subordinates believe motivates themselves and others. Motivators are numbered from one to six in order of importance. There is considerable uniformity between people's views of their own motivators. The feeling one has accomplished something worthwhile as well as having an interesting and enjoyable job are high motivators for all groups. But fascinating differences emerge in their views of what motivates others, both above and below them. Salary was the top motivator for other people, but was lower down for motivating oneself. It also shows the low priority which employees think those in authority place on the needs of the organization.

People's beliefs in what motivates themselves and others

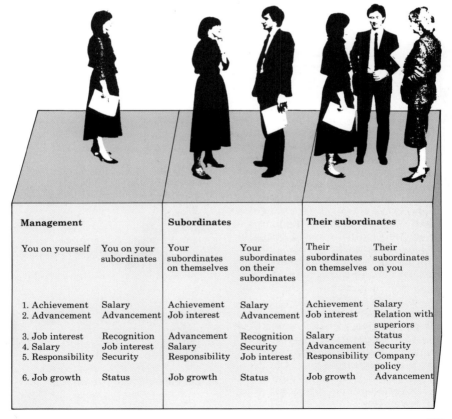

Management		Subordinates		Their subordinates	
You on yourself	You on your subordinates	Your subordinates on themselves	Your subordinates on their subordinates	Their subordinates on themselves	Their subordinates on you
1. Achievement	Salary	Achievement	Salary	Achievement	Salary
2. Advancement	Advancement	Job interest	Advancement	Job interest	Relation with superiors
3. Job interest	Recognition	Advancement	Recognition	Salary	Status
4. Salary	Job interest	Salary	Security	Advancement	Security
5. Responsibility	Security	Responsibility	Job interest	Responsibility	Company policy
6. Job growth	Status	Job growth	Status	Job growth	Advancement

Creating motivation

To motivate a team you need to investigate what motivates you. Understand this and it will help you analyse what motivates others. But remember, people will have different motivators, and these will change over time.

As a manager, it is your responsibility to ensure that your staff are well motivated and content, while making certain that they work hard and effectively and are prepared to put in extra time and effort in an emergency. Check that:

● You are doing all you can to make sure the work is interesting, challenging and demanding

● People know what is expected of them and when they are meeting your high standards

● Rewards are clearly linked to effort and results.

Unless these factors go some way toward fulfilling the organization's needs and the expectations of your staff, no lasting motivation can be achieved, regardless of your best efforts.

If pay and prospects within the organization are bad, you must seek to improve the system. Make sure that your part of the organization recognizes the improved performance, productivity and profit that would result from keeping motivated, effective staff longer.

The very act of interceding on behalf of your staff will help to increase their motivation and strengthen their commitment to you.

To manage staff effectively, you must get to know their circumstances, needs and aspirations, both within and outside work. Show that you can help them achieve their personal aims.

If you can coordinate your staff's aims with corporate objectives, by reconciling their personal aspirations with the organization's need to operate profitably, you will be running a successful team and enhancing your own reputation.

How to motivate your staff

● Get to know your staff individually. Keep up to date on what is happening to them.

● Understand what interests and motivates them in and out of work. These factors will probably change, so check on how they develop.

● Provide them with increasingly more challenging opportunities, but watch for signs that they may have reached the limit of their abilities.

● Analyse their strengths and weaknesses. Ensure that they have opportunities to use their strengths and that their weaknesses are covered.

● Coach and guide them in areas in which they are weak or are making mistakes. Ensure that they have the chance to learn from colleagues or superiors who have the strengths they lack. If appropriate, encourage them to seek formal training or qualifications.

● Give immediate recognition for good job performance as well as at a formal or annual assessment.

● Tell your colleagues, superiors,

The BPX Change Process

BP Exploration is responsible for BP's interests in oil and gas exploration, field development and production (the 'upstream' activities) as well as the processing and marketing of natural gas and the management of oil and gas pipelines. Its operations span the globe, wherever the natural resource is found.

BP Exploration has recognized that it works in a complex world and that to meet the challenges of the coming years, the entire workforce must be more dedicated and committed to success on a global scale. An ambitious strategy of frontier exploration and efficient oil field development demanded the best from a highly trained technical staff.

staff in other departments how well your team has done or is doing.

● Ensure team members get the rewards they deserve (salary, bonus, promotion, company perks etc). Risk giving a little too much, or a little too early, rather than too little, too late.

● Delegate more of your own work, especially those parts which are interesting or exciting. This will give your staff the incentive to do something new or more challenging. It will also give you more time to manage people and not the job. It is usually worth taking the risk of delegating a lot early, but be alert for signs that the person is not coping.

● Involve your staff in as many decisions as you can (don't overestimate how much secrecy you are keeping from them anyway). Seek their views; consult them on the advisability/practicality of any potential change. They will usually reward you with greater commitment and endeavour.

● Encourage them to bring up ideas on how the job can be done better. They are closer to the action than you and will usually have better knowledge of the problems and difficulties. If they wish to change their way of working, give it serious consideration. After all, it is *their* job you are dealing with.

● Share information. They will probably hear it soon on the grapevine, so it is better if they get it directly from you.

● Get them involved in your budget setting and control. Without their understanding and agreement, it will be much harder to achieve their commitment and thus any targets.

● Help them resolve their problems with other parts of the organization if their case merits it. At some point, you will want them to make sacrifices for you, so be prepared to give help when they need it.

● You can do a lot to provide the right conditions for them to work effectively and happily. However, they also have a responsibility to approach their work with a positive attitude. Make sure that they understand this.

The company realized that such commitment could not be demanded, but had to be earned through an environment of participation which both emphasizes and rewards individual effort, and values teamwork. Climate surveys sent to employees in 1989 showed a complete overhaul of the company infrastructure was needed. It was too autocratic, decisions were passed upwards, and morale and motivation were low.

A long-term programme to facilitate the move towards a new culture for the group was set up. Employee representatives were asked to comment on the organization's effectiveness. Their conclusions were presented early in 1990 at a meeting in Phoenix, Arizona. These included changes to organizational structure and management processes, ways of working and the way people related to each other.

A series of 'fitness' workshops were set up, and were attended by a cross-section of 30 to 70 people. Over two days, staff identified ways to eliminate unnecessary bureaucracy. Roles and accountabilities have now been more clearly defined and the number of committees drastically reduced. These simplified management processes encouraged a new approach based on trust and co-operation. The climate has already changed, giving power to the people closest to the job.

Preparing to delegate

Delegating responsibilities to others increases your available time to carry out important work. Delegation also develops your team which, in turn, increases the effectiveness of your operation and improves your chances of achieving departmental goals.

Willingness to delegate is one of the marks of leadership, but delegation is difficult to excercise effectively. This is chiefly because it entails getting work done in a way that appropriately balances the quality of the solution with the needs of individuals.

To delegate successfully, you need to know exactly what task has to be done and what motivates and satisfies your individual members of staff. Effective delegation involves a continued and growing relationship between you, the manager, and those to whom you assign tasks.

As a manager, you should delegate authority but not responsibility. This means that you must be prepared to accept responsibility for the action of your staff. That will sometimes be tough. You should also be prepared to let them have the glory when their actions are successful – that may be even tougher.

Effective delegation is essential for the growth and development of each member of your staff. And they must know what results are expected of them and to what extent they are accountable.

Staff need the authority and freedom to get on with the tasks in hand, knowing they have your confidence and can come to you for help.

Delegation is not:
● Dishing out parcels of work in an indiscriminate fashion
● Offloading tasks which you either do not have time for or do not want to do yourself
● Merely a question of balancing the workload between individual members of staff.

Delegation inevitably involves an element of risk. A task may not be performed as well, as cheaply or as quickly as you could do it. But once your staff get the hang of it, they will eventually end up matching your own level of expertise.

Younger managers tend to hang on to too much, especially the more exciting and responsible aspects of work. So ask yourself: 'What parts of my job can I *not* delegate?' Draw up a list, review it and then cut it down.

Now ask yourself: 'If I were ill for a month, which tasks could not be done?' If you are honest, there should be almost nothing. But if you are still left with plenty, then you are probably not delegating enough.

Do not overestimate your abilities or underestimate your team's potential. Delegating may well create new or better ideas about how solutions can be achieved. Good managers delegate a great deal, creating a team which is constantly drawn up to the next challenge. A broad base of skill and experience is thus firmly established.

You should delegate everything you need not do personally, especially tasks which you are good at yourself and are used to doing.

You will be particularly good at training your staff to perform and take responsibility for tasks with which you are familiar. Make sure you delegate some aspects of the job which stretch your staff's ability and provide challenges. Obviously, you should delegate to staff members who have better knowledge or more up-to-date information than you.

Managers are often overworked, and effective delegation frees them for work on larger, broader projects. And when tasks are delegated to you by your boss, do not assume you are the right or only person to do them. Your desire to impress must be tempered by the need to have the work performed by the most appropriate person.

Barriers to successful delegation

You may be reluctant to delegate a task for a number of reasons; the following are some of the more common ones:
● Delegated work will be done badly and you will be blamed.
● Time will be lost when you could do it quicker yourself.
● Since you have little idea how the task can be done you had better do it yourself.
● Your employees will do, and be seen doing, your job. As a result others believe your subordinates are capable of taking over from you.
● Spending time explaining to someone else how to perform a task uses up valuable time.
● Nobody else can do it as well as you can.
● There is literally nobody to delegate to. If so, who and how are you managing?
● You feel you need to be involved so as to be close to what is happening in your team.

Steps to effective delegation

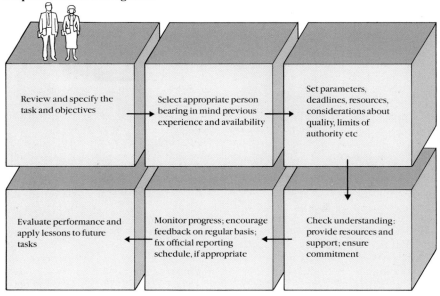

Review and specify the task and objectives

Select appropriate person bearing in mind previous experience and availability

Set parameters, deadlines, resources, considerations about quality, limits of authority etc

Evaluate performance and apply lessons to future tasks

Monitor progress; encourage feedback on regular basis; fix official reporting schedule, if appropriate

Check understanding: provide resources and support; ensure commitment

Selecting delegates

Before selecting delegates, ask yourself:
● Who would be challenged? Who would learn most? Who should not do it?
● Who has the necessary skill?
● Does the task need previous experience? Would it be useful to have someone acquire this experience to give the team greater strength in depth?
● If time/quality allows, could the task be a training exercise for a team member?
● What particular personal qualities are needed? Who has them?
● Is more than one person needed? If so, how will they work together?
● Is it a task to be delegated upward?
● What other work-loads/priorities does your delegate have? Will you need to help re-sort/change these?
● How will you monitor progress and evaluate results?

Making delegation work

Effective management relies on proper delegation. It is wrong to say to your subordinate, 'Here is the task, now get on with it', while you sit back and wait for results. Remember the slogan: delegate, don't abdicate.

Having decided exactly what the task is and having selected staff to carry it out, there are three broad stages of delegation: briefing the delegates, monitoring progress and evaluating results.

Briefing the delegates

● Specify the essential parameters: details of task, deadlines, resources.
● Explain the desired outcome.
● Allow them freedom to decide how to perform the task – but get them to explain their plan.

● Check they understand what is required – encourage discussion, suggest possible approaches.
● Sell, but do not oversell, your own approach. Be enthusiastic. If you get commitment and agreement, you all have a better chance of success.
● Be realistic about your expectations; do not underestimate the difficulties but set challenging targets.
● Indicate the need for progress reports, intermediate deadlines, and that the needs of all are served if you are kept closely informed.
● Discuss which areas of the task are sensitive to error or risk.

Monitoring progress

● Allow the delegates to proceed with the task without interference.

Briefing
Equipped with details of the assignment and tasks to be achieved, the manager delegates the role of task leader (*above*). Because it is a high-risk assignment, requiring strong commitment, she has decided to stay close throughout the process. She briefs the task leader about the aims and parameters of the assignment, and he puts forward his ideas about how he would approach and achieve it.

Planning
The task leader had decided to use a member of the team whose prior knowledge and experience would prove invaluable to this assignment. Called to a meeting with the manager and task leader (*above*), she is briefed about the task and offers her ideas in return. Delegated the specific role of 'researcher', she will liaise with the task leader and, with him, organize the means and timing of the accomplishment of the task.

● Encourage delegates to follow their own way of working if you are sure you are agreed on the desired result.
● Be alert for signs that things are going wrong, but be prepared to allow trivial mistakes to be made.
● Intervene only if delegates do not spot their errors or where sensitive areas are threatened.
● Be ready with help, advice and encouragement, but avoid doing the task yourself. Transfer the delegation only in extreme circumstances.
● Encourage frequent informal discussion rather than formal feedback.
● Stand back from the process and retain a view of the bigger picture.

Evaluation and feedback

Did the task produce the results you expected? If it was successful, say so. Give praise, recognition and credit to the people involved.

If the result was unexpected, ask:
● Was it due to a misunderstanding between you and your delegates?
● Was a delegate's performance not up to standard?
● Was a wrong delegate selected?
● Were there unforeseen problems?
● Were the mistakes preventable?

Make sure everyone concerned learns from the experience. Finally, do not blame your delegates in public, to your boss or colleagues, but accept the responsibility yourself.

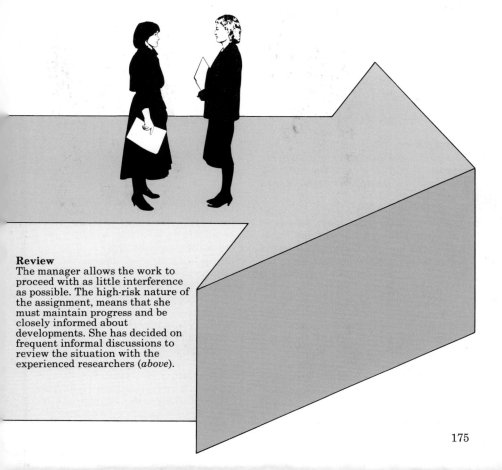

Review
The manager allows the work to proceed with as little interference as possible. The high-risk nature of the assignment, means that she must maintain progress and be closely informed about developments. She has decided on frequent informal discussions to review the situation with the experienced researchers (*above*).

Appraisal, counselling and promotion

One of the hardest managerial tasks is to appraise staff or give performance reviews.

Reasons for assessing and appraising staff include the need to: maximize performance, identify training needs, provide data for salary and promotion reviews and set targets for the future. You will also improve understanding between you and your staff.

Employees are naturally sensitive about any official process of scrutiny because they feel their integrity or responsibility is being questioned. But they need to have some idea of how effective they have been and whether more or different demands will be made of them.

An informal process of continuous review should be used to give your staff feedback on their performance and prospects: at the same time this encourages them to practise self-appraisal.

This approach will help you to judge your staff impartially without damaging team relationships. It will also simplify the task of meeting the formal requirements of the organization.

The added advantage of the on-going self-appraisal system is that, by instilling trust in your team, you will get comment on *your* behaviour and approach.

Counselling staff

As a manager, there are occasions when you need to discuss subordinates' problems. You may be required to give advice on how they can improve on personal efficiency or cope with a stressful situation.

Good counselling is an exercise in good communication on a one-to-one level. Attentive listening is important, as is the ability to talk frankly and get to the nub of the matter.

Be positive: if subordinates have come to you with problems, they will not want to go away feeling they have wasted their time and yours. Even if you cannot solve their problems, tact

---

Promoting staff

You are promoting employees for the right reasons if:
● They can accept more responsibility, allowing their superiors to concentrate on other tasks.
● Their particular skills can be developed to create greater productivity for the company.
● They have distinguished themselves in a series of well-managed tasks and projects; their talents should now be more widespread.
● A department has assumed greater responsibility and work, so new employees need experienced supervision.

You are promoting employees for the wrong reasons if you argue:
● 'She'll leave if we don't promote her.'
● 'Department X has three section managers so why shouldn't we?'
● 'He's been around a long time.'
● 'If she's pushed upstairs she won't try to change anything.'
● 'He won't make any decisions without telling us first.'
● 'Make him management, that will curb his union activities.'
● 'She'll make a good manager – she never argues.'

---

and sensitivity create trust and strengthen their loyalty to you.

Promotion and reward

If you say to your staff, 'I think you are doing a great job and if it were up to me I'd give you all a 15 per cent pay rise, but company policy does not ...' you are passing the buck.

While you should naturally praise and encourage your staff, they will become demoralized if they see that your words are not backed up with positive results. You must devote, and be seen to be devoting, sufficient time and effort to securing appropriate rewards for your team's achievements.

The appraisal

Do...

● Develop clear objectives, set goals and agree action plan.

● Prepare well beforehand. Allow sufficient time for the meeting itself.

● Appraise continuously and in a relaxed way; you will then avoid the resentment that is felt for the formal annual review.

● Talk about strengths and weaknesses objectively; beware of over-reacting to good or bad points. Feedback should be balanced. It is easy, but not smart, to run out of superlatives.

● Avoid saving up praise or criticism for the next appraisal. Try to deal with issues as they arise.

● Make criticism specific and illustrate the points you are trying to make. Where possible, indicate what should have been done.

● Complete the personnel department's appraisal forms carefully, and then discuss them with the reviewing manager to give a rounder picture.

● Be open to changes in job description: they might lead to better job performance.

● Remember that the purpose of appraisal is to motivate the appraised and send signals to those who decide on pay and promotion.

Don't...

● Approach potentially difficult appraisals as if the employee were overpaid, underworked and unreasonable.

● Believe that your assessment of a bad performance will necessarily ensure that an employee improves.

● Fail to appreciate that individual team performances are interdependent and complex; a bad or good performance may not lie entirely within the control of any single team member.

● Dictate what the employee must or must not do. You can outline the approach most likely to be effective; if the individual does not choose to adopt it, then don't press your point.

● Obscure criticism by talking around it. Get to the point, otherwise you may fail to get your message across.

● React defensively to complaints about your management style. Rather, listen to what may be valuable feedback.

● Adopt standards of appraisal different to those used in everyday life.

● Become involved in recommending solutions to private or emotional problems – specialized counselling may be needed.

● Make unrealistic promises.

Handling trouble

Teams always encounter problems. As individuals change – by, say, becoming more experienced and being promoted – so their aims and behaviour alter. This may work in the team's favour; sometimes it alters the equilibrium and reduces effectiveness.

Your team's health is your responsibility; it is your task to observe, diagnose and treat disaffection, disunity or demotivation.

Be on the alert for signs of trouble; in general, when your team cannot heal its own problems, you can be sure something is wrong.

If a person's bad behaviour or performance threatens morale, act quickly to keep your team's respect and confidence. Look for causes, enlisting help from other team members. Then talk to the dissident in private. After all, if you have been working happily together for some time you will probably want to help.

Be direct about what impact the employee's attitude is having on the rest of the team. Try to identify the problem, which may be due to:
● Personal problems or illness
● Insecurity about new structures or technology
● Disappointment at not receiving recognition/reward
● Significant disagreement with you or another team member
● Failure to relate to a new team-member
● Staleness due to, say, repetitive work
● Apparent loss of status.

Do not let the individual indulge in self-pity. Giving your full support to a rational solution to the problem is often enough to reconcile the person to the team.

Team health is best maintained by giving individuals a variety of tasks and projects. If staleness is the problem, a change of job within the team or a move to another team may help.

Differences which alienate one team member from the others call for more serious measures. First, consider whether another member of the team can help.

If the lack of commitment or the bad performance continues, confront the person again.

Give the employee every chance to explain his/her actions; discuss ways of solving the problem. Reprimands and confrontations are a test of your fairness, objectivity and strength. You may have to broach the idea of dismissal if no alternative is available.

Once the future of the individual has been settled, communicate your decision to the rest of the team. Try to be positive. It is important for the team's recovery that the problem is not seen as a team failure.

Dismissal

Going . . .
Your team is a self-protecting organism. Its first instinct will be to solve difficulties without you.

If you are aware of the problem, either because the offender is noticeable or factions have formed, show your concern.

If counselling proves ineffective, tell the individual what is expected.

Danger signs

Something is wrong in a team if individuals who have been supportive and reasonable:
● Begin to perform poorly – miss deadlines, produce substandard work.
● Expect others to solve their problems.
● Do not take responsibility for their actions.
● Break up into subgroups instead of sharing work.
● Show destructive criticism or dismissive behaviour toward others.
● Get involved in serious and unresolved conflicts.
● Show no interest in team activity.

Positive alternatives

'Obstinacity' is a word used by the Coverdale training organization to show that an employee's qualities detrimental to one environment may be helpful to another.

A quality control supervisor was taken to task for his autocratic and 'nit-picking' attitude. Team spirit deteriorated so much that it was decided he had to go.

The manager prepared a balance sheet of the supervisor's good/bad points and realized that he was also accurate and painstaking. So he was transferred to a job which meant reading complex instruments. The man's lack of human skills did not affect the instruments.

Going . . .
A formal warning is the next step. Consult Personnel and follow the company's disciplinary procedure. Give the subject a time limit in which to improve. Be reasonable; rehabilitation is your aim.

If the subject fails to improve, proceed with the next warning stage. Once all the stages have been exhausted, dismissal is the right course.

Gone
Try to find a way of allowing the person to leave with dignity. Invite the employee to resign but be prepared to fire. Be supportive.

Consult Personnel to make sure of compliance with notice periods, legal and trade union requirements, and to avoid subsequent litigation for unfair dismissal.

Exploiting opportunities

The business world is evolving so rapidly that the watchword for the modern world is change. What once took many years to manifest itself and become part of the social fabric can now happen almost overnight. Progress in technology, communications and competition has seen to that.

Political developments such as the opening up of the eastern European markets or the dismantling of apartheid in South Africa also provide new opportunities and challenges for business. Other key business trends are the moves towards globalization and privatization.

Changes have happened so fast that the present has hardly begun before the future is already upon us. And the indications are that the rate of change is accelerating.

This presents the manager with a demanding, but not insuperable, problem. Change must be welcomed, embraced and turned to good effect, even though it may be threatening. Innovation and adaptability must become part of the everyday habit of managers. They must find more efficient ways of doing things, accept new developments in their industry and seek new opportunities for generating business. If they do not, competitors almost certainly will.

As a manager, you must view change and innovation as opportunities to seize rather than as threats to fear. You will only learn to master change when you encourage, welcome and incorporate it into your professional and personal lifestyle.

There are two types of change: change you can't control but need to react to, eg the situation in eastern Europe (reactive change), and change that you can control, such as reorganizing internal processes to help you compete in a changing environment (proactive).

Fluctuations in international interest rates, changes in foreign exchange rates and technological innovations are just some of the external forces that daily shape the fate of many businesses.

As a manager you must play an important role in dealing with change. You have to:
● Interpret change, both outside and inside your organization, and create certainty and stability for your staff
● Instigate and implement changes you consider essential for your part of the organization
● Encourage flexibility and a positive outlook among your staff.
● Contribute to the discussions and decisions concerning the future of the organization.

Fixed ideas bring suffering not prosperity, whereas flexibility of outlook and purpose helps you to understand and adapt to changing environments.

Innovation and change are a way of life for some businesses, such as those in the high-tech arena. But others, often the more traditional ones, have a history of stability and may be resistant to change.

While doing what you have always done may be wise in an unchanging world, learning to be accomplished in a variety of ways is advisable in a world of accelerating change.

What you need is a personal strategy for managing change which:
● Enables you to assess potential change in the light of long-term improvement for the company
● Gives you advance feedback of likely reaction to change, particularly the possibility of resistance.
● Helps you harness the energy of those who support change and win over, or deal with, resistors to change.

If you learn to deal with change, the benefits are positive – greater creativity, better performance, increased achievement. Even if you make mistakes, they will be instructive. Change also creates situations where your talents can shine and be rewarded.

Managing change successfully

Reacting quickly to change is a key factor in the success of any business. Management at all levels needs to think in a creative and innovative way.

To help yourself and your staff to embrace change and make it work:
● Accept that dealing with continually changing situations is a normal part of your job. Don't bury your head in the sand when new or different problems arrive.
● Ensure that you plan time for the innovative aspects of your job.
● Maintain a well-informed knowledge of developments in your industry or profession. Read the part of the press relevant to you.
● Monitor the environment for signals, trends and developments in the attitudes and behaviour of competitors, customers and the market.
● Stimulate a positive attitude to change by regularly discussing new ideas and issues with colleagues.
● Encourage your staff to raise issues affecting their work. Watch for signs that accepted practice is inappropriate.
● Discuss future plans and issues with your staff, both individually and as a group, on a regular basis. Once every six months may be enough, but ensure it happens.
● Communicate internal changes to your staff unless there is a good reason not to do so in the short term.
● Be experimental and flexible in your approach to people's ideas.
● Try out new techniques and ideas whenever appropriate.
● Mobilize your staff quickly and boldly, but in a coordinated fashion.
● Create a working atmosphere in which ideas and issues do not fall between bureaucratic cracks.

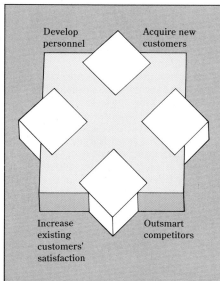

Develop personnel

Acquire new customers

Increase existing customers' satisfaction

Outsmart competitors

Customer service

Increasingly, companies need to be customer-driven. A clear customer focus will:
● Produce action on new fronts and so encourage versatility, learning and development.
● Help prioritize the key business processes.
● Help companies adapt to changing markets and fluctuating customer requirements.
● Lead to greater understanding of weaknesses, strengths, resources, and new business potential.
● Enable companies to seize more opportunities and outsmart their competitors.

Coping with major changes

Managing to encourage innovation and change is quite different from managing the consequences of unexpected and dramatic change.

In the first instance, you operate in a stable environment with a relatively secure staff; you have some notion of where your organization is heading, and you control the timing of events affecting your team.

But sudden dramatic change threatens everyone in the organization and could force you to operate without direction or a controllable timescale. You may also have to take responsibility for people whose behaviour and effectiveness are impaired by stress: they will need you to create certainty at a time when little is certain.

Events leading to sudden crises may not, in themselves, be dramatic. However, the consequences of the events may often be both unexpected and far reaching. Companies can pass into crisis because habitual bad management has led to financial distress, and banks demand reductions in borrowings. Markets may change, and lack of foresight may leave the company unprepared and exposed. Mergers or take-overs can remove security, creating uncertainty and anxiety.

Common to all these situations is an apparent lack of policy or authority. The rules have not just changed, they have disappeared; and a new set needs to be imposed.

In a crisis, you may suddenly find yourself reporting to a new boss, someone brought in by the board or by the new owners of the company. In an extreme case, this person may be a receiver, appointed by the bank to return the company to profitability or to sell it as a going concern.

This new person may be sure about what has to be done and how it will be achieved. However, he/she may need time fully to understand and deal with the problem.

Your first priority should be to determine where you and your team stand. You may be asked to supply information about your activities, your potential, and the extent to which performance has been affected by the crisis. This is particularly important if you are in a revenue-earning position, such as sales or customer service.

Try to understand what plans there are for your organization. Ask about them, and if no answers are forthcoming, watch for signs. Action should indicate the direction in which things are moving.

Encourage your team to cooperate in the formulation of plans and new direction. Avoid adding to rumour and speculation.

The new boss may want to create a new management team, and will want to act quickly; but if the crisis is financial, there will probably be a lack of funds to recruit externally. Your performance throughout this period may determine whether you have a continuing management role or not. The period of uncertainty may be an opportunity for you to demonstrate your talent.

Be alert and cautious until the operation has returned to profitability and stability. Your part of the business may recover well, only to be undermined by continuing losses elsewhere. Crises often take longer to resolve than they do to occur.

In the end, the most sensible approach to adopt is one of project management: breaking down tasks into short-term assignments that can be managed single-mindedly.

This gives your team something specific to do and, as the list of successfully completed tasks grows, it helps to rebuild confidence.

Recognize that your team members feel threatened in a crisis. They will need reassurance throughout. Make sure they are involved and consulted.

Managing crises

The formulation of a plan, the acquisition of resources to carry it out, and the building of a new team, is the object of crisis management.

To be a part of the team that comes together in crisis, and turns round an operation, can be a rewarding experience. It will test your management ability and skill – maybe even your nerve.

You should take stock of your chances of success. If you feel that your career may be endangered, it may be wise to look for another job. In a severe crisis, you must protect yourself. Be realistic, maybe even over-cautious – if in doubt, don't wait for others to make your decisions for you.

The two key areas in any crisis are, first, you and your colleagues affected by the crisis; and second, the central problem which precipitated the situation.

Regrouping
Involve key staff and resources in the construction of plans for the future. Take this outside the boundaries of your immediate operation and present your scheme to senior management.

You must ensure that you have authority in your part of the operation if you are to get the internal support essential to your team's success.

Avoid extreme reactions. Do not be rushed into hasty judgements and, above all, *look* as though you are coping.

Tending the wounded
The tasks confronting you may be daunting. People may have to change or lose their jobs.

They will need help to change or move. Act quickly and positively, if possible. The uncertainty caused by inaction can often be more painful than the eventual decision, however severe it is. Do not try to soften the blow by long explanations. Give people options and time to consider them. Then move on to the practical means of lessening the impact on the department as a whole.

The real test of a good manager is the quality of the remedies applied in a crisis. Help those who are the casualties, stay closely involved, but ensure above all that your own and their futures receive your greatest attention.

Dealing with stress

Managers are responsible for taking decisions that can make or break the organization. They contribute to the creation of the wealth on which the survival of a community may depend. They also significantly affect the environment in which the rest of the staff work. Those who have achieved the skills needed to manage must recognize the potential stress that goes with a challenging job. They must learn to cope with their own and others' stress in order to remain effective.

Managers need challenge to stimulate them and add zest to their lives. Challenge successfully dealt with is satisfying. Only when it cannot be met, when pressures become too great, does it become stressful. Stress reflects a failure to cope with certain situations. Reactions to stress are either predominantly related to mood and behaviour or they can manifest themselves in physical symptoms such as dyspepsia, skin eruptions, headaches and so on. But, because reaction occurs at a subconscious level, the symptoms are seldom seen as directly related to the cause.

Stress is 'dis-ease', involving the whole personality. Coping with it depends on a holistic approach to health. The way in which you contend with your own stress threshold depends on your basic personality, acquired skills and past experience. Thus, anxious introverts are likely to be more vulnerable to it than brash extroverts. Individual strengths and weaknesses cause different areas of vulnerability. Skilful managers thus play on their strengths and cover their weaknesses.

Coping with stress

● Know yourself: list your strengths and weaknesses; consider what you are like to work for or be married to.
● Make sure your job allows you to concentrate on your talents.
● Know what you are meant to be doing, where you are going, how you fit into the organization and what the future might hold.
● Discuss your grievances and difficulties with a sympathetic colleague or friend, or your partner. Encourage your colleagues and subordinates to do the same.
● Review your priorities regularly, change them and delegate wherever possible. Learn to say 'no'.
● If you are not succeeding with one approach, don't try harder. Think of a better way.
● Accept that you cannot do everything. Apply principles of time management.
● Plan holidays and days off in advance; protect this time and relinquish it only after all other possibilities have been considered. If you have to let it go, reschedule it immediately.
● List your outside activities and interests and plan them into your diary.
● Set predetermined eating and drinking 'rules' for yourself. Determine your optimum weight. Take action when you stray from what you know is good for you.
● Decide your minimum sleep requirement and ensure you get it.
● Ask yourself whether you are having fun. If the answer over a long period is 'no', try to work out why.
● Try to identify what is causing you to feel stressed.
● If work is a prime cause of stress, be prepared to change your job. But consult those whose opinion you respect (or who may have had the same problem) first.
● At home, stress arises from the conflict of unsolved problems. Discuss them openly with your partner and work out solutions together.

Like everyone else, managers function as whole beings and not, as they may like to think, as separate 'selves' at work and at home. In practice, good relationships are the key to minimizing stress. Conflict and frustration can be work- or home-based and each affects the other. It is thus essential that your job is structured to provide defined and achievable targets. You must be willing to discuss difficulties before they become problems.

At home, as at work, understanding each other and the way people interact is the key to minimizing stress. Relaxational activities raise stress thresholds. Ask yourself what you are like as a marriage partner and act to improve things.

A reasonable degree of physical fitness helps to keep work and home in balance, and the time needed to get fit ensures that you take time out from work. Well-balanced managers are likely to be more successful at work, happier at home and, therefore, less vulnerable to stress than narrow-minded workaholics who neglect relationships.

Equally, managers should ensure that their part of the organization provides an environment in which individuals can flourish to the benefit of the enterprise and the individuals involved. Ask yourself what you are like to work for – you should not be a cause of unnecessary stress in your subordinates. Be aware of symptoms that could be stress related. Encourage staff to achieve a balance between home and work so that they are better equipped to deal with challenge.

Stress-related symptoms

If you recognize a number of mental and physical symptoms in yourself, a member of your team, or your partner, that could be related to stress, you should tackle the problem immediately.

Danger signals at work

● Frustration over failure to get results
● Complaints about the quality of your team's work
● Inability to determine priorities
● Diary constantly full of meetings and appointments for which you are ill prepared
● Full in-tray, inability to decide what to tackle first
● Personality clashes with superiors or subordinates
● Too busy to take holidays or even a day off
● Taking work home at night and at weekends
● Unwillingness to discuss problems and prospects
● Lack of concentration and/or memory

Danger signals at home

● Not contributing to important domestic decisions
● Feeling that life is no fun
● Regularly coming home late
● Spending too little time with the family
● Reluctance to discuss problems
● Being too busy, or not inclined, to take exercise

Planning time

The manager has four major resources – people, equipment, money and time. Time is irreplaceable. One of your most challenging tasks is to discipline your own use of time and that of your colleagues and bosses.

Your purpose is not just to increase the number and quality of tasks performed, it is also to ensure that you are making the most of your career, which is, after all, a span of time devoted to the achievement of personal, financial and organizational objectives. Indeed, the most successful people often squeeze two or three different careers into one working lifetime.

Managers with domestic responsibilities need to use and respect time judiciously; career planning becomes more crucial since they may have to manage two jobs simultaneously.

Time planning depends on a methodical and disciplined approach: try breaking up your day into short segments – half-hour periods – and analysing the main uses of time. Compare this 'expenditure' with your personal and departmental objectives. If they don't match up – if you are spending time on irrelevant details – then you must switch priorities.

Be ruthless with yourself and others. If you are spending time on unnecessary tasks, you are either badly organized or somebody is 'dumping' on you. Hand work back, delegate it, or question its purpose. Most time and resource waste is a result of purposeless, unquestioned activity.

First, ensure your own department is operating at maximum efficiency:
● Create stretching but realistic deadlines for tasks; otherwise work tends to expand to fill the time available.
● Never do work yourself that can be safely delegated; subordinates may not perform a task quite as well as you, but without experience, they never will.
● Try to arrange your commitments in such a way that you have large blocks for difficult tasks such as forward-planning, report writing, problem analysis or deciding on strategic direction.
● Discover your own and others' prime time and assign the most exacting tasks to it.
● Remember the right amount of pressure brings speed and high performance; too much, and things go wrong.
● Get others – secretaries, subordinates – to protect your time. If you operate an open-door policy, consider an appointments system for non-urgent staff problems.
● Make a habit of asking 'How much time will we need?'
● Allow time between meetings to implement the solutions and plans they have produced.

Don't assume that you can only manage your own time and that of people working for you. The greatest potential timewaste can result from being badly managed yourself.

Once your department is running like a well-oiled machine, you are ready to improve the performance of your superiors:
● List the points you want to cover in meetings with the boss.
● If possible, arrange your meeting so that there is just enough time to cover the agenda, before you, or the boss, have to attend another important meeting.
● Don't try to cover too many subjects in one meeting: have short meetings more frequently.
● Always do *brief* follow-up memos; 'We agreed the following . . .' The boss will soon get the picture if long meetings produce short action lists.
● If your boss is keen to chat, or you are collared by the office bore, you should break in at the first possible pause. Politely, but firmly, indicate that you have a mountain of work to shift and must get back to your desk.

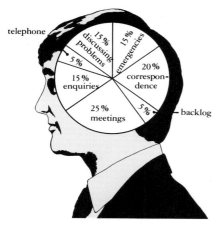

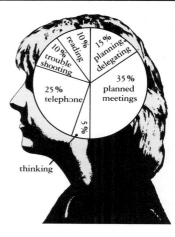

This busy manager's life is not planned. Perhaps that is why he *is* busy. His use of time indicates an entirely responsive approach to his job, with more time devoted to administration than customer service. The high level of emergency is indicative of serious problems. (Peter Drucker states in *The Effective Executive* that well-run organizations do not have crises.) This manager should ask: 'What am I here to do?' 'Do I delegate enough?' 'Had I more time to plan, would those emergencies go away?'

This effective manager delegates correspondence to subordinates and deals with major issues in person or by telephone. Her meetings are well planned: she attends only the key parts, leaving the rest to staff, and can often fit in two meetings where a busy colleague has not completed one. She is popular with customers and suppliers because she spends time getting to know them, and her reading makes her knowledgeable about the industry. She does not merely discuss problems; she solves them. She always seems to have time...

Using time

Managing time is not just about enabling your team to handle increasing amounts of work. It should also ensure that events, projects, proposals and developments are timed correctly. For example, a new investment project, introduced when a similar project is late and over budget, is unlikely to be judged favourably. You need to know what is going on in the organization before making proposals that have an impact beyond your own department.

If you can manage your own time properly, then you will, by example, inspire confidence in your staff. Search for the most *relevant* and *powerful* ways of employing time, for your department and for the company.

People respond far better to well-planned surges of activity than they do to crises or to unremitting routine. Try to survey staff needs and anticipate demand to have enough time to cope with the unexpected. Vary the pace at which you and your staff work. Remember, people need recreation for their mental and physical well-being; but try to ensure that holidays do not coincide with a surge of work.

If a member of your staff is a poor time-keeper – regularly late for work or going home early – find out why. Perhaps the job is boring or personal problems need to be discussed.

If your staff are habitually working long hours, check they are doing so for the right reasons. As long as it does not disrupt the team, it does not matter if the best creative work is done very early or very late in the day. Allow time for people to recuperate.

Committed people may work late to compare notes with colleagues or simply to enjoy being a team. But someone who works late because they don't want to go home could be heading for a personal crisis which then could affect the whole team. And teams who stay late because their work forces them to will soon lose their loyalty to you.

Larks and owls

Managers who ignore the body's natural clock may do so at their peril. Personal rhythms of wakefulness and rest differ from person to person and affect the timing of all mental and physical activity.

All teams consist of people who are larks (do their best work in the early morning) and owls (who peak at night). You should be aware of your own body rhythms and get to know those of your staff, colleagues and boss.

Avoid difficult meetings first thing in the morning if you are an owl. Don't waste valuable prime time doing routine tasks when you arrive at work if you are a lark. Leave them to the end of the day.

Take account of the effect of the time of day on others – you may or may not want them at their best.

Time-related problems can be solved by a methodical approach. Analysis can lead to more than one solution.

When choosing a course of action, remember that your own style of management may be at fault.

Problem
Routine review shows employee with possible time fault; this person works late, takes work home.

Action
Discuss with person.

Tips for good time management

Does time plus money plus skill equal achieved objectives? If not:
- Define the essentials of your job. Ensure that most of your time is spent on them.
- Analyse the use of your time frequently.
- Ration your time and that of your staff.
- Plan your time so that you deal with top priority items when you are at your best.
- Gradually allow less time for tasks as experience increases, until optimum performance is reached.
- Show that you disapprove of time-wasting.
- Always question tasks – they may be irrelevant or capable of postponement.
- Before committing yourself to a task, check to see whether you can delegate it.
- Conduct *brief* meetings; set a time limit for objectives.
- Try to protect your time from intrusions.
- Make it known that your time is precious so that others compete and negotiate for it.
- Always thank those who are brief but to the point.
- Spend time understanding the organization.
- Spend time understanding your market/industry/profession.
- Minimize the time your staff spend on unpopular tasks.
- Encourage enthusiasm – it makes people work faster.
- Create surges of activity toward goals.
- Set deadlines for yourself and others, but remember that speed is not the only consideration, particularly if quality suffers.
- Constantly question whether your present activity is the best use of your time.

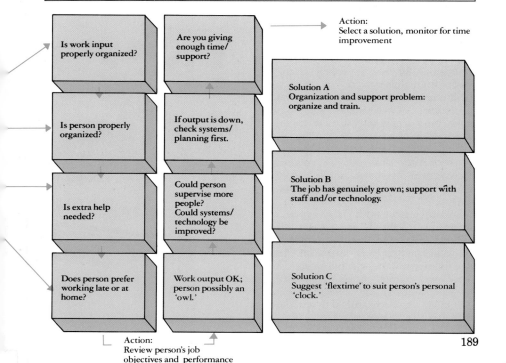

Is work input properly organized?

Are you giving enough time/support?

Action:
Select a solution, monitor for time improvement

Solution A
Organization and support problem: organize and train.

Is person properly organized?

If output is down, check systems/planning first.

Solution B
The job has genuinely grown; support with staff and/or technology.

Is extra help needed?

Could person supervise more people?
Could systems/technology be improved?

Solution C
Suggest 'flextime' to suit person's personal 'clock.'

Does person prefer working late or at home?

Work output OK; person possibly an 'owl.'

Action:
Review person's job objectives and performance

189

Managing tough situations

In theory, successful managers decide objectives, identify problems, allocate resources to solve them, organize implementation and measure results. The reality is that objectives change, problems grow, resources are not always available and solutions do not necessarily work out. And, perhaps most trying of all, there is rarely enough time to accomplish everything you would like.

Furthermore, as you gain seniority, the range of subjects about which you need to have detailed knowledge rises dramatically.

The principles of good management – proven methods of doing things – are worth knowing, but you will never have time to practise them all. They need to be coupled with a practical approach.

Accept that fictional managers 'plan, organize, coordinate and control', then look at the facts. You, the manager, have to cope, improvise, react and create certainty.

If you often feel so far out of your depth that if you blink you will drown, don't worry. All managers feel like that much of the time. The essential skill is to keep moving, but don't be too 'stylish' in your approach – it may cost valuable time.

Managers often have two broad priorities: consistently successful management of their department and completion of a 'project X'. The difference is that general management is a continuing series of problems, choices and decisions, while 'project X' is a 'one-off', with deadlines and a budget.

General management is what you do intuitively all the time: meet the sales budget, complete the monthly report, supervise and support your staff. Project management, eg planning the new head office move, is usually imposed on an already hectic routine and must be accomplished with no disruption to normal service.

Management theories

Learn how to question the plans and projects based on management theories and ask how relevant they are in the context of the organization today and to your own particular situation.
● Detailed planning may be rendered obsolete when the environment changes. Better to know where you want to take your team and to develop a flair for seizing opportunities.
● Print-outs from management information systems may be out of date by the time you read them. Get the latest information, even if it is just factory-floor gossip.
● Carefully planned projects may be conceived without accurate information. Develop ways of saying 'Why?' to senior management until the purpose of the project is clear.

Project viability

Projects are invitations to accept risk. Do not take a project briefing at face value; it may merely be to get the problem off someone else's desk and on to yours.

Before accepting a project, be sure it is viable; if not, modify it. Never be afraid to argue for its rejection if you have tangible reasons to believe it cannot be achieved.

The trick with project management is to gain enough information and knowledge to develop an instinctive approach to the task.

● Differentiate between questioning a project to obtain time, resources and authority, and 'analysis paralysis' produced by researching so closely that you no longer recognize a project's purpose.

● Understand the project's objectives and its value; can it be done more quickly or more cheaply?

● Does the organization really *need* the project?

● Have similar projects been done before by the organization? If so, can you have access to information?

● Can you pick your own team for the project?

● What time/budget constraints are imposed?

● Do you know all the possible snags? Are there any unstated conditions?

● Who is ultimately responsible – you or the senior manager delegating the project?

● Will you need specialized knowledge? Is it accessible?

● Seek clear indications of your expected input.

● Remember that the level of resources and the ease with which deadlines can be met are invariably underestimated.

The BA story

In the late 1970s British Airways was an unprofitable organization with a poor customer image. It was overstaffed, morale was low, and it was regarded as extremely bureaucratic.

Action was required. A turnaround began with the appointment of a new management team, none of whom had any previous airline experience. Sir John (later Lord) King was appointed Chairman, followed by Sir Colin Marshall, Chief Executive, and a new chief financial adviser, Gordon Dunlop. The brief was to take all appropriate action.

With recession biting during the early 1980s, the main thrust of their management plan was to modernize the company's assets, carry out financial reconstruction, reduce staffing levels and implement an intensive staff training programme. BA reduced its workforce from 50,000 to 36,000 by voluntary severance. This was followed by imaginative training for all levels of staff. Financial reconstruction involved the formalizing of clear plans in consultation with the government, and communicating them to the staff.

By the mid 1980s, the new team had achieved its primary objectives. By February 1987 when privatization was achieved, the company's financial performance had improved dramatically.

One of the key ingredients of this business turnaround was the success of the 'Putting People First' training programme. The management team and employees worked together to generate a new spirit and willingness to contribute to the company's future.

Managing problems

All managers have to deal with the problems that arise in their jobs. The classic process of solving problems is divided into four phases: diagnosis of the problem; choosing a solution; implementing the solution; and monitoring the result.

The theory is useful but difficult to apply. As managerial responsibilities increase, so do the difficulties of managing problems. Senior managers rarely deal with isolated problems. When several exist simultaneously, these problems and the issues they raise may be interrelated.

Defining the problem
Look at the managers you know who are successful. They recognize symptoms, sensing intuitively when a problem exists or is likely to arise. They do not retreat to wrestle alone with the company's problems. They are present among those who are living the problems, observing them and other people's reactions to them.

Choosing a solution
Effective managers shepherd their teams toward solutions, maintaining flexibility in order to change course when necessary. They interrelate problems so that several can be solved at the same time. If they can, they will use progress on one problem to achieve progress on a related issue.

Solving the problem
Managers tend to rank problems according to how quickly they can be solved, tackling the easier ones first. This is a useful way to link the stages of problem analysis and problem solving into implementing the solution.

Tracking the problem
Action is often part of defining the problem, not just of implementing the solution. Look for connections among the many different problems you are dealing with. Monitor interrelated problems. Just because you have chosen one course of action, don't forget the other options.

Problem solving: some common mistakes

'I must do something because that is what a manager is employed for.' Reflect and analyse the problem before taking action.

'I have seen this one before.' Don't assume that this problem is the same as a previous one just because it has similarities. Mistrust solutions that are based purely on previous problems.

'I have not got all the facts, so I can't make a decision.' Get moving: the action you take will give more information.

Managing problems via people

Confronted by a new problem, ask the team:
● Is this a potentially serious problem or a passing difficulty?
● Does it have an obvious possible solution? Is there someone well placed to solve it?
● Can we solve it by adjusting the way we work?'

Once the team is actively addressing the problem:
● Concentrate on managing the team, not the problem.
● Be sure team members are getting accurate, timely information.
● Stay above the process in case another plan is needed.
● Review progress with the team frequently.
● Encourage fresh ideas and approaches.

If the problem defies solution:
● Redefine it. Look at possible solutions first and see how they fit the problem.

If the problem remains insoluble, ascertain whether:
● Specialist knowledge is required. If so, acquire it, but square this with the team.
● More resources (people/time/ money) are required.

Once a solution begins to emerge:
● Arrange for the team to discuss action plans with you.
● Agree on time, resources, people to be committed.
● Ensure that the team gets recognition for solving the problems.

Remember that it is better to arrive at a solution everyone can accept than to persist in trying to apply a solution which appears to cover all aspects of the problem, but which some of the team will be reluctant to implement.

'My experience and understanding make me uniquely suited to finding the solution.' You will rarely be fully qualified to deal with a problem on your own. Get more brains to help.

'I must solve my subordinates' problems for them.' Encourage your team to bring to you both their problems and their ideas for solutions. Encourage subordinates to learn from their own actions.

'This problem is so urgent it must be solved immediately.' Not all problems need instant solutions. Quick solutions tend to be short lived. Procrastination can lead to improvement. Sometimes, one problem may change or solve itself, so consider whether it can hold for a while.

Making decisions

Decision-making is an inescapable responsibility. No matter how good you are at generating ideas or motivating people, you will be judged by your boss and your staff on the quality of your decisions.

Quantity can be no substitute for quality. In fact, a plethora of bad or short-term decisions will lead to a serious backlog of niggling problems.

Decisions are judgements, choices between alternative courses of action, neither of which is completely right nor wrong. Effective managers make:
● The minimum of decisions
● Decisions at the right time
● Decisions based upon the best possible information.

Managing your team's performance in a regular series of tasks and a number of various projects involves decisions relating to routine, individuals and teams. Ensure that you:
● Avoid impulsive decisions
● Seek informal reactions to situations requiring decisions in order to gauge team response
● Collect *all* information, not just that which supports your view
● Do not ignore your instincts, but do use information to test them
● Feel free to discuss decisions that will affect people with a more experienced manager – but retain responsibility for the final decision
● Do not be tempted or forced into making premature or unnecessary decisions because someone either wants something or is passing the buck.

Decision-making about routine general management should be delegated to members of your team. Not only does this encourage their growth and development but it also frees you for strategic issues.

Certain decisions need your closest attention, for example:
● Overall direction, such as which markets to be in
● Staff resources, such as employment of new people, promotion or the

---

Project management decisions

Managing projects means making hard decisions about money, materials and time. As projects have deadlines and budgets, they are put at risk by slow decisions. To minimize this risk:
● Ensure that all members of the project team know their roles.
● Frequently review progress to spot potential problems and note what time and resources are in hand.
● Arrange access to expert advice, if not permanently at least readily enough to help in any emergency.
● Report back to your boss frequently enough to prevent misunderstandings if things go wrong.
● Refer upward any decisions falling outside your sphere of authority and flexibility; accompany such referral with a clear statement of possible choices, together with your recommendation.

---

discipline of existing staff
● Structure of your department, such as whether it is properly organized to meet its objectives and cope with its workload
● Specialized skills, such as the provision of information and facilities to deliver sound technical decisions
● Planning, such as whether your team can continue to operate cost-effectively to achieve organizational objectives. Are any new projects or budgets needed?

Never remain in the rut of one technique, one style of dealing with everything. There are no hard and fast rules to decision-making, so try to learn 'unswerving flexibility'. Successful decision-makers call on an ever changing blend of experience and instinct, training and insight, independence and team expertise.

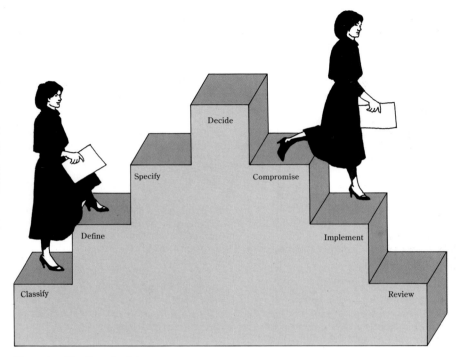

Steps to effective decisions

All managers make decisions. They are not sudden, isolated events but rather an ongoing and evolving process that can be broken down into a series of steps. These steps, based on Peter F. Drucker's sequence required to make an effective decision, are outlined here.

Classify the problem: if its generic, it is probably one of these everyday problems that has to be solved by adapting the appropriate generic rule, policy or principle. If it is extraordinary, the problem must be dealt with on its individual merits.

Define the problem: state precisely the nature of the problem and check your definition against all the observable facts. Beware the plausible but incomplete definition that does not embrace all the known facts.

Specify the conditions: clarify exactly what the decision must accomplish. These are the so-called boundary conditions, or specifications, that must be satisfied by

the solution to the problem.

Decide the right action: decide first of all what is right to do rather than what is acceptable in the circumstances. Make the ideal decision which satisfies all the specifications.

Compromise the decision: in reality there always has to be a compromise, so make the best decision possible by adapting it to the circumstances.

Implement the decision: assign the responsibility of carrying out the decision to those people capable of doing so. Make sure everyone who needs to know about the decision is informed.

Review the effectiveness of the decision: build feedback and monitoring into the implementation process. Receive reports on how the results of decisions measure up to their expectations. Incorporate any positive facts into the classifying, defining and specifying process of making decisions.

195

Managing the boss

Given education, parental influences and respect for authority figures, many managers may not realize their bosses need managing and want to be managed. Though difficult and at times risky, it can and should be achieved to the benefit of everybody.

Take time to find out about your boss by observing, discussing and talking to both him/her and his/her colleagues. Don't worry; it is legitimate and necessary, not machiavellian or sycophantic.

Do not think some areas of business are for the boss and some for you. Bosses have (arguably):
● Greater status
● Easier access to power/influence
● More experience
● More command of resources
● Broader vision.

But you may have:
● Greater or more detailed understanding of day-to-day issues
● More up-to-date information and closer contact with the customer
● Easier access to the team: where a boss feels cut off from a team, you provide the link.

Get involved and keep close to progress on issues your boss is dealing with. Bosses are not infallible; they will sometimes miss things, so always be on the lookout.

Don't rely on bosses for constant, detailed guidance. Provide them with ideas; give definitions of problems and your views on the solutions (that way you learn best): don't shirk the solution part. Always ask yourself what you would do if you were in charge and then compare your boss's solution against yours. Ask yourself which is the better course to follow and for precisely what reason.

Gradually develop a way of handling your boss by understanding what to deal with directly, what to consult on first, how to enlist his/her close involvement and when you should delegate upward.

You can legitimately expect:
● Another view on things
● More information (bosses probably know more about the overall picture)
● Advice on tricky issues
● Guidance on appropriate politics
● Support, protection (but make sure you consult or clear things with him /her).

But you should provide:
● Clear definition of issues
● Courses of action *and* your view on the one to follow
● Reasoned arguments on how/why you have arrived at your recommendations
● Your predictions about likely outcomes and contingencies if a recommended action is unsuccessful or of dubious worth
● Information on group progress.

Don't forget your boss depends on you to produce results and to organize your team. This gives you power. And the better manager you are, the more likely it is that your boss will want others to see you as the product of his/her management.

If you are considered to be good, your boss will not want to be seen as the person who prompted you to transfer to another department; or caused you to leave the organization; or impeded your progress. He/she will want to be seen to be handling you well in the eyes of his/her own bosses and, especially, peers.

Bosses will be busy with their own issues and will want you to advance those under your control. Having watched your first successful efforts closely, they will grow to trust you more.

You will eventually get to know both when you can go ahead alone, keeping the boss informed, and when you need to check beforehand. If you are unable to determine whether to check first or not, then there could well be something wrong with the way you are managing your boss.

Analyse your boss

Develop a worthwhile relationship with your boss and get to know what makes him/her tick.

Recognize the need to exchange information and ideas constructively and remember you depend on each other for progress.

Consider your own relationship with your subordinates. When it works well, what are the reasons? Are these relevant to your relationship with your boss? If so, are they present? The following analysis assumes your boss is male, but it applies equally to female managers:

1 Aims/values
● What does he want for himself?
● Is he ambitious or concerned with protecting himself from harm/criticism?
● What are his values?
● How does he measure himself?
● How does he measure you?
● Who are the people he admires?
● Does he like open discussion?
● Is he a risk taker or a protector/controller?
● Is he autocratic, expecting you to do as he says, or intuitive, expecting you to follow broad informal indications or signs?

Analyse why situations produce conflict or stalemate. Is it because your views differ or because you both manage the situations badly?
● Does this help you decide if you have the qualities he values?
● What does he expect from you?
● Do his goals and values match yours? If not, can you live with the resulting difficulties?

2 Strengths/weaknesses
● Is he quick to see essentials, keen to resolve issues?
● Does he need time and lengthy explanations?
● Is he good at one-to-one/personal communication?
● Does he contribute good ideas and practical solutions? Or does he rely on you for that?
● Does he enjoy conflict and handle it well, or does he seek to avoid it?

Seek to complement his strengths/weaknesses. Modifying your behaviour to suit your relationship with him is legitimate, not a sellout, and can be productive. But don't go too far.

Decide on your own values and how far you will go in adapting them. Avoid constant compromising of fundamentals.

3 Style
Does your boss prefer:
● Detailed written reports? If so, provide them and check orally.
● Verbal briefing? If so, provide it and confirm with a memo.
● Formal meetings with agendas?
● Preparatory memos and minutes?

4 Circumstances
● What are the pressures on him?
● What is expected of him? Where does he look for success?
● What are his own dealings with his peers and bosses?
● How are you contributing to what he is trying to achieve?
● How do his peers view him? Find out directly (by asking) or indirectly (by observing).
● What will be his reward if he succeeds? Promotion? Salary increase? Is he already a profit sharer? Does he have a bonus riding on the results – to which you are contributing?

The relationship you develop needs to recognize:
● Your individual styles, goals, strengths, circumstances.
● The need to exchange information and ideas constructively.
● Your dependence on each other for progress.

Planning your future

Success in business will never be handed to you on a plate, nor will it be achieved merely by being a good manager. Like Sir John Harvey-Jones, you must be good at your job *and* your career.

As an excellent salesperson of your company's products, you may well achieve security – with increasing financial rewards – most of your working life. However, if you aspire to top corporate posts, you must start to sell yourself.

Everyone must know you possess the skills, judgement and experience to warrant promotion to the highest levels. So:
- Know your ambitions, strengths, weaknesses.
- Review your personal values and requirements (see pp. 14–15) and ask: Do I desire high corporate office?
- You are probably right for top jobs if, like Richard Brewster of Jarvis Porter, you enjoy responsibility, seek challenges and are obsessed with creating excellence.
- You are not right for top jobs if you leave thinking about it until a vacancy occurs.
- Start planning early in your management career – 5 to 10 years is a reasonable time-scale to consider.
- Don't advertise your bid for power. No one likes power-hungry junior executives.
- Keep your own counsel, be wary of placing too much trust in others, be careful of your reputation and study the politics of your organization.

Working hard like Sir John Harvey-Jones, even in retirement, to promote your company and career requires your family's support. They must share your desire to achieve because they will have to tolerate long hours, a disrupted private life and a work-centred social life.

If you are not prepared to pay the high price nor inflict it upon your family, then don't aim for the top. And

Selling Yourself

Once you have planned a route to success, your career becomes a project to be managed. The following pointers are useful:
- Encourage a positive endorsement from everyone who meets you.
- Be well informed – read widely and discuss industry with experts.
- Make friends with the PR department and encourage them to use you as a spokesperson.
- Join the relevant professional, industrial or trade body.
- View your membership of clubs strategically; always 'trade up', not down.
- Support company social functions, but do not over-indulge.
- Get to know the person whose job you may want.
- Develop a grapevine to give you feedback on your reputation.
- Become known outside your department or firm with speech-making, community affairs, training assignments or whatever similar activity suits your temperament.
- Be interested in the company's finances – the share price, shareholders and brokers.

if power attracts you, but you value your lifestyle, a move to a smaller, less complex organization may be wise.

If you are happy to settle for a less senior job, select the role which best matches your positive characteristics and plan carefully to achieve it. Organizations need talented directors almost as much as they need leaders.

Your ambition needs a career plan and you should start charting its course early. Meteoric rises to the top are rare – executive success is more about planning, hard work, dedication, determination and, maybe, a few setbacks along the way.

Ann Gloag

Ann Gloag, the daughter of a bus driver, originally trained as a theatre sister. She started her £100 million turnover business from simple origins: she rented out caravans to tourists. When the roads between Perth, Aberdeen and Edinburgh were being upgraded, contractors needed buses to move their men. Mrs Gloag moved into the bus business and has not looked back since. She describes the onus placed upon a successful businesswoman this way: 'I'm expected to look like a lady, act like a man, and work like a dog'.

Stagecoach is now one of the largest bus companies in the UK and has expanded overseas. Following the worsening political situation in Sri Lanka where she had planned a joint venture, she expanded into Malawi, where Stagecoach acquired a controlling interest in the national bus company and introduced double-decker buses. Maintaining her earlier interest in medicine, she ensured that all outgoing buses to Africa are packed with medical supplies for refugee camps.

Ann Gloag was the Veuve Clicquot Business Woman of the Year in 1989.

Sir John Harvey-Jones

Sir John Harvey-Jones had a successful naval career until 1956, when he joined ICI's work study department. In 1967, he became a director of one of ICI's biggest manufacturing divisions. He joined the main board of ICI in 1973, becoming chairman in 1982.

With a straight-talking desire to communicate the reasons for change, fairness and unremitting hard work, Sir John led ICI to change its established way of working to overcome the world recession of the early 1980s and to succeed in an increasingly competitive environment.

As the BBC's 'Troubleshooter', he diagnoses where companies are getting it wrong and prescribes appropriate remedies.

He says, 'In business terms I learned three lessons. Firstly, beware of the allure and attraction of your own creation. Second, be very, very clear about the cash generative characteristics of the business you are in as well as the profit. Third, and the most difficult, it pays you to take decisions sooner rather than waiting until they're forced upon you.'

Richard Brewster

Richard Brewster qualified as a Chartered Accountant and soon became Chief Accountant of Bullens Transport Group, a subsidiary of Giltspur Investments.

He served as Finance Director of the Group and Deputy Managing Director. Giltspur was taken over by Unigate PLC in 1981.

In 1983 Brewster identified David S Smith (Holdings) PLC as an interesting and small public listed company. He acquired 10 per cent of its shares and became its Chief Executive. Since that time, David S Smith has expanded from a turnover of £5m from one location in South Wales to more than £350m per annum from 45 locations all over the UK. Earnings per share over this period have grown from 0.2p to over 30p.

Voted Guardian Young Businessman of the Year in April 1990, his greatest outside interest is the 'Looking Glass Appeal' of the Royal National Institute for the Blind.

Remaining as a non-executive director of David S Smith (Holdings) PLC, Richard Brewster left to take up his new post as chief executive of Jarvis Porter PLC in May 1991.

Creating the right image

When a change of top executive is imminent, the successor is often waiting in the wings. The candidate has not only been pursuing a deliberate plan to get to the top but has also developed the 'right image' for the job, the company, the industry. The development involves a reputation for:
- 'Delivering the goods'
- Achieving successful projects
- Understanding thoroughly the industry's affairs and the company's business
- Being an able manager of people
- Being respected by customers and industry partners.

These credentials are not in themselves enough to qualify you for the top job. You also need a touch of something special, 'charisma' or 'presence', which encourages others to follow you.

Properly qualified and well-experienced candidates may be passed over in favour of someone technically less suited but better connected, someone who looks the part and projects a style and confidence fitting the company ethos.

Top jobs may differ in detail from company to company, but they share certain features:
- The exercise of power over the organization
- The link between the organization and important external institutions
- The barometer of corporate reputation – how the company is doing, what its challenges are, and what its responses to opportunities and dangers will be.

A major function of the job is communication – the best reputation and image command the greatest audience and confer the most business advantages on the organization.

Confident, reliable statements, for example, by a well-respected leader can positively influence the value of the company's publicly traded shares.

Like entertainers and politicians, top business people have to become used to being public property. While there are obvious risks, there are also advantages.

Skilled business leaders, such as restauranteur Prue Leith OBE and Jan Carlzon, CEO of SAS Airlines, find that the media's reportage of their activities creates myths and legends about them.

These generate confidence, support, even fondness for a company and its products, giving it valuable prestige over its competitors.

It is essential to lay the foundations of the image you wish to project as early as possible:
- Analyse the background, culture and roots of your company and industry. Understand what the people in power feel comfortable supporting.
- Project values appropriate to your industry and support them strongly.
- Develop friendships with media people – but don't become their pawn.
- Evolve and be prepared to defend your stance on challenging issues and matters central to the well-being of your company.
- Build a strong team to complement your skills and give it challenging assignments crucial to your company's success. Make sure the results are well publicized.
- Get help and advice on making presentations to large audiences and the media.
- Seek appearances on radio, TV and at speaking engagements, but prepare meticulously.
- Ensure your appearance and surroundings look good when you give public interviews.
- Keep in touch with informed, influential people from related fields. Be a good listener as well as talker.
- Support the efforts of your junior managers – you will get the pick of the crop and strong loyalty.
- Never publicly deprecate your competitors for high office.

Pru Leith OBE

She sums up her philosophy of food as the best of English country-house cooking. Captivated late by cookery, she never went near a stove during her 'happiest of childhoods' in South Africa. Leaving home to study French history at the Sorbonne, she became instantly fascinated by French cooking. Failing to persuade any French restaurant to let her work in the kitchen, she trained at the Cordon Bleu School in London, got a job cooking lunches for a legal firm and then started her own catering service in 1962. Her successful restaurant opened in 1969, followed by Leith's School of Food and Wine, offering professional training for career cooks and short courses for amateurs. She recently added a retail division, which has contracts for the restaurants in Hyde Park, Kensington Gardens and Hampton Court Palace.

She has been a cookery writer for the *Daily Mail* and *Sunday Express*, and was cookery editor and columnist for the *Guardian* for eight years. A major contributor to radio and television food programmes, she also gives lectures and cookery demonstrations at home and abroad.

From her '£3 a throw' dinner party beginnings, she has built up a group with an £8m turnover and assets of £5m. Her secret? To produce stylish, unpretentious and truly excellent food, no matter whether it be a banquet or a sandwich.

Jan Carlzon

Jan Carlzon was born in Sweden in 1941. He earned his MBA Degree from the Stockholm School of Economics in 1967, when he also began his career as Product Manager at Vingresor, Sweden's largest inclusive tour operator which became a subsidiary of SAS (Scandinavian Airline Systems) in 1971. In 1974 he was named Managing Director of Vingresor, and as President of Linjeflyg, which owned 50 per cent of SAS, he revived that airline's flagging fortunes. He then became Chief Operating Officer of the SAS Airline in 1980 and Chief Executive Officer of the Group less than a year later.

At the time he joined the airline, it had been in the red for two years to the tune of $30m, following 17 years of profitability. Rather than launching a cost-cutting programme which he felt would be demotivating to staff and damaging to products, he invested $25m in service improvements and staff involvement programmes with the intention of getting the company on its feet again. He positioned SAS as 'the business-man's airline' and replaced the former production orientation with a strong sense of customer orientation.

Within a year SAS had more than recouped its losses with a profit of some $60m. Carlzon's philosophy is simple: 'SAS used to fly airplanes. Now we fly people'.

Although, along with many other airlines, SAS ran into operating difficulties in 1990/91, it has gained a reputation with airline travellers as a truly customer-orientated organization.

Changing jobs

Changing jobs is a major feature in the evolution of your career, and timing is critical to the moves you make if your plan is to proceed to schedule. Gone are the days when the concept of lifetime service was admired; in some fields it can be a disqualification.

No route to the top is foolproof, however. No matter how carefully you plan to become a successful executive, you may fall foul of unforeseen factors.

Your company may be taken over by another group, for example, making the route to the top of the new parent company too long to suit your needs. Alternatively, your horizons may broaden dramatically, causing you to seek even higher targets.

In any event, do not underestimate the value of the 'headhunter' in your strategy. Known also as executive search consultancies, headhunters specialize in finding and proposing qualified candidates for important executive, managerial and technical positions.

Their services are paid for by the searching organization and fees are considerable, usually around 30 per cent of the contemplated annual salary for the position they fill.

Headhunters are important to you because:
● They may be your means of escaping from a company which no longer holds your interest.
● They may present an alternative strategy which gets you to your career goal faster.
● They may offer job changes that allow you to gain broad-based experience in industry.
● They can be a rich source of contacts, useful in pursuing your career.

Your best interests are served by being helpful to headhunters. Their regard for you as a source, their sensitivity to your potential as an eventual client and their knowledge of your history make them useful friends.

When to change jobs

The route to the top often requires a spell in other industries to acquire the breadth of experience deemed necessary in a top executive. Pan-European and international companies want managers who understand the range of markets and cultures they operate in.

The following circumstances may necessitate a change of jobs:
● If you have peaked too early and face a long wait for advancement.
● When any recent success enhances your 'market value'.
● If you feel you are getting insufficient recognition where you are.
● If your company falls behind competitively and you cannot persuade it to respond.
● If reorganization or change has left your plan in tatters.
● If you develop new horizons.

Do not leave any decision too long. It is better to risk changing sooner than you would like.

Curriculum vitae

Job applications must be backed up with a good track record of achievements, endorsements from people who think highly of you, and a well-thought-out presentation. A good CV may be disproportionately useful in increasing your chances.

You can get your CV drawn up by a professional agency at a cost, but if you compile your own remember:
● Structure facts into sections: achievements, experience, responsibilities, background, education.
● Achievement should be the focus, supported by hard facts. Give a lot of time, effort and space to this.
● Use headings, short paragraphs, margins and double-spacing.
● Be distinct – vary typefaces for copy and headings, use colour, underlining and a summarized beginning.
● Give a chronological summary.

Sir Bob Reid

Sir Bob Reid, the chairman of British Rail, was born at Cupar, near St Andrews, the son of a butcher. He lost part of his arm at nine while trying to unstick dripping fat in a mincing machine.

The disability spurred his will to succeed and after reading political economy and modern history at St Andrews, Sir Bob went to work for Shell and was quickly sent abroad, to Brunei, Nigeria, Thailand and then Australia. After the Shah's downfall he was sent to Iran to secure oil supplies.

Sir Bob returned to Britain and became chairman and chief executive of Shell UK in 1985.

He began his chairmanship of British Rail in April 1990 after being offered the job by Energy Secretary Cecil Parkinson.

David Smith

Born in Scotland in 1944, David Smith graduated from the University of Glasgow with a BSc. Joining Arthur Young in 1966, he became a partner ten years later. In 1980 he took over the running of the management consultancy division in London, responsible for around 100 staff.

In 1986 he left Arthur Young to set up a sole practice. His involvement in an abortive bid by Barker and Dobson for Gateway led to his being approached by a former director of Gateway Food Markets. Their consortium, Isosceles, made a £2.2b leveraged bid and gained control of Gateway after a three-month struggle. Having won the battle in what was Britain's fifth biggest takeover, David Smith then became responsible for the third largest UK supermarket group.

Michael Julien

Michael Julien has a reputation for hard work. After doing his National Service he did his articles, and at 29 became chief financial officer of insurance broker C. E. Heath.

He made no secret of his intention to become chief executive of a large public company. It took him 20 years working for seven companies before he achieved his ambition. He was treasurer at British Leyland for one year before moving to Willis Faber, which he helped to float. Within three years, he moved to BICC as finance director, but then he moved to the board of Midland Bank and made his reputation with a key role in the Crocker affair.

A spell with Eurotunnel and on the board of Guinness led to an offer from Sir Terence Conran to become chief executive at Storehouse.

Kathleen O'Donovan

Kathleen O'Donovan joined the growing band of women in executive positions when she was appointed Finance Director of BTR, the industrial conglomerate, in June 1991, one of the youngest female executives in a UK public company.

After graduating from University College London with an economics degree, Kathleen entered accountancy. In her 13 years with Ernst & Young, she rose from trainee to partner and developed a detailed knowledge of BTR through her involvement in the BTR audit.

Getting to the top

Navigating the corridors of executive power can be exceedingly complicated. The prevailing corporate behaviour of each organizational level differs, and you need to fit in, yet stand out at the same time. And it is no good behaving like a chairman when you get your first major department or become a junior director.

'Organizational politics' is the unspoken process whereby some managers achieve greatness, while others lust unproductively after power. If you are unprepared to graduate in this obscure science, forget the walnut panelling and the Rolls Royce; they will never be your natural environment.

You would in all probability be unhappy and insecure if you did achieve such power. Without the qualification or the desire, you would be far more suited to a more modest position where you could use your talents and not worry about the 'politics'.

Appointing a top manager is a most sensitive decision, yet few organizations consistently operate a thoroughly efficient procedure for 'growing' their own senior people.

The benefit of promoting from within is recognized by behavioural analysts and business schools, but people in power in the companies may tend to resist internal appointments which could bring change.

Ostensibly there to serve the shareholders' interests, some company directors are primarily concerned with continuing to be company directors. Hence the furious desperation with which some takeover bids, clearly in the shareholders' interest, are opposed.

Reluctant to relinquish power, such opponents are unlikely voluntarily to help an advocate of change, especially if they may suffer as a result.

As an aspiring senior executive, therefore, you must present such people with a clear political message.

Acquiring organizational power

All you have read so far about selling yourself and creating the right image must be supplemented by an objective attitude about the acquisition of organizational power. You should:
- Always work for 'winners'.
- Be loyal, but do not avoid 'changing horses' if your career will be harmed by excessive loyalty.
- Reconcile the company's well being with individual needs and be ready to make firm, if unpopular, decisions.
- Communicate the reasons for such decisions if anyone suffers.
- Recruit excellent people to cover your area of professional weakness.
- Concentrate on using your talents to benefit the organization.
- Know the strengths and weaknesses of other top executives.

On the one hand, they must see you as a way to keep their power, but on the other they must realize you are not to be thwarted.

In your organization, there may be a management streaming process intended to identify talented managers and expose them to a breadth of experience appropriate to a career in the upper levels of management.

Membership of this 'elite' gives you no immunity from politics; rather it exposes you to more. For not only will you experience the 'acceptability barrier' with each step up the corporate ladder, you will also be competing with others of similar ambition.

So you must know the culture of your organization, like Sir David Scholey got to know his, and the effect it has on those around you – especially those in positions of power. But do not conclude that successful politics alone will take you to success – top managers *are* political, but they also deliver.

Sir David Scholey

He has been described as the City's Mr Big. As architect and chairman of the S G Warburg group, he is the most powerful investment banker in the land, yet he defies the traditional image of the City grandee.

He passed his Oxford entrance exam but did his national service first: 'It was very broadening and deepening – People who served in the armed forces realize their responsibility is as much to the people that report to them, as it is to the people above them.'

Leaving Oxford after a year, he had a spell at Lloyd's, spent a year as an insurance broker in Canada and then on his return to England, joined Guinness Mahon.

In 1965 he met Sir Siegmund Warburg and soon joined the firm, becoming deputy chairman in 1977 and joint chairman in 1980.

Like his mentor, Scholey is obsessive about communication. He commands respect for his judgement and skills, but his outstanding talent is with people, displaying a brilliant sense of leadership. As a director of the Bank of England, he has been seen by many as a likely future governor.

Sir Colin Marshall

In 1958 Sir Colin Marshall joined the Hertz Corporation in Chicago as a Management Trainee. In 1961 he became General Manager UK, Netherlands and Belgium.

He became president of Avis Inc in 1975 and CEO in 1976. Avis had been acquired by ITT in 1964 and Sir Colin learned management disciplines in the heyday of Harold Geneen. His experience in the travel business and as a frequent air traveller stood him in good stead for his later career.

In 1977 Avis was acquired by US conglomerate Norton Simon. Two years later Marshall assumed overall responsibility in the parent company as an executive vice-president for four Norton Simon companies. Thus a staunchly British executive became responsible for two-thirds of the assets, sales and profits of a huge US corporation. He returned to the UK in 1981 as Deputy Chief Executive and a board member of Sears Holdings plc.

Sir Colin was appointed Chief Executive of British Airways in 1983 and also joined the board. After a time as Deputy Chairman, he progressed to Chairman in 1993.

Klaus Jacobs

A German by birth but now a Swiss citizen, Klaus Jacobs has a reputation for toughness. He demonstrated his skills by buying a substantial slice of the European confectionery business, rationalizing it and then selling it.

The family business, founded in 1895, became Germany's leading coffee concern. Klaus took control in the early 1970s. In 1990, Jacobs sold his coffee and chocolate group Jacobs Suchard A.G. to the US tobacco firm Philip Morris amidst some controversy. Eventually, Jacobs negotiated the repurchase of some of the group's activities from Philip Morris and some months later took over Swiss manpower services firm Adia SA in conjunction with German retailer Asko Deutsche Kaufhaus A.G. 'I see myself not just as an investor but also as an entrepreneur,' he said at a news briefing.

This remarkable man then announced his support of the Boy Scout movement and a charity he has set up to help young people – the Johann Jacobs foundation, named for his great uncle who started the company.

Staying on top

One dilemma confronting you as you ascend to each new level of your executive career is 'how to stay on top'. While your route is fairly steady in the earlier part of your progress, it gets more precarious as you near the summit.

Your continued occupancy of an executive position may soon be inadvisable because your vision and ambition exceed the limits of your post; or because you are stagnating through lack of challenge; or because you must move to allow up-and-coming managers scope.

Yet top posts often take a long time to become vacant. Perhaps this is because:
● Senior executives' emotional attachment to the company makes moving psychologically difficult
● Senior directors or chief executives often have a large financial stake in the company, making a move inconvenient
● The departure of a crucial senior executive may adversely affect shareholders' confidence.

If such factors hold you back from the top job and you want neither to move nor be continually frustrated, then consider additional responsibilities and challenges, such as:
● Becoming a non-executive director of other companies
● Getting involved in politics
● Pursuing other personal interests, eg community affairs or sport
● Starting your own company.

The ability to find other non-competitive avenues for your management talents is a mark of a successful professional. The result, if profitable, can overcome the 'ambition gap' and round off the personality by exposure to new contacts, problems and relationships. It also enhances your claim to a senior post in your original company.

You may find, however, that your post is hard to handle because of:

Consolidating your position

If you succeed in providing yourself with a wider sphere in which to operate, you will have created some valuable factors favouring your ability to stay on top:
● Broad internal/external support for your policies
● Ability to use the media to carry your message
● External sources of information concerning your rivals
● Access to powerful influence against potential opponents
● Wide-ranging expertise from which to draw your support
● Fresh fields to conquer if bored
● An escape route if you are beaten in 'battle'

● Difficulty with unfamiliar technology. Don't let technologists rule you: hire the best consultant, set firm criteria for all new high-tech projects and run them alongside people-driven ones until they are proven.
● Lack of experience in a professional field. Remember, professionals should serve enterprise, not vice versa. Take the best course in the particular field, cultivate experts and choose experienced people carefully.
● Failure to win political battles. Information is your greatest asset, so rely on the research of your loyal supporters and gradually use it to handle all opposition.
● Inheriting an out-of-control problem. Delegate it to a team of talented experts, explain it to colleagues, update regularly. Impress upon the board it is their problem you are trying to solve.
● A 'pet project' going badly wrong. Replace pet projects with a flexible series of developments, which bring benefit if successful or can be ended if they look like failing.

Sir John Cuckney

Chairman of 3i Group PLC and of Royal Insurance Holdings PLC, Sir John likes the quote: 'I was brought up to spend a third of my life learning, a third earning, and a third serving.'

Clearly improving on the saying, he has had a distinguished career in business and in public service running parallel.

He was in charge of a financial group when he first entered public service in 1970 as chairman of the beleaguered Mersey Docks and Harbour Board. Drastic measures, including an Act of Parliament to convert it from public ownership to a statutory company, were required to clean up the mess.

The Crown Agents, who looked after the financial and procurement interests of overseas governments and administrations, were Cuckney's next assignment – unravelling financial muddles while preserving the Agents' sound traditional business.

Formerly chairman of the respected travel firm Thomas Cook, he is also on the board of Brixton Estate PLC, Glaxo Holdings PLC and St Andrews Management Institute. Sir John has reversed Parkinson's Law to accommodate the work allotted to him.

Lord Hanson

Lord Hanson has been described as the first and finest casting to emerge from the Thatcherite mould, the man who got stuck into reforming British industry in much the same way as the former Prime Minister got stuck into the trade union movement. Both did it, in a sense, from outside.

James Hanson, or Baron Hanson of Edgington in the County of West Yorkshire, is a Yorkshireman in all respects. Born into a solid Huddersfield business background in 1922, he has a reputation for straight talking and an honest approach to business and the pursuit of profit. When the family business was nationalized in 1949, he went to America and gathered a taste for red-blooded capitalism. Although knighted by Harold Wilson, he was given his peerage by Margaret Thatcher and is a dedicated Tory, donating funds to the party and placing resources behind the establishment of city technology colleges.

There is no devoted industrialist in Lord Hanson. He is neither hooked on textiles nor sold on steel. The group he has controlled for more than two decades has no central activity. Unlike most conglomerates, Hanson Trust did not start with a core activity and move out – the company's activities are as fluid as water and there is no emotional tie to any particular area. This ability to move in and out of companies – to sell as well as buy – is a crucial element in the Hanson success. Hanson as an organization exists for the benefit of the shareholders and it is one of its chairman's ambitions that the wealth created and accumulated over the years be handed over to them.

Checklist to a brilliant career

Climbing the management tree to success is not an undertaking to be left to chance. You need to know yourself down to the roots – strengths, weaknesses, ambitions, values – and to evolve a strong career plan that must be managed well.

Job excellence and clever career management are not enough, however. You should ensure your personality and public image match the organization in which you wish to succeed.

A brilliant career is rarely straightforward and often means moving from branch to branch of the management tree. Changing

Getting to the top

● Always work for winners.
● Recruit excellent people to cover your weaknesses.
● Be loyal, but don't jeopardize your career.
● Understand organizational politics.
● Be ready to make firm, if unpopular, decisions.
● Reconcile the company's well being with your personal needs.
● Discover the values of each level of organization and match your achievements to them.

Changing jobs

● Never leave decisions too long; it is better to risk changing sooner than you would like or you may get blocked.
● Change jobs if you have peaked too early; if recent success enhances your market value; if your talents are not recognized; if change leaves your career

Creating the right image

● Build a strong team to complement your skills and give it assignments crucial to your company's success. Ensure the results are well publicized.
● Support the efforts of more junior managers - you will help their careers and ensure strong loyalty.
● Never publicly deprecate your competitors for high office.
● Make sure your values relate to your

Managing your job and your career

● Be realistic about your ambitions, strengths and weaknesses.
● Don't be overambitious.
● Start outline planning early in your management career.
● Keep your own counsel; be wary of

trusting others unless you are sure of your trust; be careful of your reputation; study the politics of your organization.
● Stay well informed: read widely and discuss industry affairs with experts.
● Closely follow your company's results,

Staying on top

● Train your loyal supporters to help you win political battles.
● Ensure broad support for your policies.
● Use the media to carry your message.
● Seek new challenges, eg in politics or community affairs, becoming a non-executive director of other companies or starting your own private enterprise.
● Avoid pet projects – concentrate on your business's central issues.

plan in tatters or with new horizons.
● Regularly update an excellent CV.
● Consider experiencing other industries or countries. They often allow you to aquire the breadth of knowledge deemed necessary in a top executive.
● Never underestimate the value of the 'headhunter' in your strategy.

industry and support them strongly.
● Decide and be prepared to defend your stance on significant issues and matters central to your company.
● Develop friendships with media people but do not become their pawn.
● If you can handle them, seek appearances on TV, radio and at speaking engagements, but prepare meticulously. Get advice on making presentations to large audiences and the media.

jobs may often be a necessary feature of success, giving you the experience and flexibility to navigate corporate power.

Reaching your goal seems to grow harder the nearer you get to it. This is when you most need your experience in organizational politics and your knowledge of the industry's culture.

Staying on top of the tree means seeking continued growth and avoiding stagnation. Keeping active in various fields – politics, sport, private enterprise – will mean that you are less likely to jeopardize all you have worked for than if you are emotionally or financially attached to your position of power.

follow the share prices, know who the major shareholders are, meet the company's brokers.
● Develop a grapevine to give you feedback on your reputation.
● Keep close to the person whose job

you may want – he/she often has a lot of say about a successor.
● Join the relevant professional, industrial or trade body and become active if you enjoy it and find it progressive.

Glossary

A

Accrual Accounting:
the reporting of income and expense at the time they are earned or incurred, not when they are received or paid.

Asset:
item of value which is owned by a company or person and is expected to be of economic benefit. Assets may be divided into *fixed assets* (eg buildings), *current assets* (eg stocks) or *intangible assets* (eg patents).

Audit:
examination of a company's financial statements by an independent third party, followed by a report to shareholders of the results. (See also *Internal auditing and Management audit*.)

Average rate of return (ARR):
measurement of the profitability of a project which averages the *cash flow* or profit over its total life.

Average total cost (ATC):
Variable costs plus fixed costs divided by the number of units produced.

B

Balance sheet:
periodic (usually annual) statement of a company's financial position which summarizes what is owned (*assets*) and owed (*liabilities*) by the business.

Brainstorming:
a meeting designed to generate as many ideas as possible in an allotted time. A small group of people focus on an issue or problem and make suggestions. Criticism and comment on ideas are forbidden.

C

Capital:
money invested in a business by its owners.

Capital employed:
can be defined as either total assets, or total assets less current liabilities. The return on capital employed is most commonly calculated using the latter definition.

Capitalization:
the company's debt and equity structure (long-term debt, preferred and ordinary shares, capital surplus and retained earnings).

CASE (computer aided software engineering) tools:
automated tools used to assist the development and maintenance of information systems. Typically used to specify the information requirements of an organization.

Cash flow:
the inflow and outflow of cash through a company. It is used in the day-to-day management of funds to describe the cash needed to finance weekly or daily operating expenses and other obligations. (See also *Cash flow forecast* and *Cash flow statement*.)

Cash flow forecast:
estimation of expected *cash flow* used

to alert management to future cash shortages or surpluses.

Cash flow statement:
summary of actual or projected *cash flow* over a particular period.

Conglomerate:
company with diverse, often unrelated, business interests.

Convertible option:
an option for a lender of long-term debt to convert the debt into share capital at the end of the stated period.

Corporate culture:
unwritten set of values and rules within an organization which conditions the behaviour of those belonging to it.

Corporate strategy:
assessment of the relationship between an organization and its environment (customers, competitors, suppliers, government etc) resulting in a plan to achieve the business objectives.

Costing systems:
the collection and classification of cost information to determine the cost of a unit of output. The most common systems are process costing and job costing in manufacturing industries and operation costing in service industries.

Critical success factors:
those aspects of a business which need to be concentrated on to achieve a high degree of success.

Cross-selling:
selling additional products or services to an existing client through existing markets.

Current assets:
assets of a company which are likely to be converted into cash (eg debtors, work in progress) within 12 months.

D

Debenture:
long-term loan secured on specific assets or through a *floating charge* on the business as a whole.

Debt capital:
money loaned to a company, usually for longer than one year and, in the event of *liquidation*, the first to be repaid.

Deferred tax:
the tax attributable to the timing differences which arise as result of items of income or expenditure being either taxable or deductible against tax in periods different from those in which they are covered in the financial statements.

Depreciation:
the amount by which a *fixed asset* is diminished in a particular year through its use in the business. This amount is charged against profits.

Direct cost:
cost directly associated with a unit of production (eg the amount of steel needed to make a motor car). (See also *Indirect cost*.)

Glossary

Discounted cash flow (DCF):
measurement of cash flow which recognizes that future receipts or payments have less value than the same amounts received or paid today. This technique reduces all future receipts or payments to a common unit of measurement, ie their *net present-day value*.

Double entry bookkeeping:
accountant's device for ensuring accuracy and completeness of recording transactions. Both aspects of every transaction are recorded.

Downtime:
time during which an employee or machine is not working efficiently due to maintenance work, faults, waiting for materials.

E

Earnings per share:
the profit in pence attributable to each equity share, based on the consolidated profit of the period after tax and after deducting minority interest and preference dividends, but before extraordinary items, divided by the number of equity shares on issue and ranking for dividend in respect of the period.

Equity:
the *capital* invested in a company by its owners, together with *profits* from previous years that have not been distributed as dividend.

F

Fixed assets:
the assets of a company (eg equipment, land and plant), which are held, not for conversion into cash, but over long periods to further the main trading activities.

Fixed costs:
costs which are unaffected by changes in volume but tend to change over time (eg rent, rates).

Floating charge:
security for a loan which is granted over a range of *assets*.

Franchise:
means of distribution by which the right to sell or manufacture is sold to a company or individual within a given marketplace. The franchisee usually pays the franchisor an initial sum and thereafter a royalty in exchange for technical support and advice and the benefit of the corporate image.

G

Game plan:
overall strategy, tactics or method.

Gearing:
relationship between the amounts invested in a business by its owners (*equity*) and by outsiders (debt).

Globalization:
growth of companies until they become truly international, operating in whichever country in the world suits their purchasing, manufacturing and distribution requirements.

H

Headhunter:
consultancy service which seeks out, interests and proposes suitable candidates for executive, managerial and technical positions.

Holding company:
a member company which has a majority of the voting rights; or can appoint or remove a majority of the board; or controls alone a majority of the voting rights by agreement with other members; or has the right to exercise a dominant influence through the Memorandum and Articles or a control contract or has a participating interest and either exercises a dominant influence or manages both on a unified basis. Some holding companies' business consists entirely of holding shares or securities of other companies. (See also *Parent company*.)

I

Indirect cost (or overhead):
cost not directly associated with a unit of production and which will be apportioned across a number of activities or products (eg the cost of running a canteen in a car factory).

Intangible assets:
assets which are neither physical nor financial (eg goodwill, trademarks, licences etc).

Internal auditing:
review of operations by a special internal department within an organization.

Inventory:
list detailing stock that is kept for use as required – particularly raw materials, work in progress, supplies and finished goods.

L

Liability:
obligation of a company to make payment in the foreseeable future for goods or services already received.

Limited company:
company in which the shareholders' liability is limited by shares or guarantee.

Line manager:
employee who is responsible for the performance of a principal section of the work of the organization and for achieving its objectives.

Liquidity:
the pool of accessible funds, either in cash or in *assets* that may be transformed rapidly into cash, to meet immediate debts.

Loan stock:
type of loan/debt, usually long-term and secured.

Long-term debt:
loan repayable one year or more from date of transaction – usually secured. (See also *Debenture* and *Loan stock*.)

M

Management audit:
examination and appraisal of the quality of management action in an organization.

Glossary

Market based pricing:
pricing decision based on the perceived value to the customer, or 'what the market will bear'.

Market capitalization:
current market value per share multiplied by the number of issued shares.

Market research:
analysis of the changing market for a product/service, used to formulate *marketing plans*.

Market strategy:
analysis of the critical components in the marketing of a specific product/service and the development of a plan to achieve marketing objectives.

Marketing mix:
the balancing of a product/service with factors such as place, promotion and price to achieve customer satisfaction.

Marketing plan:
the formulation of a method to achieve profitable results from the sale and distribution of a product/service.

Marketing segmentation:
breaking up of the market for a product/service into segments.

Minority interest:
the shares in the subsidiary undertaking not owned by the parent company.

Modelling techniques:
refers in the context of information systems to specific methods employed to define a system. Typically the techniques document the inputs, outputs, processes and data files in the system.

N

Net present-day value (NPV):
the value today of future *cash flows*.

Net realizable value:
the price at which assets could be sold minus all the cost of selling them.

O

Overhead:
see *Indirect cost*.

Overtrading:
trading which exceeds the financial capacity of a business and may lead the company into financial distress.

P

Parent company:
a company which either owns or controls a majority of the voting rights; or has the right to appoint or remove a majority of the board. (See also *Holding company*.)

Payback period:
time taken for the initial investment in an asset or project to be repaid from profits.

Portfolio analysis:
breakdown of the investments that a company has made in securities held for financial gain, rather than as trade investment.

Preference shares:
form of share capital whereby the holders have a preferential right to receive a dividend out of profits of a certain percentage of the *share capital* before the owners of ordinary shares get any dividend.

Price Earnings ratio (PE):
the relationship that a company's profits bear to the publicly quoted value of its shares, usually expressed as market value of share/earnings per share.

Privatization:
the sale by a government of assets which it owns.

Profit:
what remains when costs (of producing, selling etc) have been deducted from revenues.

Profit and loss account:
compares revenue for the year against the cost of goods sold and other expenses. It also discloses revenues arising, or costs resulting, from non-operating activities.

Prospecting:
the identification of specific potential customers.

Prototyping:
a technique used to develop a simplifed working model of a new system, automation tool or product. Primary aims are to sell the idea to management and test its feasibility for continued development.

R
Research and development (R & D):
the search for improvements and innovations in a company's products/services and the solving of allied technical problems, with a view to creating new products/services.

S
Sale and leaseback:
form of financing by which a business sells an asset which it owns and then leases it back at an annual rent from the purchaser.

Selling on:
adding value and additional services, which can be invoiced separately to an existing contract.

Share capital:
the amount of money invested in a company by its risk-taking shareholders.

Share premium:
money received by a company for a share issue which is in excess of its nominal value (ie its face value).

Solvency:
maintenance of a sufficient level of *liquid assets* by a company to meet its short-term obligations.

Source language:
a programming language such as
COBOL in which systems are often
developed.

Standard costs:
scientifically predetermined
estimates of the cost of performing a
certain operation, within a given set
of working conditions and for a
given period.

**Statement of source and
application of funds (SSAF):**
analysis of the sources of funds
(financial resources) and how they
have been used, showing how and
why a company's cash position has
changed.

Strategic management:
the discipline of managing an
organization's resources to achieve
defined long-term objectives.

Strategic planning:
process by which a company aims to
reach a *strategic success position* by
setting objectives, undertaking
strategic analysis, and making
strategic choices.

Strategic success position:
point from which an organization
has the best opportunity to achieve
above average long-term objectives.

SWOT:
acronym for strengths, weaknesses,
opportunities and threats relating to
a company. These are investigated as
part of strategic analysis.

T
Turnover:
the gross revenue earned from
providing goods/services to
customers. Turnover should not be
confused with *cash flow*.

U
**Unlisted securities market
(USM):**
market which enables smaller
companies to attract public
investment without the formalities
and costs of a listing on the London
Stock Exchange.

V
Value chain:
term coined by Michael Porter to
describe the five areas in which a
company's *critical success factors* lie:
research/design, development,
production, marketing/sales and
distribution.

Variable costs:
costs that vary directly with the
level of output.

Venture capital:
investments in start-up or early stage
technology, manufacturing and other
growth-oriented ventures, often
shunned by traditional finance
sources, as being too risky.

W
Working capital:
the amount of short-term funds
available to a business to perform its
normal trading operations. Usually
defined as the difference between
current assets and current liabilities.

Ernst & Young Worldwide

Ernst & Young is one of the world's leading firms of accountants, business advisers and management consultants. With operations in over 100 countries and a strong presence in all major markets, the firm is noted for its commitment to excellence and its dedication to the success of its clients worldwide. The expertise of the firm's partners and professional staff is sought by organizations of all types, ranging from start-ups, private companies and public sector bodies to multinationals whose products and services are household names the world over.

Ernst & Young's extensive range of services includes audit, accounting, management consultancy, tax services, investigations, and assistance with acquisitions and mergers. The firm's management consultancy services focus on human resources (including recruitment, management development, organizational effectiveness and change management), financial management, information systems, operations management, privatization, and location advice.

Ernst & Young's experience in working with the world's successful organizations means that there is virtually no business problem that the firm cannot solve. If you would like to discuss any ways in which the firm could help you or your business, please contact your local Ernst & Young office and ask to speak to a partner.

Bibliography

Bolles, R. N. *What Colour is My Parachute?*; 10 Speed Press 1991

Campbell-Jounson, A. *Mission with Mountbatten*; Hamish Hamilton 1985 (UK), Atheneum 1985 (USA)

Drucker, P. *The Effective Executive*; Pan 1970 (UK paperback), Harper & Row 1967 (USA)

Drucker, P. *Managing in Turbulent Times*; Pan 1981 (UK paperback), Harper & Row 1980 (USA)

Edwardes, M. *Back from the Brink*; Collins 1983 (UK)

Ernst & Young, *UK GAAP*; Longmans 1990

Goldsmith, W. & Clutterbuck, D. *The Winning Streak*; Weidenfeld and Nicholson 1984 (UK), Random House 1986 (USA)

Handy, C. *Gods of Management*; Pan 1979 (UK paperback)

Herzberg, F. *Work and the Nature of Man*; Staples Press 1968 (UK), T. Y. Crowell 1966 (USA)

Jung, C. G. *Psychological Types*; Routledge 1971 (UK)

Katz, D. & Kahn, R. L. *The Social Psychology of Organizations*; Wiley 1978 (UK) & 1966 (USA)

Keirsey D. & Bates, M. *Please Understand Me*; Prometheus Nemesis Book Co 1984

Maslow, A. H. *Motivation and Personality*; Harper & Row 1970 (UK & USA)

Peters, T. J. & Austin, N. *A Passion for Excellence*; Fontana 1986

Peters, T. J. & Waterman, R. H. Jr. *In Search of Excellence*; Harper & Row 1982 (UK & USA)

Peters, T. *Thriving on Chaos*; Macmillan 1988

Porter, M. E. *Competitive Advantage*; Collier Macmillan 1985 (UK & USA)

Pumpin, C. *Practice of Strategic Management*; Swiss Volksbank 1981

Rackham, N. *Making Major Sales*; Gower 1987

Tannenbaum, R. & Schmidt, W. H. 'How to Choose a Leadership Pattern', *Harvard Business Review*; March-April 1958; also May-June 1973

Townsend, R. *Up the Organization*; Coronet 1983 (UK)

Vroom, V. & Deci, E. (Eds) *Management and Motivation*; Penguin 1970 (UK paperback), Penguin 1971 (Educational Series, USA paperback)

Warnes, B. *The Genghis Khan Guide to Business*; Osmosis Publications 1986

Index

Index

Index

Acknowledgements

Picture credits

Key: *l* left *r* right *t* top *b* bottom *c* centre

18/19	(excluding centre) American Express Europe Ltd
c	Ken Kirkwood
22	Clive Coote/Daily Telegraph Colour Library
23	Richard Ellis, Chartered Surveyors
25	Martin Parr/Magnum Photos
30 *l*	The Body Shop International plc
r	Virgin Group Ltd
31 *l*	The British Petroleum Company plc
r	Financial Times
37 *c*	Robert Harding Picture Library
b	Courtesy of Apple Computer, Inc (Macintosh is a trademark of Apple Computer, Inc)
106 *t*	American Express Europe Ltd
107 *tl*	Infoplan
tr	Pascal Rondeau/Allsport
b	Richiardi/Allsport
127	Allen, Brady and Marsh Ltd
146	Popperfoto
199 *t*	Stagecoach Holdings Ltd
c	William Heinemann Ltd
b	Jarvis Porter Ltd
201 *t*	Leith's
b	Scandinavian Airlines System
203 *tl*	British Railways Board
tr	Lombard Communications Ltd
bl	Storehouse plc
br	Shandwick Consultants Ltd
205 *t*	S. G. Warburg Group Ltd
c	British Airways
b	Financial Times
207 *t*	3i Group plc
b	Hanson plc

The publishers and authors received invaluable help from the following people and organizations:

Sue Armitage
Lewis Clark
Carol Copland
Sarah Coward
Kathie Gill
Nigel Halkes
Malcolm Higgs
The Industrial Society
Liz Jones
Lorraine Lewis
Sue Lintern
Lotus Cars Limited
Will Rainey
Eric Ross
Kay Sullivan

Research Assistance

Gavin Bridges
Stephen Brookson
Peter Dell
Karen Filleul
Ken Gilchrist
Phil Hilling
Neil MacKenzie
Iain Maclean
Andrew Meller
Bob Phillips
Andrew Prince
Sandra Sharrar
Colin Staples
Jan Tellick
Alaster Wilson
The Ernst & Young National Information Centre